M. John Harrison
Critical Essays

GYLPHI CONTEMPORARY WRITERS: CRITICAL ESSAYS

SERIES EDITOR: SARAH DILLON

Gylphi Contemporary Writers: Critical Essays presents a new approach to the academic study of living authors. The titles in this series are devoted to contemporary British, Irish and American authors whose work is popularly and critically valued but on whom a significant body of academic work has yet to be established. Each of the titles in this series is developed out of the best contributions to an international conference on its author; represents the most intelligent and provocative material in current thinking about that author's work; and, suggests future avenues of thought, comparison and analysis. With each title prefaced by an author foreword, this series embraces the challenges of writing on living authors and provides the foundation stones for future critical work on significant contemporary writers.

Series Titles

David Mitchell: Critical Essays (2011)
Edited by Sarah Dillon. Foreword by David Mitchell.

Maggie Gee: Critical Essays (2015)
Edited by Sarah Dillon and Caroline Edwards. Foreword by Maggie Gee.

China Miéville: Critical Essays (2015)
Edited by Caroline Edwards and Tony Venezia. Foreword by China Miéville.

Adam Roberts: Critical Essays (2016)
Edited by Christos Callow Jr. and Anna McFarlane. Foreword by Adam Roberts.

Rupert Thomson: Critical Essays (2016)
Edited by Rebecca Pohl and Christopher Vardy. Foreword by Rupert Thomson.

Tom McCarthy: Critical Essays (2016)
Edited by Dennis Duncan. Foreword by Tom McCarthy.

M. John Harrison: Critical Essays (2019)
Edited by Rhys Williams and Mark Bould. Foreword by M. John Harrison.

M. John Harrison
Critical Essays

edited by
Rhys Williams and Mark Bould

Gylphi
contemporary
writers
CRITICAL ESSAYS

A *Gylphi Limited* Book

First published in Great Britain in 2019
by Gylphi Limited

Copyright © Gylphi Limited, 2019

A CIP catalogue record for this book is available from the British Library.

ISBN 978-1-78024-077-0 (pbk)
ISBN 978-1-78024-078-7 (Kindle)
ISBN 978-1-78024-079-4 (EPUB)

Design and typesetting by Gylphi Limited. Printed in the UK by ImprintDigital. com, Exeter.

Gylphi Limited
PO Box 993
Canterbury CT1 9EP, UK

Contents

Preface
The Other Side of Some Inexplicable Disaster

M. John Harrison

1: delivering the future

In a novel I might write, an amputee will describe how he got his foot
stuck in the train line & how he had to 'wait for the train to come and
take it off', as if he accepts that losing his foot was the only way he was
going to get free. Everyone in that town, he will say, was an engineer
or came from a family of engineers. His family hoped he would be one
too, but he couldn't add up. He will present himself, at the point of
stuckness, as thirteen years old & deeply in need of a talent.

2: haunts and understandings

No one in the 1950s quite understood what the term 'global village'
would actually mean. What it turns out to mean is that village concerns become globalized. None of us who left deep Warwickshire in
utter fear & rage, in 196-whatever, looking for the many benefits of
an alienated & intellectualized modernity – that is, a city in which
no one knew your name or cared what you did, a place where plans
for a different future could be hatched – ever expected that 40-odd
years later it would all have caught up with us again. When I was in

my twenties in London I would work all night then try to sleep until six the next evening. I lived on a long sweep of bedsitters running down from Tufnell Park station towards Holloway, in a room which had been partitioned to have two-thirds of a window. Everything that happened there made me anxious. Everything I did made me anxious, even sitting still. I had little connection with the scenes in which I found myself. What connection I could manage was through a kind of terror. I valued that. It was also my condition then to believe that I was haunted, but in fact I was the haunting & understanding that eventually taught me a lot. Every book I read seemed to be published by Peter Owen or John Calder.

3: a map of moods

Even such an apparently nonsensical phrase as 'delivering the future' can contain dangerous traces of meaning. There are futures everywhere. They're at street corners. They're waiting between the buildings of an old-fashioned industrial estate, the architecture of which hasn't changed since the 50s. Or they're waiting for the train in the middle of the day, in the empty middle of an afternoon, for something important to them but invisible to you. They're in the provinces. They have a provincial nature, which is also invisible to you. They're ordinary and self-similar. They're not transparent. They have clothes, children, a job, or no job. They have ambitions. They're a gesture, a posture, an item of baggage. Futures force you to live the life that goes on in them, or used to go on in them. If you are trapped in someone's idea of the future you will end up living there, to a degree at least, the way it has always been lived in. Futures are gently demanding. They are a map of the moods & behaviours of the present. You think you are camping on the edge of a future, but all the time it is drawing you to its centre. I tried to get angry with the future but I failed. The future is always reclaimed. (In the classic New Wave sf texts reclamation is a two-way process, not simply the slow disaster eating away at the established, but the failure of the as-yet-to-be-established creeping into the present. A doubled interface, both present & future comprised of their own failure to happen, like a housing project abandoned in a desert.)

4: the future of Heritage

I await patiently the time when the Roman Wroxeter (Viroconium) site falls into ruin and far-Postmodern generations place its replica villa – built circa 2010 for a TV programme entitled 'Rome Wasn't Built in a Day' – on a historical par with the remains of the second century municipal baths, so that the Heritage experience becomes in itself heritage, as authentic as the real thing. It's the future of Heritage to replace the past, just as it is the sole known characteristic of the Analeptic Kings (*Viriconium*) to have happened in that one-word qualificatory flashback. Ironbridge World Heritage Site, just down the road: damp snow falls deep in the Gorge, on to a river one shade darker fawn than a labrador dog. Two inches of rain predicted for the Welsh uplands. Flood warnings up and downstream. A fast scum of sticks and branches on the surface of the Severn. In the car park a coach splits like a chrysalis. Puzzled by the weather, the tourists hurry away in twos and threes across the bridge & along the Wharfage, only to find flood barriers already in place down there. The river's seeping between them & the 'industrial past' they've come both to witness and to compare with that Ironbridge of the digital era, Silicon Valley. I grind my way back up the hill into Benthall Wood (where you could hear Valley rhetoric, pitch-perfect bids for a slice of the Singularity, as early as 1800) & arrive at the top just as the snow stops falling through the trees. Back in the future again.

5: shallow roots, hard routes

The central character of *Climbers* exists only to witness something he doesn't understand. The reader doesn't understand it either; not because it can't be understood, or because there is nothing to be understood, but because understanding comes at the price of reassembling the components of the book from a position – no, let's say an

3

assumption – that is only hinted-at. One way or another, everything's a clue to that point of view, but, much as a gene's most important function may be to switch on a cascade of other genes, it may be a clue only to another clue. *Climbers* isn't about somebody who 'finds himself' through climbing, or who 'becomes a climber'. It's precisely the opposite of that: it's about someone who in *failing* to become a climber also fails to find a self. What satisfies the committed climbers – the discipline, the absorption & extension of the knowledge that comprises the field, the practicality of their engagement with it, the 'community of skills' – powerfully attracts but does not satisfy 'Mike'. The last few paragraphs of the book are the *Goodbye To All That* of a flawed ephebe who rejects the ordeal and refuses 'to be newly named, newly rejoiced in' (*Divine Horsemen* [Deren, 1953]). That's what writing's been about, too. The applicant undertakes anabasis & catches a glimpse of the rites, only to drop out & break the experience up for parts. Junkman, junkyard & junkyard dog: the writer's all three; so how satisfying, in the end, to drive up to Warwick U in August 2014 & be irradiated & broken up for parts by other people & wind up bricolaged back together in a book like this.

6: how to engineer something

Provide a sense of linkage for unlinked things. The sense – the hint – of a logic of the unlinked. Place things together so that they seem embarrassed about sharing a narrative grammar. In her 2010 interview with the Tartarus Press, the closest Elizabeth Jane Howard gets to defining Robert Aickman is in her belief that he 'cheats'.[1] In fact it's in the space this essentially readerly concept fails to map that he succeeds so completely as a writer. Otherwise, his prose is often dull; and though his observation of people is good, his view of them is dully straightforward, rather old-fashioned and a bit right wing. Even his idea of what is frightening or odd can be dull. The more obvious ghost and horror stories – which play by the 'rules' Elizabeth Jane Howard refers to – are often only ghost and horror stories. As to what the cheat-space contains, that shy, sly residue that remains in occupation after his more ordinary effects have shown themselves the door, you can only shrug and point. It's in 'The Swords', 'Bind Your Hair' and 'The Same Dog'. It's in 'The Stains' but not 'The Trains'.

7: work in progress

This other character I'm writing, perhaps less amputee than orphan, never had much more than an unconscious relationship with events. His awareness always skimmed them, or worked around them, or managed to find a way of dismissing them as shallow and insubstantial even as they were happening. If the things that happened to him were taken in at all – actually engaged with or reacted to – it must have been the unconscious which did that work, because X's consciousness was never really wired up. It always seemed to be off somewhere else, living a constant present, refusing to acknowledge either the passage of life or the idea of life as a socially constructed, collegial event about the basic shape of which we can all agree. Things' effects on him had thus to be welcomed later, in symbols. Sometimes the return of the repressed was all he had to work with to understand what had actually taken place. X's author used to have him pretend he was a normal part of other people's lives (that off-stage he made – or had once made, prior to the story – some contribution to those lives, or at least that he performed some sort of add-on service): but now it must be admitted that he isn't. X is just in a temporary unstable orbit around people *who don't even particularly need him for anything*, drawn there by the obsessive-compulsive cycles of his own personality. He is of no utility. He's damaged goods. He's the drowned man, the ghost in the text looking for somewhere to wash up post-Brexit. Any port in a storm.

8: while I am waiting to be free

If you're not born in an engineering town, you may be born in a town where the population get their living from Heritage tourism. They glue themselves to a rock & sieve the water for nutrients. They plan no escape. They plan no amputation. You wonder if they had energy when they were young, or if their projects were falling into decay even then. You wonder if you're like them, if the people who come in your house think similar things about you. Anyway, while you're waiting to have your foot freed from the railway line by one visible, significant event or act of understanding, you're actually being freed by a succession of smaller, less visible ones. Like the majority of writers I spent my life anticipating the big score that would enable me to put two fingers up to everything without leaving my comfort zone. Instead, in my late sixties I experienced a cascade of change. I was untied by circumstance. Across two or three years the emotional landscape shifted completely. My expectations changed. I had a major illness. I sat on the edge of my bed in the acute assessment ward and thought: *It's quite satisfying to be set at a distance from the world I know. Soon enough another set of parameters will take effect but for now it's like a cheap comfortable hotel, air too hot, quiet conversations from the nurses' station.* I made a will. I was deeply in need of a coat of paint.

9: the resource

The house thickens inside with books. They don't just line the walls. I put on my double-pile jacket, as if I'm cold; make notes – 'Paper found in a Thai fish'. I take down a novel, retrieve a bookmark 32 years old, this torn browned bit of paper with the words 'tabolites stored in fat' scribbled on it in a handwriting not mine, which I presume to have read 'metabolites'. After that, well, the voices start, 'Buy the Pontiac', 'Avoid that shadow in the wall', usual things. So I douse the joint in gasoline & stand across the street drinking barrel proof bourbon & watching the flames etc etc. You try to break up with your library but it just follows you about whining til you hit it with a stick. Some loved writers you detach yourself from, perhaps quite gently, but determinedly too, because they're like parents or teachers you want to outgrow. Some you drift away from then bump into them with a shock of recognition forty years later, buy all their books again & discover that in the interim a hefty but laughable scholarship has grown up around them. Others, it's a grudge match: even after forty years you wouldn't piss on them if you found them on fire in Waterstone's Piccadilly – but then you do & burst into tears for no reason you can fathom. (The tears aren't quite enough to put them out.) When I was little we had three shelves of books. That was a lot for a house of engineers in the 1950s. I remember *Little Brother to the Bear, The Water Babies* & *Coral Island.* Most of the rest were popular military histories. World War Two was still very alive in the house: my father had memoirs of Operation Market Garden & biographies of General Montgomery, one of his heroes. The rest of his heroes being engineers there were engineering biographies too. Rolt's *Isambard Kingdom Brunel,* an expensive birthday present from my father to me, I was allowed to read only under supervision. I didn't mind. Though I admired Brunel's hat & cheroot & his clear sense of himself as a Master of the Singularity, I found his story had neither the sadistic punch of *The White Rabbit* nor the calming qualities of a Charles Kingsley. Stock your imagination this way when you're young & by the time you're forty those combinations will have become an exploitable resource. When they come on stream, you can begin to think solely of the other aspects of writing. Your imagination won't fail you. The stuff you dredge up from it will simply get richer & more dependable.

10: amputees

Even literary fiction is bored with the literary fiction marketing programme, all the festivals, cute little cotton bags & the *Isn't it blissful to curl up with a glass of wine and a lovely blissful book?* chat. It's a niche in crisis. Determined young women deny they ever took an MA in creative writing at UEA, reject the tasteful cover & carefully sourced endorsement, diss the discreetly-aimed marketing campaign that gives them away. They avoid the audience after the reading, & claim when cornered to do rather more than just write literature. I remember Ballard saying something to the effect of, 'Only write the parts that interest you'. I'm not interested in causality, character, motivation, a self-consistent world, empathy or *just a really wonderful story* (all staples of

7

fiction's ongoing Heritage Experience), or in explanation except inasmuch as the shape of the front-end can accidentally reveal a kind of wrenched sublimity at the back. But I was always interested in death as the big event, & if it does nothing else late life will increase your focus on that. I find I'm writing or planning stories about people who are deceased but don't know it; individuals who believe they have survived a crisis but don't really know what it was, living in societies recently arrived on the other side of some inexplicable disaster. If you work in the genre you're going to have to describe that as science fiction or something like it. It isn't, of course.

11: delivering the past

All of the things: around 500 books; bookcase made of found wood; a broken dining chair only needs a little glue; two thin ethnic rugs, rolled & cat-haired; Indian folding inlaid table 1976, hinges gone; signed copies of books by people I had fallen out with; single-spaced typewritten drafts on pink, yellow & white paper in a size fractionally larger than foolscap, 1965–1987; a good pair of jumars no one would want any more; plugs & wires from lost electrical equipment; futon, black, used-looking; handwritten journals in four colours of ink, in system binders, 1980–1987; the view from 15 Rye Hill Park, Peckham, 1988; two framed originals by Ian Miller (study for the cover of *Viriconium*, Allen & Unwin 1988; *Interzone* illustration, 'Anima', maybe a couple of years later); another picture. Some letters, Christmas cards & polaroid photographs in shoeboxes; postcards in shoeboxes; useful items found in a North London skip, 1967; box of clothes; bag of clothes; box of mixtapes w/out labels; maybe an old telephone answering machine with greasy wires; a broken Olivetti M15 laptop with a tailpipe guarantee; Walkman, pink earbuds, still plays but wonkily since I sat on it after a fall from near the top of the Mile End Wall in 1991; aluminium saucepans, kitchen things; cat bed; address books; editions of my own books & stories, glue gone, pages brown, paper smells of foecal matter or almonds depending on publisher, 1971–1998; keys to a silver Citroen BX; everything in my life that made me feel romantic at the time, nauseated later; everything I wanted to forget; a nice John Lewis table 1.5 metres on a side, two years old or less when I stored it.

12: shelter from the storm

I often wish I was still a climber & that I was top-roping a beachfront crag in the Dominican Republic. Acts like that would fit cleanly with an almost spiritual urge I've been feeling lately to make my home on an 80-year-old PBY Catalina flying-boat moored in some tiny Caribbean bay, drink Black Heart rum all day dressed in chino cutoffs, & play chess with other old guys on a cargo boat in need of a coat of paint. Every so often the ancient valve radio springs into life without anyone switching it on & a voice can be heard repeating your call sign patiently against a background of bad weather, interference & big band swing. You don't answer.

Note

1 http://tartaruspress.blogspot.co.uk/2011/10/elizabeth-jane-howard-and-we-are-for.html

INTRODUCTION
BROADLY, HARRISON

Rhys Williams and Mark Bould

The real Golden Fleece is not to be anything, to write something
that doesn't come from any side, and isn't anything.

(M. John Harrison)[1]

Maybe the fantastic is the literature of unshackled imagination, exploring the limits of the human condition and questioning our deepest-held assumptions. Or maybe it is the literature of willed naïveté: the prejudices of the present beguiling in fancy dress, an opiate haven in troubling waters. Maybe it cuts deep, demands action, stirs us from sleep; or maybe it balms, placates, provides passing relief. Either/or/and, fantasy encodes our encounters with the real, colours them blue-bleak or makes them shine gold-vermillion. (Its light, as Harrison would say, transforms all things.) Fantastic literature is our most thorough and sophisticated mode of exploring this encoding, and its potencies. Fantasy is power, and to shape fantasy is to shape people, their actions, and their worlds. Harrison's work is the elegant, fractured product of struggling with this fact and its consequences.

To read Harrison's fiction is to be aware, perhaps for the first time, of what it means to read fantasy. He wrestles with its traditions and tendencies, turning it from easy roads and calming closures, from where we, in our longing for comfort, want it to go. He evacuates it from his stories, scraping out all the fantasy to leave us with reality impressed by it like a wound or an indent in a beanbag left by the arse of someone who's played computer games all day. He deflates its pomp and circumstance until you realize a battle is just a lot of pain and guts and you could not have a drink with the elf-queen let alone a relationship and look – she's basically Thatcher anyway. He takes fantasy away to reveal our cravings for it, or lets characters overdose on it, wasting amid steroid dreams or chasing a dragon while you look on horrified from outside the twink-tank. He looks you square in the eye and you know you have just been wanking away and calling it sex because reality is hard if nothing else and needs courage and the bravest thing is giving yourself to other actual people. You might say that he is a grumpy bastard and he will not let you have any fun. But you might also start to question this idea of fun that you seem to have.

One of the editors recently had occasion to teach Harrison's classic *Viriconium* series to a host of undergraduates. Discussing the seduction and danger of fantasy-as-opiate, the students – bred on a passionately sincere diet of *Harry Potter* – became frustrated; 'I see his point,' one said, 'I do, but I *hate* him for it'. It's never easy to acknowledge your own weakness, or the desires that spring from it, or that you have invested time and, yes, yourself, in something questionable, but Harrison is relentless. His fiction demands we face up to who we are, the ways that we want, and the consequences. Not because he thinks himself better, mind (no easy fantasy of elitism here): these are warnings from someone who understands the comfort of escape intimately, and sometimes you can glimpse his own scars swelling through the printed page.

In his work, reality jags through the swaddling of fantasy. The danger of hanging from a cliff face, the mutilating consequences of desire *en passant*, the sickness that comes despite belief, the sordidness of the scene when viewed from behind a pane of glass, the fractures and ruptures and running-down of lives neglected chasing froth. Harrison paints life from a plateau that reveals us moving through our fantasies like a fog, stumbling and missing and hurting one another without knowledge. Those that do better in his world are beacons of resignation and compromise; endlessly facing and suffering their burdens, they are quiet heroes in a world where this genuine heroism is seldom recognized. There is no glamour here (or rather, we are stood outside the enchanted circle looking in and we can see the makeup and the stains and it's as if the people inside have lost their minds in their enthusiasm).

> We can never escape the world. We cannot stop trying to escape the world. (Harrison, 2005a: 144)

If the people in Harrison's works tend to the diffuse, then they are set off against a world that is dense and full of things. The title of the conference that inspired this collection – *Irradiating the Object* – comes from a comment Harrison made about Tarkovsky (whose influence upon Harrison is myriad, as Christina Sholz argues), but the sense of which applies equally well to Harrison himself. Part of Harrison's greatness lies in the beauty and the density of his descriptive power, where the landscapes of a post-industrial North (both actual, as in *Climbers*, or transposed, as in the *Viriconium* series), or the streets of London are vibrant with oscillation between the mundane and the sublime, now and then fractured by the unnerving or the grotesque. If he is elsewhere wry, brief or sharp, or deploying unerringly familiar dialogue (famously harvested from years in cafés with a pen and a pad), it is in the sweep and wealth of setting that his language soars. 'The setting is the story', he once told us.

Not that this splendid weight of place lends his worlds *duration* mind you. As one short story has it, everything is running down, passing away, flickering in and out and – as the essays of Ryan Elliott, Paul Kincaid and Graham Fraser detail – even across his works. Viriconium, the Kefahuchi Tract, England: nowhere the same twice, nowhere identical with itself, and nowhere pretending to anything more than words on a page. Harrison has no truck with tricking the reader that the map is the ground – like Brecht, he is always needling the reader with the artificiality of the construction, and refusing to let them forget that they are reading, not living, this created world. And yet this prominence of artifice is no endless clever-Dick game. He rends the veil only so the reader confronts something that feels a lot like *reality* in the midst of all this swirling incoherence. If fantasy (realism included) is typically deployed to construct a believable façade, Harrison defaces it to generate a sense of something that sits beneath (or above, or within, or, or …).

> I don't know what you're supposed to do if your urge is to break these worlds apart, torch up the local sun, and skateboard off across the universe looking for mischief. Of course, an attitude like that isn't big, or clever, or constructive … but … it's almost irresistible. (Harrison, 2005b: 227)

So why does he even write in the fantastic genres? Maybe his creativity is more heavily destructive than most. He certainly likes breaking things, is more interested in the thing breaking than the thing broken. His antipathy for closure stems from the very beginning of his career, in the sandpit with Moorcock and Delany and the other New Wave authors, all gleefully smashing their way through the genre conventions, and him in need of an iconoclasm of his own. Casting around he alights on the holy-of-holies – that satisfying click of a story closing. And so the first thing he does, with *Pastel City* (1971), is leave that door wide open, his hero refusing the queen's call to war. There has not been any real closure since, especially when you consider the way that fragments resonate across his stories, opening each onto the other again and again and again.

But to return to the dichotomy of fantasy. Harrison pierces, rends, tears, defaces. Reading him is like standing in the quiet aftermath of a volcanic eruption, as a once-familiar landscape reveals its molten underbelly, and soft falling ash obscures all around. But with escapism dead, what happens to escape? Does Harrison's revelation also paralyse us, condemn us to the bleak present? Almost, yes. There can be no easy revolution for Harrison, no quick win, no hero around which the world bends. Harrison holds dear those who are resigned and quietly courageous. There are moments of beauty, of utopian fullness, or – better – a fittingness to the world, but they are fleeting and lightly grasped. More thorough transformation is possible, but it is – in the best and most honest of utopian traditions – both inconceivable and passing monstrous, beyond our ken, and certainly beyond our fantasies. The Kefahuchi Tract, for the best example, stands as a permanent symbol of such radical change. But it is no accident that when the Tract falls to earth, and becomes the Site, it becomes a place of fetish and delusion. An image – Tract/Site – of the same impulse – Escape/Escapism – only one of which demands *everything* be given. Which is not, however, to say it is impossible.

> I'm like an alchemist that finally realizes he's not going to find the philosopher's stone, and looks back and thinks, well, 60 years! Wasted then! But on the other hand he's produced a few bits of interesting chemistry and I've produced a few books. (M. John Harrison)

Harrison's legacy, by now, is enormous. From his early years writing scathing reviews of genre fiction for the magazine *New Worlds* and publishing genre-busting stories, he has helped shaped the field from the seventies to the present. He is an author's author – without Harrison, no China Miéville perhaps, no New Weird, no contemporary post-genre or slipstream in quite the same way – and the thinker's author, lauded by the likes of John Gray and Robert McFarlane – but never, for reasons perhaps all-too-obvious, the big seller. He has never fitted comfortably into the genre market, nor the mainstream market, and for that readers everywhere should be grateful. His agitation at the borders, his catholic tastes, his contempt for the status quo, and his dream of a grand melting-pot of literature with boundaries undone have played a big part in the current situation, where Literature and Genre are less segregated than ever, and the marketing-friendly divisions become less relevant each year.

The Essays

This collection of essays falls into three rough (and roughly chronological) parts. We open with essays concerning Harrison's earlier work, especially the important *Viriconium* series, and essays that ground Harrison in his early context. We move on to work exploring some of Harrison's key interlocutors, both in the past and present, before closing with a quartet of essays that take the recent *Empty Space* Trilogy as their focus and springboard.[2] With this selection, we hope to give the reader a sense of Harrison's work as a whole, from the sediment of his foundations to his pinpoint relevance to the contemporary period. Finally, as an epilogue of sorts, we reproduce the text of a creative performance given by artist Tim Etchells in response to the work of Harrison, his long-time friend and collaborator.

First, Rob Latham's thorough contextualization of Harrison in the environment in which he cut his teeth, situating him in the flush of the New Wave, and noting the debts and differences of his early work to the interests and bugbears of that movement. Following, Paul Kincaid offers a more focused narrative of Harrison's literary development, considering how the palimpsest of stories concerned with the fantastic city of Viriconium (from *Pastel City* in 1971 to 'A Young Man's Journey to Viroconium' in 1985) allow us to track Harrison's development as an author, and his shifting relationship to fantasy as a genre. Then Graham Fraser's piece provides an elegiac reading of Viriconium as site of the hauntological, a place made of 'scraps of our desire' that work to show us how these desires never existed but in pale reflection or echo. Taking a tour through Harrison's use of Modernist techniques, Fraser draws on Walter Benjamin and T. S. Eliot to perform a reading that doubles as a mode of healing via a melancholic wander through the torn landscapes of fantasy. Finally, in this first section, Nick Freeman investigates the mundane settings and traces of realism that wind through Harrison's work, from the restlessness of cafés to the daubs of graffiti barely noticed on city walls. Focussing on his earlier work, Freeman brings out the way that Harrison dives through this mundanity, provoking a sense of the everyday that is profoundly strange and miraculous.

Ryan Elliott follows with a comprehensive overview of the technique that binds Harrison's work together – a technique he names 'versioning'. Ranging across Harrison's output, from his fiction to his blog posts and interviews, Elliott outlines this key mechanism and how it both unites and fractures Harrison's oeuvre, considering its ideological consequences, its literary meaning and antecedents, and the way it interacts with the fantastic as a mode. On the way he draws on metaphors from performance and musical resonance to provide insight into Harrison's particular approach to authorship. Then

Christina Scholz and James Machin outline two central and lasting influences on Harrison's work. Scholz brings to light (quite literally) the way that Harrison's fiction resonates with and draws upon the films and motifs of Andrei Tarkovsky, with a particular eye to inner space, notions of the sublime, and the way both artists 'irradiate' materiality to evoke a spiritual dimension beyond the mundane, which is nonetheless entangled with it. Machin draws out the shadow his Weird near-namesake – Arthur Machen – casts over Harrison's fiction, while carefully arguing for a 'profound philosophical schism between the two writers' – between Machen's belief in the fullness and potency of ecstatic immanence in the universe, and Harrison's disillusioned reworking of such immanence as, 'that vacancy which is the source of everything'. A vacancy that, 'versioned,' continues to haunt Harrison's work. This section is rounded out by Vassili Christodoulou's essay on what he calls Harrison's 'Misanthropic Principle'. Drawing on the philosophy of John Gray (also a fan of Harrison), Christodoulou argues that Harrison's work, and particularly his recent *Empty Space* trilogy, contains a deep pessimism for humanity's future, and embodies a thorough attack on the principles of liberal humanism. He demonstrates how Harrison can be understood to articulate Gray's arguments through a reworking of the conventions of space opera and psychodrama to end with a startlingly bleak assessment of humankind's place in the cosmos.

On a cheerier note, Timothy Jarvis and Chris Pak understand the *Empty Space* trilogy to be a site for thinking post-humanity, with the fears but also the hopes that transformation might bring. Through Deleuze, Gnosticism and quantum physics, Jarvis reads the trilogy as a culmination of themes from Harrison's earlier works, presenting a moment of tension between plenitude and loss, dissolution and transcendence. Pak, on the other hand, analyses the presence of animals in the trilogy, arguing that they trouble the boundaries between human, animal and other while providing a form of narrative cohesion. Drawing on recent work from animal studies, Pak proposes a new – amborg – subject that resists containment and closure.

The critical works end with two pieces that bring things full circle, with an investigation of Harrison's literary technique from the most contemporary of science-fictional angles. Nick Prescott considers Harrison's body of work as a complex system, opening with a literary scholar's guide to complexity science, and reading Harrison through ideas of strange attractors and fractal recursion. Fred Botting takes the reader through the unstable images of froth, fracture and fluttering that permeate the *Empty Space* trilogy, to consider how physics, capitalism and postmodern simulation are explicitly linked in Harrison as un-real games of chance, prediction and prophecy.

Finally, we end where Harrison himself would want us to – in chaos, with two fingers up to closure and Tim Etchells's artistic response to Harrison's work. Beginning by thinking Harrison through the work of the artist Vlatka Horvat, Etchells takes us on a conceptual, personal, and creative journey that draws on the resonances and versionings discussed so far. Etchells and Harrison are long-time collaborators, and Harrison cites Etchells's theatre group Forced Entertainment as a major influence on his work. It is fitting, then, that rather than another academic essay, we close on this transcript of a performance that Etchells gave at the *Irradiating the Object* conference, held at Warwick in August 2014 and with Harrison in the audience – the conference which provided the impetus for this collection, and of which this is but another version.

Notes

1 This epigraph, and the fourth, final one, are quotations from an unpublished interview with Harrison, conducted by the editors of this volume.

2 Although many refer to the trilogy as 'the Kefahuchi Tract novels', we have adopted Harrison's own preferred title – to judge from his blog – throughout the collection.

Works Cited

Harrison, M. John (2005a) 'The Profession of Science Fiction, 40: The Profession of Fiction', Mark Bould and Michelle Reid (eds) *Parietal Games: Critical Writings by and on M. John Harrison*, pp. 144–54. London: The Science Fiction Foundation.

Harrison, M. John (2005b) 'Worlds Apart: *The Birthday of the World* by Ursula K. Le Guin', Mark Bould and Michelle Reid (eds) *Parietal Games:*

Critical Writings by and on M. John Harrison, pp. 226–7. London: The Science Fiction Foundation.

A Young Man's Journey to Ladbroke Grove
M. John Harrison and the Evolution of the New Wave in Britain

Rob Latham

When critics write about the project of genre renovation undertaken by Michael Moorcock's *New Worlds* during the 1960s, they generally focus on the fiction the magazine published, especially the risky experiments: J. G. Ballard's disorienting condensed novels, Brian Aldiss's freewheeling 'Acid Wars' stories, Thomas Disch's bleak moral parables. The cultivation of creative alternatives to the prevailing modes of sf writing is seen as the magazine's signal contribution – a view that tends to slight the non-fiction also featured in its pages.[1] While critics at times acknowledge the role played by Moorcock's contentious editorials in articulating a fresh vision for the field, they largely ignore the many other forms of commentary – book reviews, scientific articles, literary and cultural criticism, artist profiles and more – that increasingly came to balance the New Wave fiction, particularly after Moorcock, using an Arts Council grant that saved *New Worlds* from bankruptcy in the summer of 1967, transformed the magazine into a large-format slick with a broader editorial purview. The installation of Christopher Evans as Science Editor and Christopher Finch as Arts Editor in the September 1967 issue cemented this makeover, which was capped with the appointment of M. John Harrison as *New*

Worlds's first Books Editor in December 1968, a position he held until the demise of the journal eight years later.

This growing rigour of the magazine's masthead, organized into distinct editorial departments, was not, however, reflected in its day-to-day operations, which remained notoriously casual – as Harrison's account of how he acquired his post testifies: 'it was [associate editor] James Sallis who suggested I become Books Editor. He dragged me round to Mike Moorcock's house one night at about three o'clock and said: "This chap should be Books Editor". So Mike said something like: "Oh, all right" – and I was' (Fowler, 1981: 6).[2] Despite this breezy informality, there is little question that *New Worlds* had long been groping toward a new format for literary commentary, exploring a range of coverage and deploying modes of analysis that exploded the constraints of the traditional sf review column, and that Harrison was the ideal candidate to help forge this alternative. As Moorcock (1973: 263) himself put it: 'For some years … we have been trying to form a critical vocabulary capable of dealing coherently with individual works of imaginative fiction'. Given the magazine's longstanding goal of cross-pollinating sf with avant-garde writing, what was needed was someone with catholic tastes, a passionate devotion to literature and a restless contempt for the status quo to mould and steer the section, and the youthful Harrison amply fit the bill:

> I liked anything bizarre, from being about four years old. I started on *Dan Dare* and worked up to the Absurdists. At 15 you could catch me with a pile of books that contained an Alfred Bester, a Samuel Beckett, a Charles Williams, the two or three available Ballards, *On The Road* by Jack Kerouac, some Keats, some Alan [sic] Ginsberg, maybe a Thorne Smith. I've always been pick 'n' mix: now it's a philosophy. Actually, it was a philosophy before I joined *New Worlds*. I had no way of articulating it in those days. I was just this shy, raw, undereducated, borderline personality disorder, rooting through bookshops and going, 'Shit. Wow. Look at this.' (Hudson 2002: n.p.)

Despite this rawness, Harrison was possessed of a brilliance and pugnacity that all but insured success, as Moorcock shrewdly perceived from the outset. 'He liked that I was insanely angry about everything', Harrison has said, 'so he made me one of the gunfighters at the Bar NW ranch. I was always the most hair-trigger of them because I was the newcomer and the Pistol Kid' (Hudson, 2002: n.p.).[3] His neophyte status, combined with an abiding personal shyness, kept Harrison from entering fully into the magazine's bohemian social milieu, the Ladbroke Grove counterculture that lapped at Moorcock's doorstep, but he embraced its intellectual mission unstintingly, with characteristic earnestness: 'I became immediately, completely and totally committed to it, as I commit myself to anything that I take up in that way ... I believed then and I still believe that science fiction needs to be radically changed from the inside by people who will not compromise' (Fowler, 1981: 7). It is likely that Harrison's brash intensity, arriving four years into a crusade that had already weathered a number of exhausting editorial and financial crises, served to energize the veteran members of the *New Worlds* cohort; certainly, it revitalized the magazine's literary coverage, which became both more polished and more starkly confrontational.

In his first issue as Books Editor, Harrison penned a polemical brief for the New Wave in the form of a review of two classic *New Worlds* stories that had just seen publication in book form, Moorcock's *The Final Programme* (1968) and Disch's *Camp Concentration* (1968). Affirming their 'fresh angle-of-attack' over against the 'stale and self-conscious' orthodoxies of mainstream literature, he praised their capacity 'to deal with the literary difficulties of an age in the precise terms of that age' (Harrison, 1968a: 58), with Moorcock satirizing 1960s excesses in pop-psychedelic lingo and Disch decrying militant technocracy via collage techniques, and he cited the recent work of Ballard and John Sladek as similarly urgent adaptations to contemporary realities. Perhaps slightly embarrassed by what might be perceived as cosy backscratching among the *New Worlds* crowd, Harrison cloaked this review under a pseudonym, Joyce Churchill, which he was to use on-and-off over the next several years.[4] Yet he was present also under his own byline, in an omnibus review of a number of new sf novels, applauding the incisive originality of Sladek's *The Reproductive System* (1968) and Joanna Russ's *Picnic on Paradise* (1968) while bemoaning Samuel R. Delany's reversion to space-opera formulae in

Nova (1968), which 'however finely realized, is bedded in the genre's most stifling traditions' (Harrison, 1968b: 61). Throughout both pieces, Harrison displayed a wide-ranging erudition that casually referenced Rilke and Dennis Wheatley, Rimbaud and Enid Blyton, Jean Genet and T. H. White. Rounding out the issue were several reviews, by other hands, of works of popular science, history and art criticism.

Over the next year and a half, until the large-format *New Worlds* ceased publication in April 1970, the books section thrived under Harrison's leadership. In his own reviews and review-articles – and in those he commissioned from the likes of Brian Aldiss, John Brunner, Norman Spinrad and that future powerhouse of sf criticism, John Clute – Harrison pursued several broad, overlapping agendas with vigour and panache. First, he took up and further refined the New Wave critique of traditional sf as a dull and ossified commercial genre. Writing as Joyce Churchill in the July 1969 issue, he flayed Anne McCaffrey's planetary romance *Decision at Doona* (1969) – 'her conflicts are ersatz and petty, her characters the most trivial of stereotypes, and the whole book is permeated with an odour of playroom niceness' (Harrison, 1969f: 61) – and drolly remarked of John Jakes's science-fantasy *The Planet Wizard* (1969): 'Even the heroes of this kind of fiction must be bored by now' (Harrison, 1969f: 62). In the November 1969 issue, he mocked the classic sf 'gimmick story' favoured by Robert Sheckley as 'a couple or so thousand words of featherweight characterisation, a wonderful machine, and a twist in the tail that was apparent from the third word' (Harrison, 1969g: 31). Harrison's tone throughout these reviews was scathing, reflecting an unbending refusal to accept the mediocre, the derivative, the tried-and-true.

In this regard, he was probably the most sceptical of all the *New Worlds* cohort about the genre's aesthetic viability, more dismissive in his judgments than his contemporary Clute who, while equally critical of its fumbles and failures, always had a sincere appreciation for the storytelling values of traditional sf.[5] Partly, this negativism could be chalked up to a youthful appetite for battle that had its roots in sheer bloody-mindedness; as Harrison has acknowledged, his *New Worlds* criticism was a 'polemical, anarchistic, deliberate refusal to accept almost anything that was put in front of it' (Fowler, 1981: 8). More notably, his chafing at complacency was the emotional expression of a developing aesthetic philosophy that was coming to view the basic escapism of genre-bound entertainment as psychologically and morally corrupt (more on this later). But its practical causes might simply have been the exigencies of his editorial assignment, which required Harrison to immerse himself in a monthly bath of trash, the steady stream of new titles that poured across his desk serving to confirm for him a widespread 'stasis and decay in the science fiction field':

> I would get possibly 70 or 80 books a month, which I read before they were sent out to reviewers. I prided myself on always having read the book that the reviewer reviewed, because I don't believe a literary editor's doing his job unless he knows exactly what his reviewer's talking about ... I was horrified ... because it was so bad. It was a very quick transfer from being astonished to being appalled and finally to despair. It took about three months flat ... To come across an Ace book, and to realize that the majority of the books published in science fiction were the Ace book type ... caused me to despair very quickly. (Fowler, 1981: 7–8)

Amidst this despondency, and despite his furious contempt for the field, Harrison did find it in his heart to commend on occasion a select few Old-Wave writers – Fritz Leiber, Jack Vance, Philip K. Dick – for managing to produce original, or at least moderately interesting, bodies of work despite crippling genre constraints. In some cases, as in his review of Leiber's collection *The Secret Songs* (1968) in the March 1969 issue, Harrison essentially argued for the author as a New Wave forerunner, 'consistently ahead of his time' with his incipient inner-space orientation, which had conspired to make him 'one of the most misjudged and underrated writers in the field' (Harrison, 1969e: 60).[6] Dick, on the other hand, was a classic sf ideas man whose admitted conceptual brilliance was hobbled by hasty writing and generic cliché, a fundamental inattention to structure that made even his most arresting work 'a bit of a mess' (Harrison, 1969d: 30).[7] By contrast, Vance's work was a triumph of style over substance, his fine baroque atmosphere barely disguising the threadbare banality of his space-opera plots. The abiding disjunction between topic and treatment evident in these relative assessments suggested a persistent inability on the part of traditional sf to combine ideational and formal brilliance in the same piece of writing, a goal the New Wave contingent strived for. Rare genre stalwarts such as Robert Silverberg might be able to bootstrap their way into this fraternity,[8] but most of the old-school crew was simply hopeless.

At the same time as he was criticizing sf for its rampant absurdities, Harrison (1968a: 58) was blasting mainstream fiction as 'involuted and incestuous', a tepid corpus still clinging to its quotidian certainties in the face of an avalanche of technosocial change. As he put it in a tart review of *Penguin Modern Stories 2* (1969) in the January 1970 issue, mainstream writers 'take the mundane for the durable and rake over the old, old conflicts that have simply ceased to relate' (Harrison, 1970b: 32). By contrast, the New Wave stories featured in Langdon Jones's anthology *The New SF* (1969) 'reveal that the vigour always to be found in the sf field can be channelled to produce enjoyable "hard" fiction' that is truly *modern* in its engagement with the contemporary world (Harrison, 1970b: 32). As this comment makes clear, Harrison had fully embraced Moorcock's agenda of mating sf and the mainstream to produce a new breed of writing that would, on the one hand, bring literary sophistication to a juvenile genre and, on the other hand, invigorate a decadent modernism through an infusion of futuristic topicality.

This dialectical line of reasoning was always, for the *New Worlds* partisans, a difficult balancing act to carry off, and Harrison, with his evident deep contempt for genre fiction, was perhaps in the least comfortable position to argue for sf's contribution to the emerging mutant form. But, though he later came to admit that some of his early polemical postures were adopted unthinkingly, Harrison was quite sincere in his conviction that both sf *and* contemporary literature were in desperate need of rejuvenation. He remarked in 1977:

> I still believe in one of the basic *New Worlds* tenets, which is that today's mainstream fiction is immobile, nerveless, as well as being sloppy. It lacks dynamism, and generic fiction could provide that dy-

namism, either if the mainstream began to take some of its subject matter from the generic system; or if generic fiction got good enough to compete with mainstream fiction. Both would gain. (Fowler, 1981: 17)

In his own fiction, from the classic *New Worlds* story 'Running Down' (1975) to his most recent category-busting novels, Harrison has pioneered just such a crossbreeding, using science-fictional premises to illuminate the strictures of everyday life in postindustrial Britain. No better proof of the viability of the New Wave enterprise could be asked for than those potent blends of unsparing realism and ingenious fantasy, *The Course of the Heart* (1992), *Signs of Life* (1997), and *Light* (2002).

When Harrison's reviews were not celebrating the crossover work of contemporary talents inspired by the *New Worlds* project, they were limning an evolving heritage of speculative writing that transcended the boundaries of genre. Legitimating the magazine's venturesome call for a newly relevant speculative literature, Harrison's evocation of an alternative tradition gathered avant-garde modernists, neglected mainstream fantasists and emergent postmodernists into a proto-New Wave canon that provided an encompassing context for assessing the work of Ballard, Disch, Sladek, et al. Coinciding with the publication of a short story by Thomas Pynchon in the February 1969 issue, Harrison contributed a review essay that praised books by Vladimir Nabokov, John Barth and William S. Burroughs – the latter saluted by Harrison as 'a powerful literary artist, fascinating, multivalent and visionary' (Harrison, 1969g: 60). The very first issue of the Moorcock-edited *New Worlds* had featured an editorial praising Burroughs as a preeminent example of the 'kind of SF which is unconventional in every sense and which must soon be recognized as an important revitalisation of the literary mainstream' (Moorcock, 1964: 3),[9] as well as an essay by Ballard (1964: 127) claiming that Burroughs's cut-up novels constituted 'the first authentic mythology of the age of Cape Canaveral, Hiroshima and Belsen'. Burroughs was the ideal New Wave role model because he was the perfect outsider, his work guaranteed to infuriate both genre fans, who found his imagery grotesque and his parodies of sf insulting, and mainstream critics, who were repelled by his incorporation of pulp material and his traduction of mimetic conventions.

What Harrison was doing, in this and subsequent reviews, was extending the range of exemplars to include other writers whose pathbreaking work tended to break down the opposition between sf and mainstream. Some of these enthusiasms (as with Burroughs, often borrowed from the editorial cohort, especially Moorcock) now seem rather curious – for example, the championing of British comic novelist Jack Trevor Story –[10] while others were boldly prescient, such as the passionate rehabilitation of Mervyn Peake.[11] Thanks largely to Harrison's reviews, the range of literary reference in the books section expanded enormously, and it soon became unsurprising to find J. P. Donleavy rubbing shoulders with Avram Davidson, Anthony Burgess with James Blish, Norman Mailer with James Branch Cabell. The overall sense conveyed was of a restless intelligence searching down every scrap of speculative imagination available in the sprawling landscape of modern literature.

And not only literature – following the lead of authors like Ballard, who wrote for *New Worlds* on everything from Surrealism to popular sex manuals,[12] Harrison also devoted reviews to non-fiction titles covering a variety of topics. Under his Joyce Churchill byline, he reviewed William Manchester's *The Arms of Krupp* (1968), a study of Germany's major arms manufacturer, and a series of reprint titles brought out by Paladin, including Timothy Leary's *The Politics of Ecstasy* (1970) and Richard Thayer's *The War Business* (1969).[13] An uneasy alignment of the New Wave with the contemporary counter-culture was evident in these pieces, and in similar reviews by other hands, as the books section began to tackle such issues as the growth of modern militarism and technocracy, the rise of popular pseudoscience and cult religions, and the ongoing psychedelic revolution. The December 1969 issue was perhaps the most interestingly varied and provocative in terms of its coverage, featuring reviews not of fictional works but of Hitler's *Mein Kampf* (1925) by Ballard, of Erich Von Däniken's *Chariots of the Gods* (1968) by Sladek, of Chris Booker's anti-modern screed *The Neophiliacs* (1969) by Moorcock, of an anthology of writings from the underground newspaper *International Times* by Charles Platt, and of David Solomon's *The Marijuana Papers* (1968) by Harrison himself. This book section, combined with the issue's photomontage layouts and the collage-inspired short stories, made it clear that *New Worlds* had travelled far from its sf roots, becoming something rich and strange.

But unfortunately, the journal's days were numbered, and it managed to eke out only four more regular issues (and one subscriber-only issue) before suffering another of its perennial fiscal crises and ceasing publication as a monthly magazine in the spring of 1970.[14] The following year, it was revived as a paperback series, its planned quarterly schedule soon becoming intermittent and eventually petering out in 1976. Harrison continued as Books Editor throughout, from *New Worlds Quarterly #1* to *New Worlds 10* (actually whole number 211, including the original magazine), and although the review section tended to lose its urgent immediacy and its broad range of commentary due to its delayed and more infrequent appearances, Harrison cleverly adapted to the new situation by soliciting – and himself producing – more in-depth literary essays that expounded at length on the aesthetics and politics of speculative literature. Freed from the pressures of monthly coverage, he and the handful of reviewers he employed could be both more judicious in their selection of targets and more expansive in their critiques. At the same time, because the paperback series was being categorized as science fiction by its publishers, Harrison was compelled to turn his attention back to the genre after over a year of building a broader cultural-critical conspectus. Far from feeling constrictive, the effect was positively galvanizing.

It was during this period that John Clute came into his own as a critic, generating for Harrison a number of quirky, penetrating and ambitious articles that have since been gathered into his first collection of non-fiction, *Strokes* (1988). Until the publication of *Parietal Games* (Bould and Reid, 2005), Harrison's similarly audacious and incisive review essays were neglected, which is unfortunate because, taken all-together, they amount to one of the most seriously purposed, broadly synthesizing arraignments of genre sf ever committed to paper. In essence, Harrison used these pieces to work out in fuller detail the implicit aesthetic philosophy that had always underpinned his writing for the magazine. Earnest yet simmering with irony, these essays grapple with the difficult question that lay at the heart of the *New Worlds* project: can science fiction possibly be redeemed?

Reading them in their original sequence is illuminating because it reveals the steady evolution of a first-rate critical mind building a sweeping cumulative indictment against the genre. 'A Literature of Comfort' began the bill of particulars by asking how it was that a field of writing claiming to trace its roots to intellectual giants like H. G. Wells could have 'degenerate[d] so quickly into a literature of shoddy, programmed pap' (Harrison, 1971b: 183). The answer was simple: both its authors and its audience preferred the pleasant repetition of story formulae – 'a body of warm, familiar assumptions, reiterated from book to book and serving the same purpose as "once upon a time"' (Harrison, 1971b: 183) – to the harsh light of contemporary reality. For all its pretence of tough-mindedness, sf was ultimately craven and soft, soothing its readers instead of challenging them. The failure of books like L. P. Davies's *Genesis Two* (1969) and Poul Anderson's *Tau Zero* (1970), titles here under review, was as much ethical as aesthetic – a preference for comforting fantasy over the painful truths of life. By contrast, Ballard's *The Atrocity Exhibition* (1970), while undeniably fantastic, had 'an unshakable basis in observed reality': 'Ballard constructs his fantasy from elements to be found all around us, the architectures and cultures and life-styles of the twentieth-century: his end product may be thoroughly alien, but it sends disturbing pseudopods and nerve-fibers back into the world we inhabit' (Harrison, 1971b: 188).

This notion that 'fantasy' writing should be judged ultimately as a kind of refracted mimesis, grounded in and authenticated by experience, gained substance and resolution in subsequent essays. In 'By Tennyson Out of Disney', Harrison tackled the cult of Tolkien then sprouting up around him; acknowledging that he himself had enjoyed *The Lord of the Rings* as a boy, he now, upon mature reflection, believed its readerly pleasures to be petty and corrupt: 'Like Disney, Tolkien presents us with stability and comfort and safe catharsis'

rather than 'the beautiful chaos of reality' (Harrison, 1971a: 188).
Like all heroic fantasy, it achieved its effects by a process of emotional
abstraction from the mundane truths of human struggle and suffering; pretending to ennoble experience by idealizing it, it in fact systematically falsified in a particularly dangerous way, as may be seen
in the trilogy's many scenes of majestic combat: 'you can't construct
a bloodletting from stirring speeches and splendid but vaguely-delin-
eated charges; and if you haven't the foundation of a palpable battle,
an affair of torn arteries and maimed horses, then your heroisms are
void, your battle-songs hollow' (Harrison, 1971a: 187). By contrast,
Peake's *Gormenghast* drew its sustenance from the real, however distorted the representation; it offered not a pleasing wish fulfilment,
but a metaphorical displacement, via Gothic fantasy, of believably
human flaws and foibles.

Harrison's next essay, 'The Black Glak', took up this idea that fantasy was inherently suspect unless embedded in the actual. What
became clearer in this piece was Harrison's firm conviction that the
credibility of fantastic literature resided finally in its fidelity to character, to the conscious goals and unconscious motives of recognizably human beings – 'no mouthpieces for philosophies, no fascination with gadgets ... We are eavesdropping, not listening to a lecture.
Because the story comes out of the characters' (Harrison, 1972a:
217–18).[15] The following essay, 'The Problem of Sympathy', powerfully expanded this argument. Here, Harrison argued that the tactic
of inviting readerly 'identification' with viewpoint characters, a narrative technique sf shared with other forms of popular writing, did
serve to engender a sympathetic orientation towards that character,
but this emotional attunement was vague and etiolated by comparison with the honest empathy provoked by a less manipulative, more
humanely observational approach: 'While sf is amply provided with
hero-identification ... it is relatively – and tragically – free from any
sympathy with, for or between real human beings' (Harrison, 1972b:
6). Indeed, many sf readers were likely to 'feel more compassion for
a machine – Asimov's robots, the sentient bomb of Van Vogt – than
a human being' (Harrison, 1972b: 11). This was the ultimate moral

poverty of the genre: its embrace of gleaming hardware expressed an escapist urge to reject the messy flux of embodied life.

While Harrison's intellectual foils up to this point had been individual works of genre sf, which he rebuked and ridiculed with a kind of lugubrious relish, his next essay, 'To the Stars and Beyond on the Fabulous Anti-Syntax Drive', took on a text that fought back – or tried to. Donald A. Wollheim's *The Universe Makers* (1971) was, in part, an attempt to defend 'genuine' sf against what this long-time fan and professional editor saw as the depredations of the New Wave cohort, which had introduced into the field a pessimistic anti-science subjectivism – not to mention 'shock words and shock scenes, hallucinatory fantasies, and sex' (Harrison, 1973b: 105).[16] Unfortunately, Wollheim's basic illiteracy – his muddled thinking and mangled prose – rendered this attack fundamentally toothless, and indeed, watching Harrison take the book apart with glib efficiency, one almost begins to feel sorry for this 'uncouth clannish lout lumbering about the confines of the genre' (Harrison, 1973b: 238), tilting at the windmills of change.

Yet Harrison was after bigger game here – the entire genre mindset that Wollheim's tortured manifesto evoked. The routinized pleasures of the 'habitual consumer', who 'admits that his world is small, but will permit no widening of his horizons', and who lashes out at outsiders in a misguided 'defense of the nest' (Harrison, 1973b: 236–7), was easy prey, according to Harrison, to the corrupt blandishments of cynical hacks monotonously churning out product. More disturbingly, both were linked in a tribal subculture that fled from the world into messianic delusions based on quack science and technocratic mysticism; convinced of their destiny to colonize the stars in an exalted arc of posthuman striving, these geeky overmen harboured borderline-fascist fantasies of omniscient empowerment: 'finally the great body of science fictional evidence, this incredible pulp encyclopedia, points the way to Universal domination, racial and personal immortality and The Answer' (Harrison, 1973b: 237). Though his tone was mocking, Harrison was deadly serious; in future his own fiction would persistently take up, and meditate upon, this dubious ambition to transcend mortal experience, from Isobel Avens's radical surgery in *Signs of Life* to Seria Mau Genlicher's fusion with a K-Ship in *Light* – a grandiose but ultimately self-mutilating longing Harrison sensed in Wollheim's 'militant, evangelistic, faintly embarrassing' (Harrison, 1973b: 234) mash-note to traditional sf.

In his next essay, 'Filling Us Up', Harrison dismantled another key contention of Wollheim's tract: that 'true' sf maintained at its core a faithfulness to science. As Harrison showed through caustic demolitions of novels by John Rackham, Michael G. Coney and Charles Eric Maine, the scientific references in most sf amounted to little better than 'a muck of colloquialisms and jargon words used outside their proper context' (Harrison, 1973a: 254).[17] Rather than the open-minded, sceptical posture characteristic of rigorous inquiry, these texts operated via 'pontification, achieved through disembodied mouthpieces' (Harrison, 1973a: 257). While his targets were perhaps sitting ducks, Harrison's point was telling: the main claim sf had to realism, its nominal grounding in science, was bogus; in fact, this pretence merely rationalized the genre's endemic vacuity of character, since the people in its stories were programmatically secondary to the half-baked ideas. Based on this reasoning, Harrison, in his essay 'Absorbing the Miraculous', chastised Anne McCaffrey's *To Ride Pegasus* (1973) for its subordination of human interest to the palliatives of pseudoscientific drivel; indeed, the mass of humanity is treated in the book 'with a chilling absence of interest unless some obstructive stupidity or dancing bear antic of theirs is necessary to the plot' (Harrison, 1974: 225).[18]

Harrison was clearly coming to believe that sf in fact despised real human beings. His next essay, 'Coming to Life', argued that mundane experience was being systematically effaced in the genre, growing 'progressively more streamlined and vestigial as the Great Research bears its fruit and the genre manufactures formula after magic formula' designed to 'solve' (i.e., wish away) the ineradicable problems of mortality (Harrison, 1975a: 212).[19] Faced with the cheerful inhumanity of Robert Heinlein's *Farnham's Freehold* (1964), which reduced its characters to mere puppets of the author's imperial will, Harrison's aesthetic sensibilities – though not his critical faculties – all but quailed in horror. 'At times', he bleakly remarked, 'there can be sensed at the hub of the genre something so repellent, so intolerably fixated and vacuous that you don't know quite whether to choke or laugh' (Harrison, 1975a: 217).[20] Yet as the title of his essay suggested, there were yet reasons for hope, especially in the short fiction of New Wave stalwart Disch, whose collection *Getting into Death* (1974) effectively counterbalanced Heinlein's nihilism with the compassionate irony of a truly humanist sf.

Harrison's final essay for the paperback series, 'Sweet Analytics', was a fitting capstone, since it was the most wide-ranging and synthetic of the entire sequence.[21] In some of his recent pieces, the reviewing function had basically become vestigial, subordinated to Harrison's broader aesthetic and ethical concerns; here, he abandoned the review format entirely in favour of a small treatise on the mounting 'misuse of fantasy' (Harrison, 1975b: 214) in contemporary culture. His target was two-fold: on the one hand, the tendency of certain works of sf and fantasy to become, for their obsessive fans, all-consuming substitutes for reality; and on the other hand, the increasing incidence of science-fictional ideas metastasizing into popular cult religions. Both trends took genre escapism to its logical conclusion, erecting wholesale alternatives to the real, whether in the form of fictions 'so lavish, so detailed and so long that they provide a complete "world" for their audience' (Harrison, 1975b: 212), replete with phony maps and imaginary languages, or of blueprints for fringe-culture fanaticism, including 'Geller's telekinesis, Von Daniken's visiting aliens, Manson's open use of elements from Heinlein's *Stranger in a Strange Land*' (Harrison, 1975b: 211). Whether 'crank-cult' or 'crank-fiction', the outcome was the same: a rejection of life as it is lived, in all its randomness and complexity, in favour of 'some more or less easily-grasped handle by which to pick up the universe' (Harrison, 1975b: 212).

What began as an indictment of sf's specific evasions of reality had grown, by this essay, into a critique of the widespread social embrace of comforting myths. In a fascinating move, Harrison traced the roots of this propensity to a growing disillusionment with modern science and the materialist culture it had spawned; its despoliation of the earth, and its abdication of spiritual values, had driven a large sector of the public into the soothing arms of crackpots and hacks. Reflecting the unsparing character of his critique, Harrison not only faulted Moorcock for his complicity in this scenario, his Elric fantasies rivalling Tolkien and *Star Trek* in their production of dreamy devotees, but also blamed himself for his youthful credulity, his adolescent fondness for Arthurian daydreams. The fiction Harrison began to write at this time, especially the stories that would later be gathered in *The Ice Monkey and Other Stories* (1983), expressly thematized this issue of the dubious allure of fantasy, its seduction of vulnerable individuals into fraudulent mindscapes, where they were immured and ethically neutralized. Clearly, he had found, in his relentless interrogation of sf's characteristic delusions, a way to write *about* fantasy without succumbing to its blandishments and shams.

In his 1989 *Foundation* essay, 'The Profession of Fiction', Harrison summed up the mature aesthetic credo incubated in his writings for *New Worlds*. Given that the production of fantasy was by definition an act of falsification, the only way to write it honestly was to subvert its spell – hence, the narrative disruptions in the later Viriconium stories, the seeping of mundane life between the cracks of otherworldly illusion. This subversion was an ethical duty fantasy authors owed their readers, given the escapist pitfalls built into the enterprise. Traditional sf had abdicated this responsibility: rather than endowing readers with a fresh perception of the real, it instead provided 'a cheap relaxing substitute for the excitement that has gone out of life through usage' (Harrison, 1992: 149).[22] There was something inherently sinister about genre fiction's appeal to juvenile minds, its cultivation of a blissful neverland as an alternative to the cares and rigours of adult experience. Some fans stayed trapped in these romantic fancies forever: 'A permanent escape, a feeling that you have given life the slip, is pathological, or anyway very sad' (Harrison, 1992: 148).

This richly analytic and passionately argued essay, one of the most thoughtful self-examinations ever offered by a practicing sf writer, would almost certainly not have been possible absent Harrison's eight-year stint at the helm of the *New Worlds* book section, where he was able to test out and refine his hardnosed vision of the field. Yet Harrison, ever the wary anarchist, had by the 1980s begun to look askance at the whole New Wave project and his role within it, to question its certainties as he had those of old-style sf. Lamenting the youthful romanticism of his erstwhile comrades-in-arms, Harrison acknowledged that genre fiction had proven much more intractable to change than the *New Worlds* cohort had imagined: 'popular fiction had an inertia, a doggedness, we could never have predicted' (Harrison, 1992: 141). In contemporary interviews, Harrison was even more sceptical about the putative achievements of the New Wave, remarking that his own fiction, since the mid-1970s, had deliberately moved away from *New Worlds* topics and styles. 'The range of subject matter which it was acceptable to write about if you were a new-wave author had become very limited', he has said, 'and I found that cramping' (Kincaid, 1986: 32). Always an enemy of literary orthodoxies, Harrison wanted to be seen as a *writer* rather than as a '*New Worlds* writer.

In more recent interviews, Harrison's perspective has mellowed, and he has come to a greater appreciation for what the New Wave set out to accomplish, even if its purposed renovation of the genre was ultimately modest in its effects.

> *New Worlds* helped make me who I am: but relatively little of *New Worlds* survives in who I am. I took a lot away from the New Wave – we all did – and I'm fantastically grateful for the experience. But very few of us survivors are dependent on that experience any more. That's the nature of life. *New Worlds* published some of the best generic – and the earliest post-generic – fiction of its day. The New Wave exploded F/SF out of the grip of a tired regime of control-freaks who were terrified of everything from foreigners to their own sexuality. I'm proud to have been a small part of that. But because I was an enthusiast and a latecomer, I rather got absorbed by the myth of it, which later came to seem stifling. (Chouinard, 2002: n.p.)[23]

In essence, Harrison had allowed the New Wave to become his own personal fantasy, a dream of insurrection into which he entered with all the inchoate passion of youth, but which eventually collided with the obdurate lineaments of the real. Yet in his dogged commitment to a more ethically committed and aesthetically sophisticated sf – expressed as much through his reviews and essays as through his fictional work – he has contributed immeasurably to the maturation of a popular genre which, while it still nurtures fantasy, has been compelled more and more, willy-nilly, to speak about (and to) the world we live in.

Acknowledgement

A slightly different version of this essay appeared in Mark Bould and Michelle Reid (eds) *Parietal Games: Critical Writings by and on M. John Harrison* (London: SFF, 2005). We are grateful to the author and to the Science Fiction Foundation for permission to reprint it here.

Notes

1 Not to mention the poetry and visual material. Greenland (1983), still the only book-length study of the New Wave, focuses almost exclusively on the fiction published in *New Worlds*, bringing in other work only to shed light on this primary corpus – as when he discusses Ballard's essay on Surrealism, 'The Coming of the Unconscious' (published in the July 1966 issue), in relation to the author's own literary methods (Greenland, 1983: 106). For a discussion of the magazine's highly innovative visual design, see Latham (2011).

2 Such impromptu decisions were not unusual in the laid-back environment Moorcock sustained around the magazine. During her visit to London for the 1965 World Science Fiction Convention, Judith Merril (1966: 42) reported on the scene for *The Magazine of Fantasy and Science Fiction*: 'Mike Moorcock, of *New Worlds*, holds virtual open house for his contributors in the living-room-office of his London flat ... and sometimes still picks up the guitar ... and wails a wild stomping blues'. Harrison has acknowledged that 'there was a certain amount of rock 'n' roll lifestyle, obviously' (Hudson, 2002: n.p.) – a lifestyle that would find its way into his fiction when he based one of the starship crews in his space opera *The Centauri Device* (1975) on a hard-rock band, Hawkwind, with which Moorcock was sometimes associated.

3 Unlike Harrison, Moorcock had emerged from the ranks of fandom, and many of his editorial decisions – such as appointing the cantankerous Harrison as books editor, where he was sure to infuriate fans with his uncompromising attacks on traditional sf – were deliberate provoca-

tions designed to generate an outraged response. For a discussion of how Moorcock's avant-garde agenda reverberated within the fan community at the time, see Latham (2005c).

4 Perhaps reflecting the messianic nature of their project, the magazine's editors tended to favour *noms-de-plume* with the portentous initials JC – as in Moorcock's alter-ego James Colvin, which he used for reviews and some fiction. The most celebrated JC in *New Worlds* was the journal's redoubtable mascot, Jerry Cornelius, whose chameleonic adventures were chronicled by most of the editorial enclave, including Harrison (see Moorcock and Jones, 1971).

5 For more on this point, see Latham (2005a). Harrison has admitted that he was 'not as balanced' in his attitudes towards sf as 'most of the other *New Worlds* writers and editors' (Fowler, 1981: 8), and Clute (1995: 431) has remarked upon Harrison's 'long campaign to strip his fantasy and sf of all the dreck and maya that clog its origins – of all the garish and risible escapism which makes laughingstocks in the real world of those of us who, long after we've managed to survive puberty or menarche, still read the stuff".

6 Harrison would later dedicate the American edition of his 1982 novel *In Viriconium*, retitled *The Floating Gods*, to Leiber, who is usually seen as the pioneer of the moody, picaresque breed of sword-and-sorcery that several *New Worlds* writers, from Moorcock to Harrison himself, would essay. For a discussion of the Viriconium series as a metafictional take on genre models, see Latham (2002).

7 Harrison was reviewing Dick's *Our Friends from Frolix 8* (1970).

8 See Harrison's (1970: 32) review of Silverberg's novel *Thorns* (1967) as a model of 'careful prose, discerning sympathy and tight control'.

9 Moorcock's championing of Burroughs extended back to a testy letter to the *Times Literary Supplement* protesting a negative review of *Naked Lunch*; the review, and the heated exchange it generated, have been reprinted in British editions of the novel and are also available in Skerl and Lydenberg (1991: 41–51).

10 Harrison's (1972b: 9) defense of Story's work as the persistent 'location, isolation, and subsequent refining of the fantasies implicit in reality' appeared in *New Worlds Quarterly 4* – issue 205 of the journal, now published in book form (in the UK by Sphere). Moorcock had serialized Jack

Trevor Story's marginally-sf novel *The Wind in the Snottygobble Tree* in the November 1969 to February 1970 issues of *New Worlds*.

11 Harrison's coverage of Peake may be found in Harrison (1969e), which reviews the *Gormenghast* trilogy (1946–59), and Harrison (1969b), which treats Peake's novella 'Boy in Darkness' (1956). Moorcock's long-standing advocacy had been instrumental in getting Peake's work, which had lapsed into obscurity, reprinted during the 1960s, as a neo-Gothic counterweight to what he saw as the cloying sweetness of Tolkien's *The Lord of the Rings* (1954–55), then enjoying a heyday in paperback. For his idiosyncratic views of modern fantasy in general, see Moorcock (1987).

12 Ballard (1969) is, for example, a review of Stephan Gregory's book *How to Achieve Sexual Ecstasy* (1969).

13 See Harrison (1969c) and (1970a), respectively.

14 Moorcock (1979) details this sad and trying history.

15 A similar argument for the centrality of character in a fully mature sf is made by Ursula K. Le Guin (1976).

16 For a discussion of the reaction against the *New Worlds* movement, of which Wollheim's book was a signal example, see Latham (2005b).

17 This review appeared in the US in *New Worlds 5*, published as *New Worlds 6* in the UK, indicating a further breakdown in the publishing schedule and precipitating a mess for bibliographers.

18 This essay appeared in the US in *New Worlds 6*, published in the UK as *New Worlds 7*. As he had done a few times during its publication as a large-format slick, Moorcock, burned out by the constant pressure of having to revive the foundering journal again and again, surrendered the editorial reins, this time to Charles Platt and Hilary Bailey.

19 This essay appeared in *New Worlds 8: The Science Fiction Quarterly*, edited by Bailey; by this point, the 'quarterly' designation in the book's subtitle was merely a cruel joke.

20 Harrison had earlier vented his fury in a symposium on 'Heinlein After 30 Years' published in the great British fanzine *Speculation*: 'One could forgive the rotten prose, forget the whole sordid bag of "professional" gimmicks, even regard his blatant crypto-Fascist militarism with a certain amount of amusement, if it were not for the tragic receptivity of his audience – their adolescent *need* for this sort of comfort ... How many little plastic models of himself has Heinlein created, and each one

primed to zip out and implement the savage bipolar creed? The answer is Chicago' (Harrison, 1969a: 31). The entire diatribe, which runs to several paragraphs, is a breathtaking display of invective.

21 This was the critical piece by Harrison that Moorcock selected for inclusion in the retrospective anthology *New Worlds* (1983).

22 Harrison was here drawing explicitly on Russian Formalist ideas regarding the operation of poetic estrangement; indeed, many of Harrison's stories of the 1980s – such as 'The Horse of Iron and How We Can Know It and Be Changed By It Forever' (1989) – were expressly informed by structural-linguistic theory.

23 For a similar assessment of the achievements of the *New Worlds* enterprise, see Morgan (2003).

Works Cited

Ballard, J. G. (1964) 'Myth Maker of the 20th Century', *New Worlds* 142: 121–7.

Ballard, J. G. (1969) 'Use Your Vagina', *New Worlds* 191: 58–60.

Bould, Mark and Michelle Reid (eds) (2005) *Parietal Games: Critical Writings by and on M. John Harrison*. London: SFF.

Chouinard, Gabriel (2002) 'A Conversation with M. John Harrison', *SF Site*, accessed 20 June 2018, http://www.sfsite.com/12b/mjh142.htm

Clute, John (1988) *Strokes: Essays and Reviews 1966–1986*. Seattle, WA: Serconia.

Clute, John (1995) 'M. John Harrison', in *Look at the Evidence: Essays and Reviews*. Liverpool: Liverpool University Press.

Fowler, Christopher (1981) 'The Last Rebel: An Interview with M. John Harrison', *Foundation: The Review of Science Fiction* 23: 5–30.

Greenland, Colin (1983) *The Entropy Exhibition: Michael Moorcock and the British 'New Wave' in Science Fiction*. London: Routledge & Kegan Paul.

Harrison, M. John (as Joyce Churchill) (1968a) 'The Angle of Attack', *New Worlds* 185: 58–60.

Harrison, M. John (1968b) 'A Devil of a Job', *New Worlds* 185: 60–2.

Harrison, M. John (1969a) Contribution to the 'Heinlein After 30 Years' symposium, *Speculation* 24: 31.

Harrison, M. John (1969b) 'The Boy from Vietnam'. *New Worlds* 191: 60–1.

Harrison, M. John (as Joyce Churchill) (1969c) 'The Cannon Kings', *New Worlds* 189: 59, 61–2.

Harrison, M. John (as Joyce Churchill) (1969d) 'Come Alive – You're in the William Sansom Generation', *New Worlds* 194: 30–1.

Harrison, M. John (1969e) 'Mr. Throd and the Wise Old Crocodile'. *New Worlds* 188: 59–60.

Harrison, M. John (as Joyce Churchill) (1969f) 'Paperbag'. *New Worlds* 192: 61–2.

Harrison, M. John (1969g) 'The Tangreese Gimmick'. *New Worlds* 195: 31–2.

Harrison, M. John (1969g) 'Trouble at t' White House'. *New Worlds* 187: 59–60.

Harrison, M. John (as Joyce Churchill) (1970) 'Broaden Your Horizons', *New Worlds* 199: 28–9.

Harrison, M. John (1970) 'The Wireless School', *New Worlds* 197: 32.

Harrison, M. John (1971a) 'By Tennyson Out of Disney', in Michael Moorcock (ed.) *New Worlds Quarterly 2*, pp. 185–9. New York: Berkley.

Harrison, M. John (1971b) 'A Literature of Comfort', in Michael Moorcock (ed.) *New Worlds Quarterly 1*, pp. 182–90. New York: Berkley.

Harrison, M. John (1972a) 'The Black Glak', in Michael Moorcock (ed.) *New Worlds Quarterly 3*, pp. 214–19. New York: Berkley.

Harrison, M. John (1972b) 'The Problem of Sympathy', in Michael Moorcock (ed.) *New Worlds Quarterly 4*, pp. 5–11. New York: Berkley.

Harrison, M. John (1973a) 'Filling Us Up', in Michael Moorcock and Charles Platt (eds) *New Worlds 5*, pp. 253–61. New York: Avon.

Harrison, M. John (1973b) 'To the Stars and Beyond on the Fabulous Anti-Syntax Drive', in Michael Moorcock (ed.) *New Worlds Quarterly 5*, pp. 234–9. London: Sphere.

Harrison, M. John (1974) 'Absorbing the Miraculous', in Charles Platt and Hilary Bailey (eds) *New Worlds 6*, pp. 221–7. New York: Avon.

Harrison, M. John (1975a) 'Coming to Life', in Hilary Bailey (ed.) *New Worlds 8: The Science Fiction Quarterly*, pp. 211–17. London: Sphere.

Harrison, M. John (1975b) 'Sweet Analytics', in Hilary Bailey (ed.) *New Worlds 9*, pp. 206–14. London: Corgi.

Harrison, M. John (1992) 'The Profession of Fiction', in Maxim Jakubowski and Edward James (eds) *The Profession of Science Fiction: Writers on their Craft and Ideas*, pp. 140–53. London: Macmillan.

Hudson, Patrick (2002) 'Disillusioned by the Actual: M. John Harrison', *The Zone*, accessed 20 June 2018, http://www.zone-sf.com/mjharrison.html

Kincaid, Paul (1986) 'M. John Harrison', *Interzone* 18: 31–2, 58.

Latham, Rob (2002) 'M. John Harrison', in Darren Harris-Fain (ed.) *British Fantasy and Science-Fiction Writers Since 1960*, pp. 227–38. Detroit: Gale.

Latham, Rob (2005a) '"The Job of Dissevering Joy from Glop": John Clute's *New Worlds* Criticism', in Farah Mendlesohn (ed.) *Portals: A Festchrift for John and Judith Clute*, pp. 28–39. Baltimore, MD: Old Earth Press.

Latham, Rob (2005b) 'The New Wave', in David Seed (ed.) *A Companion to Science Fiction*, pp. 202–16. Oxford: Blackwell.

Latham, Rob (2005c) '*New Worlds* and the New Wave in Fandom: Fan Culture and the Reshaping of Science Fiction in the Sixties', *Vector: The Critical Journal of the British Science Fiction Association* 242: 4–12.

Latham, Rob (2011) 'Assassination Weapons: The Visual Culture of New Wave Science Fiction', in Rudolf Kuenzli and Kembrew McLeod (ed.) *Cutting Across Media: Interventionist Collage and the Politics of Appropriation*, pp. 276–89. Durham, NC: Duke University Press.

Le Guin, Ursula K. (1976) 'Science Fiction and Mrs. Brown', in Peter Nicholls (ed.) *Science Fiction at Large*, pp. 13–33. London: Gollancz.

Merril, Judith (1966) 'Books', *The Magazine of Fantasy and Science Fiction* 30(1): 39–45.

Moorcock, Michael (1964) 'A New Literature for the Space Age', *New Worlds* 142: 2–3.

Moorcock, Michael (1973) 'Afterword', in Michael Moorcock and Charles Platt (eds) *New Worlds 5*, pp. 263. New York: Avon.

Moorcock, Michael (1979) '*New Worlds*: A Personal History', *Foundation* 15: 5–18.

Moorcock, Michael (1987) *Wizardry and Wild Romance: A Study of Epic Fantasy*. London: Gollancz.

Moorcock, Michael and Langdon Jones (eds) (1971) *The Nature of the Catastrophe*. London: Hutchinson.

Morgan, Cheryl (2003) 'Interview: M. John Harrison', *Strange Horizons*, accessed 20 June 2018, http://strangehorizons.com/non-fiction/articles/interview-m-john-harrison/

Skerl, Jennie and Robin Lydenberg (eds) (1991) *William S. Burroughs At the Front: Critical Reception, 1959-1989*. Carbondale: Southern Illinois University Press.

Wollheim, Donald A. (1971) *The Universe Makers: Science Fiction Today*. New York: Harper & Row.

'THERE HAVE BEEN MANY VIRICONIUMS'
FROM THE PASTEL CITY TO LONDON

Paul Kincaid

We begin with ruins. In 'A Shropshire Lad' (1896), A. E. Housman wrote:

> The gale, it plies the saplings double,
> It blows so hard, 'twill soon be gone:
> To-day the Roman and his trouble
> Are ashes under Uricon. ('A Shropshire Lad', XXXI, 17–20)

'Uricon' reappears in Wilfred Owen's 'Uriconium: An Ode' (1913):

> Under the sun is nothing wholly new
> At Viricon today
> The village anvil rests on Roman base. ('Uriconium: An Ode', 74–6)

The same place acquires yet another name in Mary Webb's 'Viriconium' (1928):

> Virocon – Virocon –
> Still the ancient name rings on
> And brings, in the untrampled wheat,
> The tumult of a thousand feet. ('Viriconium', 1–4)

The place referred to as Uricon, Viricon, Virocon, Uriconium and Viriconium was once the fourth largest town in Roman Britain,

Viriconium Cornoviorum. By the fourth century the name had transmuted into Uriconium, and today it is known as Wroxeter, a form of the name that has not, I think, been appropriated by M. John Harrison. Viriconium was founded as a fortification in the middle of the first century AD to control the local Cornovii people, whose main base seems to have been a hillfort on the Wrekin. It quickly grew into a town, but went into sharp decline once the legions left and was abandoned in the seventh century. The site remained farmland until antiquarians began to take an interest in the mid-nineteenth century, so there are no later accretions to muddy the picture, but there is not much left: a part of one wall, the foundations of a large bath house, a latrine and part of a forum. Near where the furnace heated the bath house, there remains a small amount of pastel-coloured plaster adhering to one wall. It is, in other words, a blank canvas, though one that has, as Housman, Owen and Webb attest, proved mutable and appealing to the imagination.

This mutability, this blankness upon which any shape might be inscribed, is the key characteristic of Harrison's Viriconium, a setting he used for a sequence of three novels and ten short stories written over some twenty years. The earliest, 'Lamia Mutable' (1972), was written in March 1967, a year before his first acknowledged story, 'Baa Baa Blocksheep' (1968), appeared in *New Worlds*; the most recent, 'A Young Man's Journey to Viriconium' (1985), appeared during a transitional moment when, as he later conceded, 'I had been ready to give it up' (Harrison, 2005a: 149). Viriconium is the one constant throughout the formative period of his career, yet it is the very inconstancy of Viriconium, the denial of familiarity and continuity, that makes these stories such a remarkable mirror within which we might glimpse the emerging shape of Harrison as a writer.

The inconstancy extends beyond the ever-shifting cast, chronology and landscape of the stories to their very presentation. The ten stories that constitute a quarter of the sequence are gathered in two overlapping collections; both are called *Viriconium Nights*, but there are significant differences not only in the contents of each,[1] but also in their order.[2] In other words the sequence in which we encounter these stories, the expectations we might take from one to the next, are deliberately disordered. Though the name Viriconium (with transparent variations) continues across all of them, though we regularly visit the Bistro Californium or meet tegeus-Cromis, we cannot assume that the names apply to the same place or person. Rather, each iteration is a complete reinvention, restructuring, remaking of what has gone before. Harrison describes Viriconium as 'a theory about the power-structures culture is designed to hide; an allegory of language, how it can only fail; the statement of a philosophical (not to say ethological) despair' (Harrison, 2005b: 246). In this light, I will explore how a city built of words can be never the same and is always the same, and thus reflect the evolution of Harrison's writing style.

Across all the stories, we see the city imagining itself into existence. It constantly tries different combinations of the same ingredients, with no concessions to history or geography, and the result is ever the same and ever different. Harrison most admires fiction that 'refuse[s] to explain itself and subvert[s] traditional understandings of purpose and closure, expecting its readers to become active participants in the creation of meaning' (Freeman, 2005: 277). Emphasizing the literary character, the constructed nature, of the work, Harrison says of the great modern fantasies: they 'were books, which means that the one thing they actually weren't was countries with people in them' (Harrison, 2005b: 245). Commercial fantasies despoiled this by literalizing the realm of fantasy, making it safe and controllable, more like a country than a book. Harrison's enterprise, therefore, was anti-fantasy, destroying the comforts of commercial fantasy by deliberately making Viriconium unstable, unlearnable, 'never the same place twice' (Harrison, 2005b: 245). In keeping with modernist ideas derived from Freud and Einstein that the world is relative not absolute, fictional creation can therefore only ever give a partial impression. For Harrison, then, writing fiction is a method of uncovering what the fiction itself is trying to disguise, to 'reveal – for a fraction of a second, to yourself as much as the reader – the world the fictional illusion denies' (Harrison, 2005a: 144). In the Viriconium sequence, Harrison exploits the simple fact that the city is made out of words, words that are infinitely malleable, that can be reshaped and remade each time they are used. And what changes as a consequence is not just the city of Viriconium but also the writer.

At the beginning there was a sense of practising earlier forms: the deconstructed heroic fantasy of *The Pastel City* (1971), the disconnected narrative forms of 'Lamia Mutable' and 'Events Witnessed from a City' (1975), the new wave sensibilities of *A Storm of Wings* (1980). But in that second novel, a passage such as 'A thin skin only, taut as a drumhead, separates us from the future: events leak through it reluctantly, with a faint buzzing sound if they make any noise at all – like the wind in an empty house before rain' (Harrison, 1982b: 33) eerily prefigures *The Course of the Heart* (1992), and Fay Glass, 'wrapped from head to foot in a thick whitish garment and turning aimlessly this way and that like something hanging from a privet branch' (Harrison, 1982b: 130) suggests Anna trapped in *Empty Space* (2012). 'Viriconium Knights' (1981) and 'The Luck in the Head' (1984) share a nightmarish quality with near-contemporary non-sequence stories, for example 'The Incalling' (1978), while 'Strange Great Sins' (1983) and 'The Lords of Misrule' (1984) introduce the Mari Lwyd, the image of the horse's skull that would become the Shrander in *Light* (2002).

I suspect that one of the things that first drew Harrison to this name was that Viriconium had experienced the end of time. It ended its days as a ramshackle Saxon settlement with signs of its former Roman glory inescapable though perhaps incomprehensible all around, and then one day it existed no longer, abandoned to the grass and the sheep. That is the Viriconium we first encounter in Harrison, approaching its end but unable to escape its past, changing yet unable to understand what it has changed from or is changing into:

> Viriconium was never intended to be the same place twice. New kings come and go, new philosophies spring up overnight. The very streets shift from story to story. All that remains, as the earth grows older and the fabric of reality forgets what it is supposed to be, is a whisper of continuity: place names which seem familiar; characters we seem to have heard of before; the imperfect repetition of this or that significant event. Even the name of the city changes. The world is a muddled old woman, obsessed with the futility of action in the face of contin-

gency and an absurd universe. What seemed clear to her yesterday she remembers today only by remaking it. (Harrison, 1984d: ix)

I do not intend to impose a chronological pattern upon the Viriconium stories; in fact, there can be no such pattern.[3] Nor, despite that 'whisper of continuity', do I suggest that the Viriconium of *The Pastel City* is necessarily the same as that of *In Viriconium* (1982); they are necessarily different. But I do want to look at how the shifting character of this inconstant city intimates the changing nature of Harrison's approach to fiction.

Throughout the Viriconium sequence, we are pointed towards the past. The first published iteration of Viriconium as *The Pastel City* is carefully situated in the evening of the world, after the last of the Afternoon Cultures left 'certain technologies that, for good or ill, retained their properties of operation for well over a thousand years' (Harrison, 1974: 5). It is a culture built out of the ruins of a more accomplished age, and the 'wealth of its people lay entirely in salvage' (Harrison, 1974: 5). The emphasis is on the huge sweep of time past, a far future that could as easily be a distant past. It is a world of knights in armour riding on horseback, also of airships and strangely powered weapons. It is a universe that is 'beginning to forget itself, it's beginning to forget how to do, as it were, temporal narrative' (Harrison quoted in Kincaid, 1986: 9). *The Pastel City*'s sense of detachment from time does not just extend throughout the sequence, but is in a way the defining characteristic of the city. This atemporality, even more pronounced in some of the stories, is a deliberate strategy: 'It forces the reader to look for the closure of the story somewhere other than in the narrative' (Harrison quoted in Kincaid, 1986: 9). As we learn towards the end of the novel, resolution of a sort can be achieved only by releasing figures from the past; but it is very much 'of a sort'. The past offers no more of a solution than the future, the absence of time only implies a stalemate, an inertia that is not yet quite the entropy so central to Harrison's best early fiction but prefigures its use as 'a metaphor for the condition that people find themselves in' (Harrison quoted in Kincaid, 1986: 10).

The landscape of dales and crags and meres within which most of *The Pastel City* plays out recalls the north of England. It is a landscape of industrial despoliation, with its 'umber iron-bogs, albescent quicksands of aluminium and magnesium oxide' (Harrison, 1974: 47), foreshadowing the grim, post-industrial wastelands that stand as other planets in *The Centauri Device* (1974). But in our very brief visit to the city of Viriconium we are introduced to 'the Gate of Nigg ... the great radial road Proton Circuit ... the Pastel Towers, tall and gracefully shaped to mathematical curves' (Harrison, 1974: 24). It is a place that shows no great signs of despoliation, despite the fact that in the opening pages of the novel we saw the city being burned. It is a place where streets and strasse, via and rue betray an indiscriminate Europeanism; it contrasts to the bleak northern landscape outside the deliberate cosmopolitanism of T. S. Eliot's 'The Waste Land' (1922), a poem about another 'Unreal City' (Eliot, 1922: 60) that hovers like a tutelary deity over the entire sequence. Such names – *In Viriconium*'s Margarethestrasse and rue Serpolet, for example, and the spot near Mynned where the shrubberies of Hoadenbosk merge with the sinister Montrouge – detach the city from its landscape. It is unanchored in space and time, and 'In miniature, the end of the world' (Harrison, 1974: 97). As in the work of Michael Moorcock (whose *Dancers at the End of Time* (1972–6) trilogy began only a year after *The Pastel City* appeared), the end of time seems to be a point at which all times are recreated. Viriconium is, inevitably, everything and nothing, everywhere, and therefore nowhere. As Harrison explained, 'I never wanted there to be a recognisable period of Viriconium's history as it were. These things should suggest to the reader that it is a temporal collision really' (Kincaid, 1986: 9).

The Pastel City and its pendant story 'The Lamia and Lord Cromis' (1971) are suffused with images that suggest entropy, then so popular among British new wave writers, without yet embracing the concept. The story repeats a passage from the novel, with very slight changes, notably in the names of characters (Birkin Grif becomes Dissolution Kahn; Tomb, Rotgob). It is an early example of Harrison's 'versioning':

like the lamia, their forms are likely to shift; and those who have not yet read the novel may look forward to alterations of name and fate in it. It seems he wrote the short story first, and then, unlike most omnipotent creators, decided to make some amends. (Kushner, 1980: 97)[4]

But, despite their entropic character, neither story nor novel can properly be described as new wave fantasy; rather they are fantasy lightly dusted with new wave sensibility.[5] However, the fact that the entire aesthetic of the novel works against the traditions of fantasy may not always be obvious. In a peculiarly wrong-headed review, John Hobson (1981: 20) described it as a 'thinly disguised tract on behalf of fascism' in which 'the characters are like shadows, fleeting across a background of purple void: sexless, humourless murderers who exist only from one inevitable battle to the next'. What Hobson does capture, though, is an evident dis-ease with the traditions and appurtenances of fantasy without fully escaping them; that can only be achieved as the idea of Viriconium itself breaks down in subsequent works.

We come closer to a true new wave aesthetic in the two stories, 'Lamia Mutable' and 'Events Witnessed from a City', published in the long interval between the first two novels. By far the earliest of the Viriconium stories, 'Lamia Mutable' was eventually published in Harlan Ellison's *Again, Dangerous Visions* (1972) five years after it was written; the city it conceives is, despite some shared landmarks, a very different place from that encountered in *The Pastel City*. Birkin Grif (who is killed in *The Pastel City*) and Lamia (who is killed by Grif's avatar, Dissolution Kahn, in 'The Lamia and Lord Cromis') are reborn as eternal monsters, reminiscing about the horrors they have witnessed, including Pompeii, Gomorrah, Hiroshima and Buchenwald. When Grishkin kills a guard,[6] we are told: 'He has a mother in Australia. He was exported' (Harrison, 1973: 386). In all of this, therefore, there is none of the detachment from our world suggested by the passing of the Afternoon Cultures; indeed Harrison's 'Afterword' explicitly links Viriconium to the here and now, describing it as 'a snide parody of London intellectual life. You can find a Bistro Californium on every

49

street corner in swinging Chelsea or with-it Hampstead: and each one is crowded with aging ravers like Birkin Grif' (Harrison, 1973: 390). *A Storm of Wings* (1980) reiterates this view of the Bistro Californium as a place of 'Philosophers and tinkers; poetry, art, and revolution; princes like vagrants and migrant polemicists with voices soft as a snake's; the absolute beat and quiver of Time' (Harrison, 1982b: 28). Though it is the beat and quiver not so much of ongoing time, but time at a standstill, echoing and repeating itself, time grown stagnant as we will shortly see it in *In Viriconium*.

The philosophers and polemicists, the bravos and mercenaries of the Bistro Californium, in whatever guise it might appear, are all abstract entities struggling to keep their metaphysics warm. Such metaphysics often find expression in direct quotation from Eliot, as when Alstath Fulthor, 'consumed by the feeling that there was nothing to choose between the fevers of his skull and those of the world outside it' hears a voice saying 'I can connect nothing with nothing' while contemplating a Rue Sepile tenement whose 'stairways wound like a tedious argument' (Harrison, 1982b: 54). Nick Freeman (2005: 282) argues that Harrison's echoes of Eliot (here, 'The Waste Land' and 'The Love Song of J. Alfred Prufrock' [1915]) initiate 'chains of association and interconnection throughout [*In Viriconium*], reinforcing the atmosphere of melancholia and listlessness'. I would suggest that Harrison's use of Eliot throughout the sequence represents something broader and more significant. 'The Waste Land' is generally recognized as one of the pre-eminent modernist texts, and one of the key features of the new wave enterprise, particularly as undertaken by Harrison and his fellow *New Worlds* writers, was importing the forms and devices of modernism into sf. Therefore, I read the Viriconium sequence, among other things, as an attempt to express Eliot's Unreal City in terms of the fantastic. It is, at least until *A Storm of Wings*, an exercise in approaching modernism.[7]

The unreality of Viriconium is emphasized by its orthogonal relationship to the familiar world of today, so that eventually it is no surprise that, in 'A Young Man's Journey to Viriconium', someone might contemplate making the passage from Huddersfield to Viriconium. Indeed, although this flatly contradicts the detachment in time suggested by *The Pastel City*, there is a suggestion that others have already made that passage; for example, *In Viriconium*'s Barley brothers are first encountered singing of being 'ousted out of Birmingham and Wolverhampton' (Harrison, 1982a: 17). However, this same specificity, this sense that Viriconium is part and parcel of the mundane world, is accompanied by a loss of understanding, a growing inability to locate one's own place in the world. In the Ash-Flats of Wisdom in 'Lamia Mutable' we are told that 'Long ago there was a war here; or perhaps it was a peace' and that 'Time is overthrown in Wisdom: its very mutability is immutable' (Harrison, 1973: 386, 387).[8]

In 'Events Witnessed from a City' repeated characters are now recognizably archetypes. There has, for instance, to be a dwarf: *The Pastel City*'s Tomb, Rotgob in 'The Lamia and Lord Cromis', Choplogic here, and *In Viriconium*'s The Grand Cairo, but all fulfil the same martial, short tempered role. And the tegeus-Cromis we encounter in this story is in a semi-organic tower that he has tended for seven centuries. These are not the same characters, though they fit into roughly the same part of the narrative.

That Dissolution Kahn and Choplogic begin the story 'discussing the peculiarities of time and the uncertain nature of events' (Harrison, 1984a: 59) tells us that Viriconium is once more detached from time and certainty. There can be nothing solid here. The events witnessed are, in the very first sentence, undermined by uncertainty. Entropy is almost too sure and particular a term for Viriconium; in fact there is something anti-entropic in being told that 'After four millennia motionless on its axis, the Earth had begun to turn again' (Harrison, 1984a: 60). But the resumption of this motion is also the resumption of time; the four millennia of stasis are peculiarly measureless. As in *The Pastel City*, we assume some separation between our here and now and the time of the story, a vast interruption filled by the Afternoon Cultures or by the millennia of motionlessness, and yet within this distant setting we encounter the same characters, Dissolution Khan, Grishkin and the dwarf (whatever name he might go by), that we met in 'Lamia Mutable' where their playground is clearly the familiar landscape of Hiroshima and Buchenwald, Blackpool and Wolverhampton. What separates us is not actual time, because time is just a peculiarity of words, but rather the conscious fictionality of the story. That words are used not to convince us with their verisimilitude but rather to deny such conviction, at once to push us apart and draw us close, is what marks this (and 'Lamia Mutable') as a self-consciously experimental new wave story.

The breaking down of character and narrative continues into the next novel, *A Storm of Wings*. Although the story is placed precisely in time, eighty years after *The Pastel City*, such certainty is instantly undermined. A rapid series of images emphasize the tenebrous nature of the setting: Alstath Fulthor 'stumbled through the arteries of his home, his brain buzzing and vibrating with a new vigor, discovering chambers and oubliettes he had never seen before' (Harrison, 1982b: 14); Viriconium 'attracted him not as a refuge (although he saw himself as a refugee), nor by its double familiarity, but by its long strangeness and obstinacy in the face of Time' (Harrison, 1982b: 17); 'The City is a product of her own dreams, a million years of them' (Harrison, 1982b: 25). And when Hornwrack leaves Rue Sepile he 'bore too obviously the signature of the City, the impassive self-indulgence, the narcissism which precludes compassion' (Harrison, 1982b: 50). Viriconium is starting to change from being a place to being an affect. In broad terms, the geography of the city – the Low City, the Artists' Quarter, and so on – stay roughly the same from one story to the next,[9] but that is no guarantee of solidity. When Tomb returns to the Low City,

> he had for a moment (it was a moment only) a sense of *two* cities, overlapping in a sprawl of moonlit triangles and tangled thoroughfares. This conceit caused him to smile but remained with him nevertheless, quite distinctly, as if he had seen the future as a composite city uninhabited by human beings ... 'As you walk,' the dwarf tried to explain after a single clandestine excursion to the Artists' Quarter, 'the streets create themselves around you. When you have passed everything slips immediately back into chaos again.' (Harrison, 1982b: 144, 149)

Against this disintegrating background, it is perhaps inevitable that the plot should also disintegrate. The story re-enacts that of *The*

Pastel City, but the exoskeleton worn by Tomb the dwarf does not work now, and the reluctant hero tegeus-Cromis is replaced by the unheroic Hornwrack (although he carries Cromis's sword and is seen bearing the metal bird as Cromis had done), and their foe is not a fierce northern army but an invasion of space insects who have no more long-term chance of surviving on Earth than do H. G. Wells's Martians. On their journey north to face this threat, replicating the journey in *The Pastel City*, 'each of us suffered during this northern transit an emptying or bleaching of the identity in preparation for a future we could not describe' (Harrison, 1982b: 103). In fact, as with so much else in this novel, the threat dissipates.

Where *The Pastel City* was heroic fantasy with a new wave overlaying, *A Storm of Wings* is a new wave story that interrogates the affect of heroic fantasy but discards it. Resolution is replaced by dissolution, and the novel ends in the broken speech of Benedict Paucemanly who had 'tried to become something else and failed' and who, teetering 'between two realities ... could perceive neither of them except as an agonizing dream' (Harrison, 1982b: 171); in the disintegrating minds of Fay Glass and Alstath Fulthor, whose 'strange, almost unemotional sexual contacts' (Harrison, 1982b: 137) prefigure the ghostly shapes that haunt *The Course of the Heart*'s Lucas and Pam; and in the dissolving landscapes where 'coast lines had taken on new forms, plastic, curious, undependable' (Harrison, 1982b: 155). Thus the doubling and remaking of Viriconium as witnessed by Tomb, the dislocation in time suggested when we are told 'They prefer now to drift, to surrender themselves to the currents of that peculiar shifting interface between Past, Present, and wholly imaginary' (Harrison, 1982b: 34), are emblematic of the novel as a whole. Indeed this shifting interface marks a change for Harrison: Viriconium had always been a place of temporal uncertainties, but now we find a move towards the unstable currents between time and the imagination that we encounter in *The Course of the Heart* and *Empty Space*.

But even if Viriconium seems less solid in *A Storm of Wings* than it did in *The Pastel City*, it does feel far more substantial than in the third novel, *In Viriconium*. This is no longer the city of warriors like Tomb or Cromis, or even of bravos like Hornwrack. While Ashlyme is entitled to wear a sword, 'he never bothered' (Harrison, 1982a: 9). This is not a city of disintegration and fragmentation but of romantic decay, a city informed by the aesthetic not of the new wave but the new weird (of which *In Viriconium* is perhaps the founding text). It is a city that resists appearance, that remains forever indeterminate. When Ashlyme looks down on the Low City he notes 'some odd quality of the moonlight giving its back and foreground planes equal value, so that it had no perspective but was just a clutter of blue and gamboge roofs filling the space between his eyes and the hills outside the city' (Harrison, 1982a: 10). The doubled city that Tomb glimpsed in *A Storm of Wings* is dissolving. As the plague advances, it is associated with a fog – recalling the fog spread by *A Storm of Wings*' insects – that makes each neighbourhood in turn obscure, and when it finally reaches the High City, Ashlyme notes: 'This psychological disorder of the city was reflected in a new disorder of the streets. It was a city I knew and yet I could not find my way about it' (Harrison, 1982a: 113). Alstath Fulthor's distinction between the fevers in the skull and the fevers in the world has become meaningless; now the fevers of the skull *are* the fevers of the world. Thus when Ashlyme sees the Grand Cairo being chased by his own police, the event soon fades: 'By the time he found himself on familiar ground, the whole event had taken on the distant, unreal air of a scene in an old play' (Harrison, 1982a: 97). The unreal city makes memory impossible, and in Fat Mam Etteilla's fortune-telling pack, the City is equated with Nothingness.

Not just cut loose from geography and appearance, Viriconium is cut loose from time – or perhaps has too much of it. In 'Lords of Misrule', the Yule Greave's house is 'one of those places where the past speaks to us in a language so completely of its own we have no hope of understanding' (Harrison, 1985a: 126). The past is so rich, so full, that it overwhelms the present, rendering the here-and-now no longer fully comprehensible: 'If you stood at the window in the studio at Mynned and looked out towards the Low City, you felt that time was dammed up and spreading out quietly all around you like a stagnant pond' (Harrison, 1982a: 83). Thus we keep coming across passages in which time is distorted, broken up, recombined in new shapes, never whole or consistent. For example, 'In Montrouge the

great characteristic towers of the city, with their geometrical inscrip-
tions and convoluted summits, had been allowed to fall into disrepair
after some long-forgotten civil war' (Harrison, 1982a: 19), presumably the civil war of *The Pastel City*, now so long in the past that it
is forgotten. Yet Audsley King's companion is the fortune teller and
cardsharp, Fat Mam Etteilla, who was killed towards the end of *A
Storm of Wings*. And when Buffo takes Ashlyme to meet an old man
who 'claims to have found living birds whose every feather is made of
metal' (Harrison, 1982a: 28), we are of course reminded of Cellur in
the previous novels, an identification pressed home by the fact that
the only word intelligible on his shop sign is 'Seller'.

This disintegration of time comes to a head with the Grand Cairo's
explanation of the Barley brothers: 'all that remain of a race of magi-
cians or demiurges driven out of Viriconium hundreds or thousands
of years ago in a war with "giant beetles"' (Harrison, 1982a: 73). This
confuses the Reborn Men raised to end the civil war in *The Pastel City*
with the war against the interstellar insects in *A Storm of Wings*, by
which time the Reborn Men had decayed into communal madness.
And this is all placed so far in the past that it has become more myth
than history. Yet the presence of Fat Mam Etteilla and Cellur suggests
that these events are within living memory if not actually contemporary. What the Grand Cairo's story tells us is that the city we encountered in the first two novels was imagined into being. As the poet
Ansel Verdigris puts it, 'Viriconium is a world trying to remember
itself. The dumb stones perform an unending act of recall' (Harrison,
1982b: 83). Trying, and clearly failing; the imagination, the memory,
is faulty. The 'peculiar shifting interface between Past, Present, and
wholly imaginary', first alluded to in *A Storm of Wings* and now the
entire guiding principle of Viriconium, means that bits of the present
float into the past, bits of here relocate to there.

Though *A Storm of Wings* is carefully positioned as a sequel to *The
Pastel City*, the two works have a curiously ahistorical relationship:
The Pastel City is a heroic imagining against which *A Storm of Wings*
is the tawdry and less heroic reality. However, *A Storm of Wings* is itself the imagined, ahistoric past of *In Viriconium*. Each iteration of the
city does not add more detail and make more solid, but rather makes

more tenebrous, more fragile, more like a story of which the teller himself is unsure of the details. As 'Viriconium Knights' explains,

> The world is so old that the substance of reality no longer knows quite what it ought to be. The original template is lost. History repeats over and again this one city and a few frightful events – not rigidly, but in a shadowy, tentative fashion, as if it understands nothing else but would like to learn. (Harrison, 1984c: 50)

And when, in the same story, Ignace Retz sees himself in the tapestry as Lord Cromis, the response is: 'There have been many Viriconiums' (Harrison, 1984c: 51).

In Viriconium marked a change of pace, a change of direction, in Harrison's relationship with fantasy. It coincided with a series of experiments, from 'Running Down' (1975) to 'The New Rays' (1981), which established the shape of his subsequent fiction, and with a time when, he reports, 'I suddenly became me' (cited in Freeman, 2005: 276). The novel, therefore, occupies a slightly uneasy position, looking backward to the other Viriconium stories and forward to the new direction of his fiction. But it remains a fantasy, a secondary world that would be redundant if the new direction had been fully embraced. That approach to fantasy had been comprehensively abandoned by the time Harrison came to write 'A Young Man's Journey to Viriconium'. Despite the title, this is a story that has less to do with Viriconium than with the world of 'The Incalling' or 'Egnaro' (1981) or *The Course of the Heart*. It is not the story of a journey to Viriconium but of an escape from it. The veils of fantasy behind which Harrison's earlier work delves are here ripped away, 'a mediating metaphor no longer technically necessary or philosophically desirable' (Harrison, 2005a: 149), in order to discover how fantasy is a way of writing about the ways we cope with here and now.

Except for one brief and possibly apocryphal account, 'A Young Man's Journey to Viriconium' is not set in Viriconium. It is, rather, a story of post-industrial northern England, Buxton and Huddersfield and Manchester, the sorts of places whose graveyard is crossed in *The Pastel City*. Rather than a landscape trying to remember itself into existence, this is a place where 'People are always pupating their own disillusion, decay, age' (Harrison, 1985b: 149). Viriconium, therefore, becomes a dream of escape from the failures of real life, but it is a dream that itself fails. It is significant that when the story was reprinted in *Things That Never Happen* (2002) the title was changed to 'A Young Man's Journey to London', and every occurrence of the word 'Viriconium' in the story was replaced with 'London'; everything else remained the same. We glimpse the Plaza of Realized Time, Yser Canal and Rue Serpolet, but these are now placed in the familiar city of London rather than the imagined city of Viriconium. Viriconium has become indistinguishable from London, and London and Manchester and Huddersfield are as much cities of the imagination as Viriconium ever was.

In the various and varied iterations of Viriconium, Harrison was not so much writing fantasy as writing about fantasy, and the literary evolution traced through these fictions was a way of finding out what it was he wanted to say about fantasy, and to discover, in the end, that he did not need fantasy to say it.

Notes

1 'Lamia Mutable', 'Events Witnessed from a City' (1975) and 'In Viriconium' (1982) appear only in the 1984 US edition; 'The Dancer from the Dance' (1985) and 'A Young Man's Journey to Viriconium' only in the 1985 UK edition.

2 'The Lamia and Lord Cromis' (1971) comes first in the US edition, second in the UK edition; 'Strange Great Sins' (1983) comes last in the US edition, third in the UK edition.

3 Although there is a suggestion of movement from the distant – whether past or future is irrelevant – to the present in 'A Young Man's Journey to Viriconium', the story that emphatically rounds off the sequence, it is as tenuous, and tenebrous, as the city itself.

4 On versioning, see Ryan Elliott's essay in this collection.

5 The repeated, almost ritualistic descriptions of tegeus-Cromis as 'a tall man, thin and cadaverous ... [who] ... imagined himself a better poet than swordsman' (Harrison, 1974: 9), or 'sometime soldier and sophisticate ... who imagined himself to be a better poet than swordsman'

(Harrison, 1971: 50) provide a clear echo of the disenchanted aesthete who populated Moorcock's Eternal Champion fantasies.

6 The name Grishkin alludes to Eliot's 'Whispers of Immortality' (1919), whose title clearly resonates with the atemporality of Virconium. Though Eliot's poem insists that 'Grishkin is nice'.

7 From *In Viriconium* until 'A Young Man's Journey to Viriconium', Harrison is clearly moving in a new direction, but Eliot is part of Viriconium's DNA and therefore his influence is inescapable.

8 This immutable mutability is what makes Viriconium such fertile ground for Harrison's experiments. In Wisdom, for instance, where 'Eidetic images of ghosts flit on the wind; women weeping weave shrouds at ebb tide; famine-children wail to old men at twilight' (Harrison, 1973: 386), do we get a first taste of the zone we later enter in *Nova Swing* (2006)?

9 Although 'The Luck in the Head' suddenly introduces a gorge: 'On the western side of the gorge (which from above can be seen to divide Uroconium like a fissure in a wart) rise the ruinous towers of the Old City' (Harrison, 1984b: 89).

Works Cited

Eliot, T. S. (1919) 'Whispers of Immortality', accessed 20 June 2018, https://www.poetryfoundation.org/poems/52563/whispers-of-immortality

Eliot, T. S. (1922) 'The Waste Land', accessed 20 June 2018, https://www.poetryfoundation.org/poems-and-poets/poems/detail/47311/the-waste-land

Freeman, Nick (2005) '"All the Cities That There Have Ever Been": *In Viriconium*', in Mark Bould and Michelle Reid (eds) *Parietal Games: Critical Writings by and on M. John Harrison*, pp. 275–89. London: The Science Fiction Foundation.

Harrison, M. John (1971) 'The Lamia and Lord Cromis', in Michael Moorcock (ed.) *New Worlds 1*, pp. 50–69. London: Sphere.

Harrison, M. John (1973) 'Lamia Mutable', in Harlan Ellison (ed.) *Again, Dangerous Visions, volume 2*, pp. 381–90. New York: Signet.

Harrison, M. John (1974) *The Pastel City*. London: New English Library.

Harrison, M. John (1982a) *In Viriconium*. London, Gollancz.

Harrison, M. John (1982b) *A Storm of Wings*. New York: Pocket Books.

Harrison, M. John (1984a) 'Events Witnessed from a City', in *Viriconium Nights*, pp. 59–66. New York: Ace.

Harrison, M. John (1984b) 'The Luck in the Head', in *Viriconium Nights*, pp. 67–95. New York: Ace.

Harrison, M. John (1984c) 'Viriconium Knights', in *Viriconium Nights*, pp. 36–58. New York: Ace.

Harrison, M. John (1984d) 'Author's Note', in *Viriconium Nights*, p. ix. New York: Ace.

Harrison, M. John (1985a) 'The Lords of Misrule', in *Viriconium Nights*, pp. 123–35. London: Gollancz.

Harrison, M. John (1985b) 'A Young Man's Journey to Viriconium', in *Viriconium Nights*, pp. 137–58. London: Gollancz.

Harrison, M. John (2005a) 'The Profession of Science Fiction, 40: The Profession of Fiction', in Mark Bould and Michelle Reid (eds) *Parietal Games: Critical Writings by and on M. John Harrison*, pp.144–54. London: The Science Fiction Foundation.

Harrison, M. John (2005b) 'What Might It Be Like to Live in Viriconium?', in Mark Bould and Michelle Reid (eds) *Parietal Games: Critical Writings by and on M. John Harrison*, pp. 245–6. London: The Science Fiction Foundation.

Hobson, John (1981) 'The Pastel City', *Vector* 104: 20.

Houseman, A. E. (1896) 'A Shropshire Lad', accessed 20 June 2018, http://www.theotherpages.org/poems/housm03.html

Kincaid, Paul (1986) 'A Young Man's Journey from Viriconium: An Interview with M. John Harrison', *Vector* 135: 9–10.

Kushner, Ellen (1980) Introduction, 'The Lamia and Lord Cromus', Ellen Kushner(ed.) *Basilisk*, p. 97. New York: Ace.

Owen, Wilfred (1913) 'Uriconium: An Ode', accessed 20 June 2018, https://www.poemhunter.com/poem/uriconium-an-ode/

Webb, Mary (1928) 'Viriconium', accessed 20 June 2018, https://tspace.library.utoronto.ca/html/1807/4350/poem3211.html

Viriconium Ghostwalk

Graham Fraser

> a breath of the past followed him a little way beyond the
> gate ... overflowing into the alleyways and peeling demimonde av-
> enues of the suburbs where geranium leaves were turning ochre and a
> faint smell like cat's urine issued from the mouldy brick. Viriconium,
> sump of time and alchemical child, sacrificer of children and com-
> forter of ghosts.
>
> (Harrison, 2005f: 151)

> The pathos of this work: there are no periods of decline ... By the
> same token, every city is beautiful to me (from outside its borders).
>
> (Benjamin, 1999: 458)

> Excuse me if I prefer the haunting.
>
> (Harrison, 2014b: n.p.)

Viriconium exists – insofar as it exists – as a series of nested para-
doxes, an intentionally shifting series of incompatible impressions.
Indeed, Harrison argues that Viriconium – like all other literary
'worlds' or 'inscapes' – cannot exist, except as a rhetorical, textual
construct: 'Like all books, Viriconium is just some words' (Harrison,
2001: n.p.). And yet Viriconium *is* a world of sorts. Harrison is explicit about his efforts to write a world that sabotages a reader's efforts
to substitute it for a real one:

I made that world increasingly shifting and complex. You can not learn its rules. More importantly, Viriconium is never the same place twice ... And if its landscapes can't be mapped, its threat of infinite depth (or at least infinite recessiveness) can't be defused, but must be accepted on its own terms. (Harrison, 2001: n.p.)

These terms are emotional, textual and metaphysical, not realistic or cartographic: Viriconium is a topography of desire, nostalgia and inference, constantly overwriting itself and emerging from between its own cracks. Should Viriconium be mistaken by a reader as a destination for an escapist fantasy, the desire to go there is thwarted precisely by the instability of Viriconium's 'there-ness'. There is no there to go to. Viriconium is not so much a place as a condition, even precisely the condition of unattainability itself.

Yet, while such critical pronouncements explain Harrison's intentions in writing the Viriconium texts, they do not fully capture the experience of reading them. Despite abjuring the illusions of knowable realism – in fact, because of it – the city exerts a seductive charisma that must be understood, paradoxically, as a caution against seductive charisma. To navigate this inscape demands not that we resolve its contradictions, but that we embrace them and enter into the spaces between them. There may be no 'there' to go to but by reading these works we do – imaginatively, provisionally – visit.

While Harrison's antipathy towards worldbuilding has commanded attention, less has been paid to the pervasiveness of haunting in his work, especially as a formal, rather than simply thematic, concern. Yet haunting preoccupies his post-Viriconium writings. In a recent blog post titled 'ghost fictions', Harrison's position retroactively resonates (right down to the T. S. Eliot quotation) with Viriconium's spectral nature:

Excuse me if I prefer the haunting. The haunting comes layered up in time. It slips about, guilted and dirty. You can't focus on a thing like that. ... It's inherent in the worn out babble of events. You aren't meant to be able to locate it. 'I do not know whether a man or a woman/But who is that on the other side of you?' The inevitable companion evading itself as hard as it's evading you. (Harrison, 2014b: n.p.)

Unlocatable, constantly eluding perception and memory, the experience of Viriconium is hauntological. The stories may have less explicitly ghostly content than some of Harrisons' subsequent writings,[1] yet they offer a fundamentally spectral *form*. A 'ghost fiction' could be either a fiction about ghosts or a fiction which operates ghostily, regardless of its thematics; as Harrison notes, a flickering, fragmentary story structure can produce 'a story of ghosts, if not an actual ghost story' (Harrison, 2015: n.p.). Taking ghostliness to be a structural quality – a question of narrative and epistemology – resonates with Avery Gordon's insight into the 'ghostly matter' that haunts narratives of the sociological imagination:

> the story must be told in the mode of haunting. ... which is also willy-nilly a mode of experience. Why must the story be told this way?
> Because the story, which is very much alive, is happening in and through haunting. (Gordon, 1997: 131)

Not ghosts but ghostliness is Viriconium's signature: the text itself – the place itself – does the haunting.

To haunt, of course, need not be strictly spectral; 'haunt' is a word rich in meanings as noun, verb and metaphor. One 'haunts' by frequenting a place, by returning to one's 'old haunts'. If that space is a literary 'inscape', then those visits are made by reading. And to be 'haunted', independently of ghostly subject matter, is to be unsettled or obsessed – to have one's imagination endlessly return to the unavailable object of that desire. If what it might be like to live in Viriconium is 'an inappropriate question – a category error' (Harrison, 2001: n.p.), a more apt question may be: what is it like to haunt Viriconium, or be haunted by it?

Viriconium comes to us as a ghost. Haunting its streets and spaces, especially through repeated readings, is a kind of knowing, and the things we discover through such haunted haunting – those things excluded, lost, unacknowledged, shifting, 'guilted and dirty' (Harrison, 2014b: n.p.) – can only be known this way. These are not the things one seeks to 'know' in the 'worldbuilding' model, nor does one know them in the same way. To wander Viriconium's streets by reading them is to undertake a ghostwalk.

***

Walter Benjamin, oddly enough, offers a way in to Viriconium more helpful than Mr Ambrayses' lavatory mirror. His exhaustive, fragmentary *Arcades Project* – the touchstone text of the theory of the flâneur – provides the literary entradista with a surprisingly illuminating guidebook to the dynamics of Harrison's Viriconium Project.[2]

Both Benjamin and Harrison write from a modernist appreciation of the suggestive, epiphanic power of the fragment and montage. Benjamin writes that *The Arcades Project* must 'develop to the highest degree the art of citing without quotation marks. Its theory is intimately related to that of montage', and explains: 'Method of this project: literary montage. I needn't say anything. Merely show. I shall purloin no valuable, appropriate no ingenious formulation. But the rags, the refuse – these I will not inventory but allow, in the only way possible, to come into their own: by making use of them' (Benjamin, 1999: 458, 460). Benjamin's modernist historiography of nineteenth-century Paris recalls Harrison's admiration for the deftness of modernist narrative: 'Katherine Mansfield could "build a world" in thirty words & a couple of viewpoint changes ... Chekhov could cram more into four thousand words than Dickens got into three hundred thousand' (Harrison, 2007: n.p.). While Benjamin's uncompleted work is essentially fragmentary, Harrison's much more polished Viriconium fictions are also collations and juxtapositions of fragments, over-writings and textual echoes. Like Benjamin, Harrison's montage method relies heavily on 'citing without quotation marks', and Viriconium itself is montaged out of bits and scraps of other places, times and energies.[3]

Harrison's scavenger–montagist practice echoes Benjamin's equation of the poet, flâneur and rag-picker. He quotes Baudelaire's description of the ragpicker:

> Everything that the big city threw away, everything it lost, everything it despised, everything it crushed underfoot, he catalogues and collects. ... He sorts things out and makes a wise choice; he collects, like a miser guarding a treasure, the refuse which will assume the shape

of useful or gratifying objects between the jaws of the goddess of
Industry

and remarks that it 'is one extended metaphor for the procedure of
the poet in Baudelaire's spirit. Ragpicker or poet – the refuse concerns both' (Benjamin, 1983: 79–80). Harrison shares a predilection
for the shabby, discarded and lost objects of our lives. His fiction lovingly attends to waste ground, rubbish tips and the contents of Oxfam
shops, and he frequently draws on the junkshop for his aesthetic metaphors, often, provocatively, connecting them to spectrality:

> The naïve, the unconstructed, the accidental ghost. The ghost from
> the faded polaroid found in a shoebox of letters from someone else's
> life. Things that might not be there; things that have no existence
> other than possibly not being there ... Reading should be as close as
> possible to discovering those letters and seeing something in them
> that might not be there. The writer should offer the shoebox, or better
> still the stall at the flea market on which the shoebox might be found.
> (Harrison, 2014a: n.p.)

Gordon (1997: 8) would agree: 'The ghost or apparition is one form
by which something lost, or barely visible, or seemingly not there to
our supposedly well-trained eyes, makes itself known or apparent to
us, in its own way, of course'. What better vehicle for the 'mode of
haunting' (Gordon, 1997: 131), then, than in the arrangement of the
already neglected and overlooked?

Harrison (2011: n.p.) writes, 'We think of ghosts as haunting places. What if places can haunt places? I bet they can'. In the Viriconium
Project – a place which is, after all, 'just some words' (Harrison, 2001:
n.p.) – texts haunt texts. Harrison declares of *In Viriconium* (1982)
that 'There are so [m]any buried allusions worked into the surface
of the book that it's an absolute palimpsest' (Fowler, 1993: 11).
Harrison's art of silent citation relies, with modernist intensity, on
intertextual allusions, but, still more disorientingly to the returning
textual flâneur, it relies on setting up often self-contradictory *intra*textual references to other Viriconium texts. The result is a palimpsestic, unstable imaginative space ridden with what Laura Oldfield Ford

(2011: n.p.), in her psychogeographic documentation of London, refers to as 'semiotic ghosts'.

A predictable early response to Viriconium's intertextuality has been to identify the sources of those 'citations without quotation marks' despite Harrison's warning that his work 'shouldn't be mined simply for this sort of thing' (Fowler, 1993: 11). As the modernists well knew, the Easter egg hunt-like sourcing of allusions is at best peripheral to (if not a distraction from) the aesthetic purpose of such intertextual collage. A more productive line of questioning, however, is to ask what the *effect* is of this intertextuality as a compositional strategy. How does one respond to a text – or an 'inscape' – which so self-consciously alludes to its own fabrication from literary scraps instead of cultivating a seamless,[4] convincing illusion of the real?

The semiotic ghosts haunting Viriconium underscore the essential *textuality* of the Viriconium experience and defuse the pull towards an illusory 'realism', even as they create the peculiarly second-hand, shoebox-of-photos tone of the Viriconium inscape. Appropriately, T. S. Eliot provides a primary stream of allusion for Viriconium, offering not only thematic resonances with Harrison's work but also a touchstone to the modernist idea of the writer as the catalyst for intertextual collage. Just as Eliot (1972b: 431) wrote 'These fragments I have shored against my ruins', so Harrison shores up fragments from Eliot to create an Eliotic tone and form for Viriconium. Alstath Fulthor, adrift in Viriconium's streets, reflects that 'The tenement in the Rue Sepile filled him with disgust. ... Its stairways wound like a tedious argument, luring part of his brain along with them until he found himself thinking, apropos of nothing, if the dead have a city it is like this, and it smells of rats and withered geraniums' (Harrison, 2005f: 145).[5] This silent citation of 'Streets that follow like a tedious argument' from 'The Love Song of J. Alfred Prufrock' (Eliot, 1972a: 6) sets up the further resonance with the rat motif of 'The Waste Land', as well as its 'unreal city' refrain in which London is seen as a city of the dead (Eliot, 1972b: 60–76). The point of the allusion, however, is not to bury a bookish reference but to invoke a tone of Prufrockian apathy and the 'wasteland' themes of sickness, decay and constantly deferred healing that inform both Eliot's poem and the psychogeographic inscape of Viriconium (Freeman, 2005: 280–2).[6]

Perhaps most explicitly, *A Storm of Wings* (1980) transforms lines from 'The Waste Land' in the disjointed ramblings of Fay Glass, a Reborn Woman whose voice otherwise reads much like that of the aristocratic Marie/hyacinth girl in the first part of Eliot's poem. She begins ventriloquizing Eliot by saying, 'Venice becomes like Blackpool, leaving nothing for anybody'; she repeats this, several pages later, as 'Blackpool and Venice become as one'; and finally, in a third super-inscription, sings that 'Blackpool and Chicago become as nothing' (Harrison, 2005f: 134, 158, 231). Having appended Viriconium to Eliot's catalogue of collapsing, reforming and mutually haunting cities, she offers an endgame where they 'become as nothing', 'leaving nothing for anybody' (Harrison, 2005f: 231) – a mirage-like vacuity towards which the Viriconium Project ultimately inclines.

Despite this propensity to blur, other elements of Viriconium, paradoxically, appear to have been crisply scissored out of some lost original context and reassembled as a Viriconian streetscape/inscape. As the narrator of 'A Young Man's Journey to Viriconium' (1985) explains, quoting – appropriately – a fragment of an unidentified 'famous novel':

> In Viriconium the light was like the light you only see on record covers and in the colour supplements. Photographic precision of outline under an empty blue sky is one of the most haunting features of the Viriconium landscape. Ordinary objects – a book, a bowl of anemones, someone's hand – seem to be lit in a way which makes them very distinct from their background. The identity of things under this light seems enhanced. Their visual distinctness becomes metonymic of the reality we perceive both in them and in ourselves. (Harrison, 2005h: 450)[7]

Clarity without context – a sense of pre-existing and incipient fragmentariness to the components of the world – reinforces the feeling of montage: that things are juxtaposed but not unified. Harrison's narrator-within-the narrator here, significantly, identifies this property as a 'haunting' feature of Viriconium, and it is spectral in at least two ways: the place is uncanny – the familiar reappearing in an unfamiliar context – and there is the persistent sense that every *thing* is limned by a gap, the seam of its scissoring. Like the disjointing of time around the apparition of a ghost, the space between and around words, quotations and things is also the sign of their evanescence, the space of haunting.

Harrison amplifies the haunting sense of returning fragments through the intratextual self-borrowings that shuffle between the Viriconium texts. He has always reworked previously published materials into new contexts, but the Viriconium texts add to this an internal haze of recycling from intradiegetic texts and memoirs quoted and circulated between the novels and stories.[8] In the déjà vu that results, we are never certain where we may have read a passage before. This textual blurring reflects an ontological blurring endemic to the Viriconium experience: as Ansel Verdigris is said to have written, 'Viriconium ... is a world trying to remember itself. The dumb stones perform an unending act of recall' (Harrison, 2005f: 167). For Jacques Derrida (1994: 11), the spectre is 'a question of repetition: a specter is always a *revenant*. One cannot control its comings and goings because it *begins by coming back*'. The déjà vu quality of the Viriconium texts' self-quotation participates in this spectral return.[9]

An especially apt example occurs when words attributed in *In Viriconum's* epigraph to Ansel Verdigris – 'I have heard the café philosophers say, "The world is so old that the substance of reality no longer knows what it ought to be."' (Harrison, 2005b: 309) – are uttered, spontaneously and verbatim, by an old man in 'Viriconium Knights' (1981), who goes on to add that 'The original template is hopelessly blurred. History repeats over and again this one city and a few frightful events – not rigidly, but in a shadowy, tentative fashion, as if it understands nothing else but would like to learn' (Harrison, 2005g: 373). What makes this example so apposite is, of course, the fact that the old man himself blurs the originality of the earlier quotation by repeating it. Authority and stability are undercut, but the words – the fragment – remain, semiotic ghosts slipping between speakers, times and texts.

The old man's philosophy of history and reality is a model of the eternal return, clearly an essential ontological and aesthetic principle of Viriconium. Again, *The Arcades Project* sheds light on Viriconium: 'In the idea of eternal recurrence, the historicism of the nineteenth century capsizes. As a result, every tradition, even the most recent, becomes the legacy of something that has already run its course in the immemorial night of the ages' (Benjamin, 1999: 116). Benjamin (1999: 419) concretizes this metaphysical stance in the flâneur's strolling: 'We know that, in the course of flânerie, far-off times and places interpenetrate the landscape and the present moment'. Alstath Fulthor shares this notion, considering Viriconium's 'long strangeness and obstinacy in the face of Time ... Its histories, as forgotten as his own, made of the air a sort of amber, an entrapment; the geometry of its avenues was a wry message from one survivor to another; and its present, like his own, was but an implication of its past' (Harrison, 2005f: 116).

What 'frightful events' are repeated in a 'shadowy, tentative fashion'? In Harrison's spectral theory of history, several motifs and actions recur with archetypal obsession: *A Storm of Wings* reprises the narrative arc of *The Pastel City* (1971), as a group of heroes (themselves products of the same blurred template – melancholy warrior-aesthete, cynical dwarf, and so on) strive to save Viriconium from an alien threat. Beetles and locusts return, first in *A Storm of Wings'* alien invasion from beyond the moon and then, apparently centuries later, as icons for street gangs or the subject of a popular play in 'Viriconium Knights'. The killing of Mammy Vooley is repeated in 'Viriconium Knights' and 'The Luck in the Head' (1984), the latter also providing an alternative death for Ansel Verdigris, who died rather differently in *A Storm of Wings*. Recurrence trickles down into the very details of Harrison's fictions – fish masks, horse skulls – and his reservoir of images and events is deep, but it is not so much the recurring fragments that matter as the sense of recurrence itself. This dynamic is best embodied in the tarot deck, one of Harrison's recurring motifs and a key metaphor for his fictional practice. Of the disjointed, prophetic speech of *A Storm of Wings'* Reborn Men, Harrison writes:

It was only that they hoped to manipulate Time, as we know: believing that by combination and recombination of a few common images – which are themselves only the symbols rather than the actual memories of acts peculiar to the Afternoon Cultures – they might obtain the 'code' which would liberate them from the Evening. Thus Mam Etteila, shuffling her pasteboard cards. (Harrison, 2005f: 232)[10]

The tarot expresses in microcosm the haunting principle of eternal return: these elements resurface, distorted and half-forgotten, as history becomes more symbolic than literal in 'the worn out babble of events' (Harrison, 2014b: n.p.).

Although there is a basic chronological sequence to the novels, there is none of the world-building accretion of history that one finds in Tolkien (or even Faulkner). One could no more write a history of Viriconium than one could draw a topographical map of it, and for the same reasons: when the chronological facts of the matter are not vague, they are actively contradictory. 'Viriconium is never the same place twice' (Harrison, 2001: n.p.), and with no continuity of identity, there can be no continuity of history. Instead, Viriconium creates a destabilizing awareness of this lack. While occasional, vague chronological references indicate that the events of previous novels are receding into the past, these temporal coordinates are often more disorienting than historicising.[11] Each Viriconium text remains a disconnected present moment – a fragment of space in a fragment of time with only the most tenuous relations to those fragments that surround it. The effect is one of equivocal timelessness. Derrida (1994: 39–40) remarks that ghosts trouble our sense of time: 'Before knowing whether one can differentiate between the specter of the past and the specter of the future, of the past present and the future present, one must perhaps ask oneself whether the *spectrality effect* does not consist in undoing this opposition'. Viriconium likewise moves, ghostlike, across temporal boundaries. What one might call the 'Viriconium Effect' – a disconnected, eternally returning, equivocal present – is the sign of the ghost in the fictions.

Taken as a whole, Harrison's montage strategies draw attention to the essential interstitiality of the Viriconium Project: to the gaps between the 'facts' – the space of their juxtaposition and contradiction – rather than to the facts themselves. Here again, Viriconium holds a mirror up to its own practice in the opening paragraphs of 'The Lamia and Lord Cromis' (1971):

> The apologists or historians of the city – Verdigris, Kubin, Saent Saar – tended to describe it at that time in terms of its emblems and emblematic contradictions. *An ace in the gutter, a leopard made of flowers,* says Verdigris in *Some Remarks to My Dog,* hoping to suggest a whole comprised of hints, casual lacunae, reversing hierarchies: *Where the city is at its emptiest we find ourselves full.* (Harrison, 2005c: 343)[12]

Haunting the space between the terms of Verdigris's surrealist metaphors, in the intangible territories opened up by the 'hints' or the gaps of the 'casual lacunae', we find Viriconium. The vision of Viriconium as emerging from the gaps between juxtaposed or even paradoxical terms is reprised, once again, by *In Viriconium*'s metaphor of the tarot deck when Ashlyme gathers the cards scattered by the Fat Mam, including 'THE CITY *(Nothingness)* – a dog between two towers' (Harrison, 2005b: 329). Here the city is emblematized by the space between structures, not the structures themselves. That the 'City' card can also be read as 'Nothingness' both underscores the notion of Viriconium as a composite of negative spaces and recalls the sense of 'city-as-nothing' voiced by Fay Glass. Once more, we are shown, there is no there there.

Again, the equation of reading these texts with walking the streets of Viriconium recalls Benjamin (1999: 425) characterizing 'the peculiar irresolution of the flâneur. Just as waiting seems to be the proper state of the impassive thinker, doubt appears to be that of the flâneur'. Uncertainty – or rather, a patient openness to a shifting not-knowing – marks the epistemological stance of both the flâneur and the visitor to Viriconium. Benjamin declares that 'The "colportage phenomenon of space" is the flâneur's basic experience' (Benjamin, 1999: 418), quoting Odilon Redon to clarify this phenomenon: 'The sense of mystery ... comes from remaining always in the equivocal, with double and triple perspectives, or inklings of perspective (images within images) – forms that take shape and come into being according to the state of mind of the spectator. All things more suggestive just because they do appear' (Benjamin, 1999: 429). The 'equivocal' experience of reading the Viriconium texts – the 'mystery' or the 'colportage phenomenon' of shifting intertextuality and self-contesting fact – subverts the accumulation of facts into a stable, knowable 'world'. Like the modernists' reliance on epiphany and suggestion, Harrison's Viriconium is an evanescent world that happens both between and after the terms of his statements about it. Evoked rather than depicted, it evades and fades away from any effort to hold it fast or take as 'real' its ghostliness.

***

> Like all books, Viriconium is just some words.
>
> (Harrison, 2001: n.p.)
>
> Viriconium.
> Its achingly formal gardens and curious geometries; its streets that
> reek of squashed fruit and fish ... how can one deal with it in words?
>
> (Harrison, 2005f: 252)

Gordon (1997: 8) contends that, 'haunting is a very particular way of knowing what has happened or is happening'. To understand haunting as a way of knowing, rather than a thing to be known, opens a way to grasp Viriconium's ghostliness. While that 'way of knowing' informs the shifting textuality of the Viriconium works, the characters who dwell there, and who haunt its streets, experience it as well. Perhaps the only way to entertain the 'inappropriate' question of 'what it might be like to live in Viriconium' is to solicit the perspectives of the characters who actually do.

Unlike the detailed and stable secondary worlds of conventional fantasy, Viriconium shape-shifts between its textual incarnations. In *The Pastel City*, Viriconium appears as a semi-familiar, medievalized fantasy setting (albeit a medievalism that has already anachronistically collaged with the distant future). The city here exists primarily as a collection of majestic and strange pseudo-medieval, post-technological landmarks, such as the Proton Circuit that spirals up to the pastel towers where its Queen dwells, overseeing the quests of her court of

Methven knights. Harrison otherwise pays very little attention to the details of the city. It remains in the background; the action primarily occurs in the wastelands beyond Viriconium.

As the Viriconium Project unfolds, however, Harrison focuses more intently on the city as a city. Abandoning heroic-fantasy plots, Harrison instead begins to follow the incompetent, quotidian scrambles of Viriconium's inhabitants, while at the same time discarding the high fantasy, pseudo-medieval setting in favour of a sensibility increasingly reminiscent of an eighteenth- or even nineteenth-century Europe,[13] which makes for still more sympathetic resonances with Benjamin's reconstructions of Baudelaire's Paris.

Harrison's movement to de-fantasize or pseudo-modernize Viriconium parallels his increasing emphasis on the linguistic nature of the city. There 'is a particular voluptuousness in the naming of streets' (Benjamin, 1999: 517) that Harrison clearly indulges to build a city of evocative semiotic ghosts. To Benjamin (1999: 516), Paris is 'the city that never stops moving. ... Such is the movement of the streets, the movement of names, which often enough run at cross-purposes to one another'. Viriconium is likewise a city of unending movements, the linguistic among them. Harrison scavenges the linguistic 'afternoon cultures' of nineteenth- and early twentieth-century Europe to collect a polyglot, cross-temporal montage of street and place names: the Bistro Californium, the Luitpold Café, the Margarethestrasse, the Haadenbosk, Boulevard Aussman and Rue Serpolet, Minnet-Saba, the Pont de Nile, Thing Alley, the Gabelline Stairs and Line Mass Quay. Other names draw their evocative power from their surrealist collisions of ideas, such as the Plaza of Unrealised Time or the Piazza of Inherited Tendencies. Benjamin (1999: 522) tells us that 'Through its street names, the city is a linguistic cosmos',[14] and *The Arcades Project* provides a useful gloss to the impossible contents of a *Viriconium A to Z*:

> in fact, street names are like intoxicating substances that make our perceptions more stratified and richer in spaces. One could call the energy by which they transport us into such a state their *vertu evocatrice*, their evocative power – but that is saying too little; for what is

decisive here is not the association but the interpenetration of images. (Benjamin, 1999: 518)

'The interpenetration of images' – 'the colportage phenomenon' of language – is key to the evocation of Viriconium as an uncanny and seductive palimpsest. Like the intertextuality that marks the Viriconium Project as a whole, the montaged street names never settle into a coherent cultural milieu but instead jostle one another and, through their very familiarity, constantly unsettle the space in the reader's imagination.

Harrison's increasingly fine-grained appreciation of the urban space of Viriconium is often expressed through a sense of presumed, even anecdotal, familiarity. The reader wanders through many passages such as this, in which Galen Hornwrack travels on horseback through the city:

> Now, the Plaza of Unrealised Time and its shabby dependencies behind them, they shepherded him through the Low City. Alves passed like a dream, its breached copper dome and sprawling rookeries lapped in the silence of the desuetude. Along the Camine Auriale a drizzling rain commenced. The earthly wounds of the Cispontine Quarter opened before them like a freshly dug graveyard.
>
> Eastward, where the Artists' Quarter huddles up to the skirts of the High City (and Carron Ban, it's said, deserted by her sour daughter, still waits for Norvin Trinor in the inexpressibly sad shadows beneath the heights of Minnet-Saba) dawn had filled the streets with faces Hornwrack knew. (Harrison, 2005f: 142)

As one district of the city yields to another, landmarks rising and falling away, Harrison weaves the illusion of a stable – even potentially mappable – topography, complete with a pseudo-familiar fragment of local folklore. And yet on close inspection that solidity fails. The spatial relations of the topography remain as unclear as the legend of Carron Ban, and for the same reason – the words offer only a pretence of meaning which ultimately evaporates, leaving behind only a topographical mood of haunted melancholy.

Harrison also cultivates the tone of knowing familiarity through use of the second person, as in 'The Dancer from the Dance' (1985):

Every winter years ago, little girls would chalk off the ground for 'blind Michael' in a courtyard off the Plaza of Realised Time. (It was on the left as you came to the Plain Moon Café, where even in February the tables were arranged on the pavement, their planished copper tops gleaming in the weak sun. You turned down by an ornamental apple tree). (Harrison, 2005a: 427)

Harrison again relies on the suggestive power of the fragment and montage bathed in a tone of familiarity which paints over the city's deep unknowability (and instability – if we're familiar with the plaza at all, it is under its previous and more frequent appellation, the Plaza of *Un*realised Time). Harrison writes of the streets and prospects of Viriconium as if we could recollect them – yet they go largely undescribed, presented only as evocative street-corner details and certain slants of light.

While the city's details come into focus as its streets and neighborhoods are named, traversed and inhabited, these streets never coalesce into anything more than a kaleidoscope of fragments.[15] Often, the characters' perspectives reflect Benjamin's (1999: 429) 'colportage phenomenon of space', which 'comes from remaining always in the equivocal, with double and triple perspectives', as when Tomb the Dwarf perceives that,

> The mosaic of [Viriconium's] roofs, whited by moonlight and last week's frozen snow, lay like the demonstration of some equivocal new geometry. The Low City had retreated from him even as he entered it ... so that he seemed always to view it at a distance. ... He had for a moment (it was a moment only) a sense of two cities, overlapping in a sprawl of moonlit triangles and tangled thoroughfares. (Harrison, 2005f: 216–17)

Ashlyme has a similar experience as, descending the stairs from the High City, he sees Viriconium as a cubist canvas:

> From here he had a view of the Low City, some odd quality of the moonlight giving its back and foreground planes equal value, so that it had no perspective but was just a clutter of blue and gamboge roofs filling the space between his eyes and the hills outside the city. (Harrison, 2005b: 258)

At other times, the instability of perspective becomes explicitly spectral, as when Ashlyme,

> found himself on the seeping periphery of Cheminor, that suburb of flaking brick walls where the streets are lined with graveyards, old churches, and boardinghouses. At night the lamps there give off an orange glare which muddles the sense of perspective and gives the blank faces of the people a suffering look. They seem to float towards you in their cheap sober clothes, then away from you again like ghosts. (Harrison, 2005b: 319).

Emerging and receding figures against a fractured perspectival ground, the inhabitants of Viriconium become as ghostly and inaccessible as the city itself.

From *A Storm of Wings* onward, the novels present a constant *moving through* the city, to the point where Viriconium comes to feel less like a background than a *medium*. As Viriconium's inhabitants traverse the city they often sense a reciprocal motion, as if the city flows and reshapes itself around them:

> Leaving the palace for the city was like entering a dark crystal …; the shape of things became irregular, refracted; sudden astonishing mirages swallowed the Pastel Towers or engulfed the denizens of the streets beneath them. It was as if Viriconium (the physical city, that is, the millennial artefact which sums up a thousand dead cultures) had suffered some sort of psychic storm, and forgotten itself. Its very molecules seemed to be creeping apart. 'As you walk', [Tomb] the dwarf tried to explain after a single clandestine excursion to the Artists' Quarter, 'the streets create themselves around you. When you have passed, everything slips immediately back into chaos again.' (Harrison, 2005f: 221)

Not all who haunt Viriconium's streets remain as composed in the face of its disorienting spectralizings. *In Viriconium's* Ashlyme becomes mildly lost one evening: 'he found himself on Clavescin Crescent, a street whose name was not familiar to him. … It was already late, and a heavy blue twilight had set in, confusing him as to distances' (Harrison, 2005b: 310–11). Here he encounters a panic-stricken, hallucinating Paulinus Rack: '"I'm lost," whispered the entrepreneur helplessly. "I'm lost." ... Suddenly he shivered and hissed: "Livio, all these roads are the same! Livio, *they don't lead anywhere!*" (2005b: 312). Later, in the Luitpold Café, Ashlyme gives Rack the best advice one could offer to a wanderer in the plague zone, or in Viriconium more generally: 'You will always get lost in there ... [B]ut you must never panic. ... You get used to it in the end' (Harrison, 2005b: 313). Complicating the kaleidoscopic propensity of its streets is Viriconium's tendency towards reflections and self-mirroring. Benjamin devotes an entire section of *The Arcades Project* to the prevalence of mirrors in Paris, remarking on 'the way mirrors bring the open expanse, the streets, into the café – this, too, belongs to the interweaving of spaces, to the spectacle by which the flâneur is ineluctably drawn' (Benjamin, 1999: 537). Similarly, the flâneur's wanderings in Viriconium often dissolve into a self-deferring maze of reflections. Typically, there is a tension between beauty and squalor, reminiscent of Benjamin's vision of the Baudelairean poet as ragpicker, as in Tomb the Dwarf's excursion:

> A red stain grew in the sky above the Haunted Gate. Against it floated the airy towers, suspended as if in water glass, while below were conjured shabby reflections – a glitter of fish scales, olive oil, broken glass, and the west wind shivering the wide shallow puddles in the empty squares. (Harrison, 2005f: 150–1)

However, the city begins to lose its psychogeographic stability in this self-mirroring colportage of perspectives, as Ashlyme discovers:

> This psychological disorder of the city was reflected in a new disorder of its streets. It was a city I knew and yet I could not find my way about in it. Avenue turned into endless avenue. Alleys turned back on themselves. The familiar roads repeated themselves infinitely in rows of dusty chestnut trees and iron railings. If I found my way in the gardens of the Haadenbosk, I lost it again on the Pont des Arts, and ended up looking at my own reflection dissolving in the oily water below. (Harrison, 2005b: 331)

That Ashlyme ends up seeing his own reflection amid the reflections of the city recalls another instance in which the 'psychological disorder of the city' reflects the desires and lacks of those who wish to go there: the quest in 'A Young Man's Journey to Viriconium' for the lavatory mirror which will provide the entry point to the city. Like Ashlyme, the Young Man's journey dead-ends with his own fugitive reflection: 'Mr. Ambrayses was right: the mirror is of no use to me. I went down there; I stood in front of it. Except perhaps myself, I saw no one trapped and despairing in it' (Harrison, 2005h: 462). Benjamin (1999: 537) writes of the nineteenth-century Parisian Arcades that 'where doors and walls are made of mirrors, there is no telling outside from in, with all the equivocal illumination'. His observation could apply equally well to the predicament of both Viriconium's inhabitants and the thwarted entradistas who seek to join them. One recalls Mr. Ambrayses' account of how, mistaking a reflection from the inside of a café for a figure in the twilit gardens outside, he 'ran straight into the plate-glass window and was concussed' (Harrison, 2005h: 455).

Benjamin's beautiful description of the unsettling, mirrored arcades of Paris could as easily have been written to describe the hauntology of the streets of Viriconium:

> For although this mirror world may have many aspects, indeed, infinitely many, it remains ambiguous, double-edged. It blinks: it is always this one – and never nothing – out of which another immediately arises. The space that transforms itself does so in the bosom of nothingness. In its tarnished, dirty mirrors, things exchange a Kaspar-Hauser-look with the nothing. ... Odilon Redon ... caught, like no one else, this look of things in the mirror of nothingness, and ... understood, like no one else, how to join with things in their collusion with nonbeing. The whispering of gazes fills the arcades. There is no thing here that does not, where one least expects it, open a fugitive eye, blinking it shut again; but if you look more closely, it is gone. (Benjamin, 1999: 542)

Benjamin's arcades recall the furtive optics of Harrison's 'ghost fictions', where 'The haunting comes layered up in time. It slips about, guilted and dirty. You can't focus on a thing like that ... evading itself as hard as it's evading you' (Harrison, 2014b: n.p.). Like the tarot card which can be read as either The City or Nothingness (Harrison,

2005b: 329), the mirror world of Viriconium is 'the mirror of nothingness' (and the desire of the entradista is, fatally, the desire 'to join
with things in their collusion with nonbeing'). The 'whispering of
gazes' that haunts the arcades also speaks to the self-reflective optics
of spectrality; as Derrida remarks:

> The specter is also among other things, what one imagines, what one
> thinks one sees and which one projects – on an imaginary screen
> where there is nothing to see. ... The perspective has to be reversed,
> once again: ghost or revenant, sensuous-non-sensuous, visible-invisi-
> ble, the specter first of all sees us. From the other side of the eye, *visor*
> *effect*, it looks at us even before we see *it* or even before we see period.
> (Derrida, 1994: 100–1)

Viriconium's mirror world joins Benjamin and Derrida in a triangulation of ghostly gazes. Where Benjamin looks into a 'mirror of nothingness' and Derrida sees ghosts on a 'screen where there is nothing to
see', the Young Man has his lavatory mirror and Ashlyme and Tomb
their oily canal and puddles. In each case, the ghosts come forth as
the haunted (or self-haunted) and bewildered beholder exchanges 'a
Kasper-Hauser-look with the nothing'. For, as Derrida (1994: 156)
writes, 'How do you recognize a ghost? By the fact that it does not
recognize itself in a mirror'.

***

> Yearning has its ghosts, Ashlyme. I painted such ghosts, as you well
> know. Not for pleasure! It was an obligation.
> (Harrison, 2005b: 262)

In both form and content, Viriconium comes to us not as a world but
as a haunting. And there is a reciprocity – even a mirroring – between
haunter and haunted. Gordon (1997: xvi) writes that while haunting is a mode of knowing, 'haunting ... is distinctive for producing
a something-to-be-done'. Harrison likewise recognizes this demand
of haunting: in a blog entry about returning to a strangely empty
London streetscape, he writes: 'It didn't look like that last time I was
here. It was a dark fraught place & I was in a poor state too ... It was

my condition then to believe that I was haunted: but I was the haunting, & understanding that eventually taught me a lot' (Harrison, 2009a: n.p.). Viriconium, 'a dark fraught place' if ever there was one, holds up a similar mirror to those it ostensibly haunts, and makes a similar demand that we sort the haunted from the haunting.

Like the Young Man seeing only himself despairing in the mirror, Viriconium is a ghostly reflection of our own misplaced, thwarted, haunting desires. Each Viriconium is different, both in Harrison's texts and in the imagination of each reader or character haunted by it. And this is the source of Viriconium's charisma – how can we not be drawn to a city constructed out of the scraps of our own desire?

If a haunting is a sign of 'something-to-be-done', how do we read the sign of Viriconium? In a notebook entry, Harrison offers a theory of haunting couched in the sketch of a ghost story, which may, retrospectively, offer a resolution. The inhabitant of a house, 'A', increasingly troubled by supernatural eruptions, discovers that what she took to be a single traumatic event in need of exorcism is actually only 'a record of habitation' and a series of 'fragmentary, palimpsestic, meaningless' phenomena:

> The past is only the past: we do not owe it any guilt, we cannot even recognise anymore what constitutes it. ... When we 'learn' from it, all we are doing is rewriting it according to what we need at the time.
>
> As soon as A understands this, she gets well. The hauntings stop. She has laid the past to rest not by understanding it but by consigning it to the past where it belongs. (Harrison, 2009b: n.p.)

If Viriconium reflects our desire to escape our lives into a fantasy world, the resolution to that haunting – which is a self-haunting – lies in relinquishing that desire. Harrison scathingly declares that fantasies of escape, control and stability are precisely what Viriconium chews up in its visitors:

> No character ever 'survives' Viriconium: the best they can hope for after they have been sucked in is to be spat out whole (if changed). Recognise this procedure? It's called life. This is one of Viriconium's many jigsawed messages to the reader. You can't hope to control

things. Learn to love the vertigo of experience instead. (Harrison, 2001: n.p.)

Or, as Ashlyme coldly (yet more gently) comforts Paulinus Rack, 'you will always get lost in here ... But you must never panic ... You get used to it in the end' (Harrison, 2005b: 313). Gordon (1997: 57) writes that, 'To be haunted in the name of a will to heal is to allow the ghost to help you imagine what was lost that never even existed, really'. Viriconium does not exist. It is 'just some words'. But the fact that it 'never even existed, really' is exactly what its ghostly streets are trying to help us know.

Notes

1 *Empty Space* (2012) is subtitled 'A Haunting', but the entire *Empty Space* trilogy transposes hauntological principles into the key of quantum physics. *The Course of the Heart* (1991), however, is ghostly in ways that arise directly from the hauntedness of Viriconium. Harrison's recent collection *You Should Come With Me Now*, subtitled 'Stories of Ghosts'. testifies to his affinity for the genre.

2 Reversing the lens, one might also think of *The Arcades Project* as a kind of entradista text to a Paris that has slipped through Benjamin's grasp. In his nostalgia for that irrecoverable city, nineteenth-century Paris becomes Benjamin's Viriconium.

3 Viriconium is introduced in *The Pastel City* as arising from a scavenger culture, collecting the refuse and artefacts of the Afternoon Cultures to assemble a sense of itself: 'The wealth of its people lay entirely in salvage. They possessed no science, but scavenged the deserts of rust that had been originally the industrial complexes of the last of the Afternoon Cultures' (Harrison, 2005e: 3).

4 In critiquing the illusions of world-building fiction, Harrison argues that 'the reader, it's assumed, wants to receive the events in the text as *seamless* & the text as unperformed ... This experience is somehow unmediated, or needs to present itself as such: any vestige of performativeness in the text dilutes the experience by reminding the reader that the "world" on offer is a rhetorical construct' (Harrison, 2007: n.p., emphasis added). Harrison's desire to flaunt the seams in his texts bespeaks an almost Brechtian commitment to anti-illusionism.

5 This quotation is preceded by the words of the old man, who says 'I can connect nothing with nothing' (Harrison, 2005f: 145), a citation without quotation marks of Eliot's Thames daughters who sing 'On Margate Sands./I can connect/Nothing with nothing' (Eliot, 1972b: 300–2).

6 Harrison also borrows Eliot's sense of the city as an allusive and elusive space. Like Eliot's 'Unreal city', of which it seems to be an iteration, Viriconium drifts spectrally between times and incarnations: it is 'all the cities there have ever been' (Harrison, 2005b: 275); its name shifts (Uriconium, Vriko, Vira Co), thus highlighting that Viriconium is 'just words'.

7 Compare Benjamin (1999: 539) on the equivocal illumination of the arcades: 'Actually, in the arcades it is not a matter of illuminating the interior space ... but of damping the exterior space'. Like the Parisian arcades, Viriconium is a sealed space, an interior, mirrored world cut off from any external 'reality' it might reflect.

8 To further destabilize the boundaries and ontologies of texts, Harrison freely intermixes quotations from historical literary sources with those from texts composed by the inhabitants of Viriconium. The chapter epigraphs of *In Viriconium*, for instance, draw on the work of Rilke and Jesse L. Weston as well as Audsley King and Ansel Verdigris, enacting on the textual level the interpenetration between worlds said to occur between Viriconium and our own – the tree that Ambrayses says exists in both Viriconium and York (Harrison, 2005h: 453), or the Isle of Dogs which seems shared between Viriconium and London (Harrison, 2005g: 369). Places and words are shared indiscriminately, which is only appropriate for a place that is 'just words'.

9 An unusually powerful instance of this is the re-publication of 'A Young Man's Journey to Viriconium' as 'A Young Man's Journey to London' (Harrison, 2003), with only the name of the city changed. The gesture enacts at the level of Harrison's canon the notion that, to paraphrase Fay Glass, 'Viriconium and London become one' to the escapist imagination, but this effect is appreciated only when one has read both stories. The point is made, in effect, in the *space between* the stories.

10 An intertextual ghosting of Eliot's Madame Sosostris.

11 For example, references to revived swordsman fashions in *In Viriconium* place the actions of tegeus-Cromis and the events of *A Storm of Wings* 'two or three centuries' earlier or perhaps even 'hundreds or thousands of years ago', if the garbled legend about the Barley Brothers is to be be-

lieved (Harrison, 2005b: 284, 303), yet 'The Lamia and Lord Cromis' has tegeus-Cromis living after *In Viriconium's* Audsley King (Harrison, 2005c: 348).

12 It is another ghosting between worlds to include Alfred Kubin – author of *The Other Side* (1909) – among the historians of Viriconium. Kubin's fantastic novel of a man's journey to the mysterious city of Perle, a city created from dreams, similarly deconstructs the *entradista* fallacy. In Harrison's deft intermixture of the Austrian Kubin with the Viriconian Verdigris and Saent Saar, Perle and Viriconium become as one.

13 In advance publicity, *In Viriconium* was dubbed 'pre-Raphaelite sword and sorcery' (Freeman, 2005b: 282).

14 Freeman (2005: 281), who also catalogues such street names in light of Eliot's 'Unreal City', finds the effect to be 'omniurban' and that as a result 'the distance between "textual" and "real" universes is narrowed or even erased'. While this may be the case, Harrison's street-naming primarily draws and holds our attention to the level of the signifier and the semiotic montage that constitutes this 'linguistic cosmos'. Viriconium is composed not of scraps of the 'real' world, but of scraps of the language we use to speak of it.

15 Just as the zones of the city have a mobile relation to one another, so do the texts that constitute the Viriconium Project. While *The Pastel City, A Storm of Wings* and *In Viriconium* fall into a loose (albeit vague and inconsistent) chronological order, the collection *Viriconium Nights* is a wildly fluid textual kaleidoscope in its own right. Aside from offering stories that contradict the historical 'facts' of the novels (and one another), the collection itself is unstable, the selection, number and order of stories varying between the American Ace edition (1984) and the British Gollancz edition (1985), an expression at the textual level of the shifting and shuffling that happens at street level in the city itself.

Works Cited

Benjamin, Walter (1983) *Charles Baudelaire*, trans. Harry Zohn. London: Verso.

Benjamin, Walter (1999) *The Arcades Project*, trans. Howard Eiland and Kevin McLaughlin. Cambridge, MA: Harvard University Press.

Derrida, Jacques (1994) *Specters of Marx*, trans. Peggy Kamuf. New York: Routledge.

Eliot, T. S. (1972a) 'The Love Song of J. Alfred Prufrock', in *The Waste Land and Other Poems*, pp. 9–14. London: Faber and Faber.

Eliot, T. S. (1972b) 'The Waste Land', in *The Waste Land and Other Poems*, pp. 25–51. London: Faber and Faber.

Ford, Laura Oldfield (2011) 'Elephant and Castle. Oct/Nov 2005', *Savage Messiah*. London: Verso.

Fowler, Christopher J. (1993) 'On the Edge: The Last Holmfirth Interview with M. John Harrison', *Foundation* 57: 7–26.

Freeman, Nick (2005) '"All the Cities That There Have Ever Been": In *Viriconium*', in Mark Bould and Michelle Reid (eds) *Parietal Games*, pp. 275–89. London: Science Fiction Foundation.

Gordon, Avery F. (1997) *Ghostly Matters: Haunting and the Sociological Imagination*. Minneapolis: University of Minnesota Press.

Harrison, M. John (1993) *The Course of the Heart*. London: Flamingo.

Harrison, M. John (2001) 'What It Might be Like to Live in Viriconium', *Fantastic Metropolis* (15 October), accessed 27 September 2017, https://www.warwick.ac.uk/fac/arts/english/currentstudents/undergraduate/modules/ch369/fantastika/bibliography/2.7harrison_mj._200/what_might_it_be_like_to_live_in_virconium.pdf

Harrison, M. John (2003) 'A Young Man's Journey to London', in *Things That Never Happen*, pp. 167–85. San Francisco, CA: Night Shade.

Harrison, M. John (2005a) 'The Dancer from the Dance', in *Viriconium*, pp. 427–44. New York: Del Rey.

Harrison, M. John (2005b) *In Viriconium*, in *Viriconium*, pp. 257–39. New York: Del Rey.

Harrison, M. John (2005c) 'The Lamia and Lord Cromis', in *Viriconium*, pp. 343–60. New York: Del Rey.

Harrison, M. John (2005d) 'The Luck in the Head', in *Viriconium*, pp. 381–400. New York: Del Rey.

Harrison, M. John (2005e) *The Pastel City*, in *Viriconium*, pp. 3–108. New York: Del Rey.

Harrison, M. John (2005f) *A Storm of Wings*, in *Viriconium*, pp. 111–254. New York: Del Rey.

Harrison, M. John (2005g) 'Viriconium Knights', in *Viriconium*, pp. 362–78. New York: Del Rey.

Harrison, M. John (2005h) 'A Young Man's Journey to Viriconium', in *Viriconium*, pp. 447–62. New York: Del Rey.

Harrison, M. John (2007) 'very afraid', *Ambientehotel* (31 December), accessed 11 August 2015, https://ambientehotel.wordpress.com/2007/12/31/very-afraid/

Harrison, M. John (2009a) 'a dark fraught place', *Ambientehotel* (29 July), accessed 17 June 2015, https://ambientehotel.wordpress.com/2009/07/29/a-dark-fraught-place/

Harrison, M. John (2009b) 'notebook entry, 1993', *Ambientehotel* (25 August), accessed 17 June 2015, https://ambientehotel.wordpress.com/2009/08/25/notebook-entry-1993/

Harrison, M. John (2011) 'a fresh start', *Ambientehotel* (10 December), accessed 17 June 2015, https://ambientehotel.wordpress.com/2011/12/10/a-fresh-start/

Harrison, M. John (2012) *Empty Space: A Haunting*. London: Gollancz.

Harrison, M. John (2014a) 'anti surrealism', *Ambientehotel* (5 April), accessed 17 June 2015, https://ambientehotel.wordpress.com/2014/04/05/anti-surrealism/

Harrison, M. John (2014b) 'ghost fictions', *Ambientehotel* (8 November), accessed 17 June 2015, https://ambientehotel.wordpress.com/2014/11/08/ghost-fictions/

Harrison, M. John (2015) 'a story of ghosts', *Ambientehotel* (19 October), accessed 11 May 2015, https://ambientehotel.wordpress.com/2015/10/19/a-story-of-ghosts/

Harrison, M. John (2017) *You Should Come With Me Now: Stories of Ghosts*. Manchester: Comma Press.

Kubin, Alfred (1909/1973) *The Other Side*, trans. Denver Lindley. Harmondsworth: Penguin.

'SOUTHEND WILL FOLLOW YOU WHEREVER YOU GO'
M. JOHN HARRISON AND THE FICTION OF EVERYDAY LIFE

Nick Freeman

Familiar Objects?

The BBC's quiz show *Ask the Family* (1967–84), which ran from Harrison's *New Worlds* period to *The Ice Monkey and Other Stories* (1983), insisted on the fundamental strangeness of 'a familiar object, seen from an unfamiliar angle'. Eric Illet's close-up photographs of vacuum cleaner attachments, childproof medicine bottles, tootbrushes and soda siphons fascinated and startled in equal measure, giving the apparently harmless details of everyday existence – a scraping of burnt crumbs on a butter knife, strands of greasy hair in a tortoiseshell comb – the miraculous menace of things seen through an electron microscope. Anxious and bewildered contestants struggled to recognize their own possessions, their ever-more bizarre misidentifications taking the discussion further and further from the materials purportedly at issue. Illet's images, one assumes, were never supposed to acquire the diagnostic status of Rorschach's or Holtman's ink-blots, but they offered an oddly profound index of domestic alienation, showing how perceptions of the world often fail to extend beyond superficiality. One hesitates to attribute a lesson of any kind to *Ask the Family* and its cast of chartered surveyors and suburban housewives, but it did demonstrate how 'normal life' is only precariously and partially 'known', and can be at any time supplanted by the terrifying, the marvellous or the absurd.

This essay looks at the ways in which Harrison's fiction frequently has a similar, albeit vastly more sophisticated, effect in exposing the contingent and fragile hermeneutic systems of its characters and readers and making them see (or exposing their inability to see) life from those 'unfamiliar angles'. As Robert Macfarlane (2013: xi) has remarked in his introduction to the latest edition of Harrison's *Climbers*, 'Again and again ... those who are tasked with interpretation find themselves baffled, frustrated or worse. Theorists, detectives, scientists and code-breakers are all left intellectually concussed by their attempts to construe complexity'. Such a condition is often induced by being unable to draw a clear line (or any line, come to that) between the subjective and the objective (is the world we perceive the world as it truly is?), and by a failure to realize or appreciate the symbiotic relationship between 'everyday' and 'visionary' experience. From his early Jerry Cornelius adventures onwards, Harrison sought to interrogate these terms, fusing, shifting and always resisting the accretion of complacency that they have attracted.

Peter Greenaway once remarked that the world was comprised almost entirely of two types of people: those who saw zebra as black animals with white stripes, and those who saw them as white animals with black stripes. Much discord could be avoided, he went on, if each could accept that the zebra was both at the same time, but only a very few individuals were able to adopt such perspectives.[1] Unless they recognize simultaneity, no reader of Harrison can be secure, let alone complacent, in the textual habitats he creates. At times, he pulls them up short with a direct question, as when the narrator of *The Course of the Heart* asks himself and, by extension, us: 'At what point do you recover your self?' (Harrison, 1992: 111). At others, his perceptions of the inherent ambiguity of language create comedy and estrangement, as in *Signs of Life*, when Choe Ashton is confronted with the menu in a Chinese restaurant and, 'bored with Hot and Sour', orders some 'Bitter and Unfulfilled' (Harrison, 1997: 24). In 'The Horse of Iron and How We Can Know It' (1989), an adept making a journey determined by Tarot cards reads the instruction 'PRESS WHEN ILLUMINATED TO OPEN' on a train door, and adds that 'Illuminati everywhere should know about this sign' (Harrison, 2003d: 246). In *Climbers*, two characters find themselves in a Cornish café with a sign reading 'WE SERVE RAY WING' and ask 'Who's he?' 'I don't know, but you get a lot,' the waitress replies (Harrison, 2013: 135). In the café's toilets they encounter gnomic graffiti, 'someone had signed himself "Psycho" and drawn to go with it a cap-and-bells; or perhaps it was a crown – '. The scene finishes at that point. No further knowledge of Psycho is vouchsafed; nor can it be.

Through this uncommon focus on common things, Harrison refuses to allow readers to settle into a familiar groove. Instead they are poked, prodded, inveigled, questioned, teased. Spaces and places are seen anew; nowhere is safe or comfortable. Many of Harrison's characteristic moments of alienation occur in precisely those run-of-the-mill settings such as cafés and public lavatories, sites which, at least in the latter's case, rarely receive much novelistic attention. These are spaces through which people pass (or piss), rather than in which they dwell, and they offer plentiful opportunities for students of human behaviour and (mis)communication to develop their skills. Cafés seem always to attract writers, or at least, those who might be writers when occupying the window-seat, notebook partially concealed, partially flaunted as they observe the constant shifting of human tides and the often peculiar creatures left behind in the rock pools. It is clear that Harrison – who admits to spending most of his time in the 1980s 'in cafés and pubs and on tops of buses, listening to people talk' (Bould, 2005: 332) – has taken a great many notes in them, using them as an ornithologist would a hide. In *Climbers*, Mike and Pauline first meet in 'a dull café in the provinces' where 'Curd tart is the "specialte maison"!' (Harrison, 2013: 79), appropriately neutral ground for a relationship that never quite manages to find its true home: 'With its wooden chairs just too small for adults and polished with use the place looked like the classroom of an old-fashioned infants' school from which the children had run away' (Harrison, 2013: 78–9). The wallpaper's pattern 'gave an impression of stealth' (Harrison, 2013: 79), while in a subtle foreshadowing of tragedy that we only later connect with the image of the absent children, a cemetery is visible from the window. 'Dull ironic laughter' issues from Viriconium's Luitpold Café (Harrison, 2000a: 448). *Signs of Life* opens with China and Isobel in another café, this one 'full of mismatched wooden furniture, cracked melamine trim and the hot steamy air of an era before true fast food' (Harrison, 1997: 7). Their relationship will soon cease to be 'hot and steamy' as Isobel's obsession with modifying her body leads her from the grubby café to the menacing sterility of Dr Alexander's private clinic. In *The Course of the Heart*, Yaxley sneers at tourists over espresso 'too hot to taste of anything' (Harrison, 1992: 27) in the Tivoli near the British Museum, and Lucas Medlar's creation, 'Michael Ashman', lunches in The Naked Man near Burrington Combe to a backdrop of day-trippers from Bristol muttering 'Seafood platter? Seafood platter?' (Harrison, 1992: 140).

The frequent depiction of such venues in Harrison's work gives an overarching feeling of transient and contingent relationships, as well as of a profound restlessness. The pilgrims put down their packs for an hour or so, eat stale sandwiches, fail to finish their flavourless coffee, and then plod onwards in search of holy wells they will probably not recognize even if they should ever arrive at them. Here the everyday is quotidian because it is unexamined, its oddness unaddressed. 'Our failure is to form habits,' wrote Walter Pater (1986: 152): 'habit is relative to a stereotyped world, and meantime it is only the roughness of the eye that makes any two persons, things, situations, seem alike'.[2] Although one hesitates to attribute Pater's 'carpe diem' imperative to Harrison, they seemingly share a belief in the importance of subtly recognizing and appreciating their surroundings, their perceptions offering a bulwark of sorts against numbing homogeneity imposed by the political and economic conditions of contemporary existence.

In this environment, it is vital, Harrison suggests, to read and observe, though to do so has its own dangers. 'Those who go beneath the surface do so at their peril', says Oscar Wilde in *Dorian Gray* (1891), and 'Those who read the symbol do so at their peril' (Wilde, 2006: 3). Graffitied lavatory walls – from the cover of the Rolling Stones' *Beggars' Banquet* (1968) with its cryptic allusions to the album's contents, to the bluntly terrifying announcement 'I FUCK ARSES' read by a urinating Paul McGann in *Withnail and I* (Robinson, 1988) – serve as a dead letter office, a site in which identity is proclaimed and insisted upon in an uncaring world ('Kilroy was here'), one where coded (and not so coded) messages are left for initiates with accompanying requests for telephone numbers. Rendezvous are arranged, loves proclaimed, threats uttered. Similar in some ways to ancient shrines, where requests for divine intervention were scratched on shards of pottery, the toilet wall is a rich palimpsest of cryptic found utterance, a mode of discourse crucial to the Harrisonian aesthetic. The Grand Cairo's men daub slogans in their own fluids while waiting to die: 'We are the boys from the second floor!' (Harrison, 2000a: 527). In *Signs of Life*, Choe claims to have been spoken to by a hand-drier in a London restaurant's lavatory. He is amused by a sign advertising 'CONTINENTAL EXCITER CONDOMS – USE FOR FUN ONLY', and sees 'DAVE WAS HERE FROM EASTBOURNE' carved into the wall of a New York drinking den (Harrison, 1997: 52, 152). Throughout Harrison's work, there is a fascination with these moments, in which identity (and existence itself) is asserted and inscribed while at the same time providing an all-but unreadable narrative trace for those who encounter it. On one level, the inclusion of such detail enhances the believable nature of Harrison's settings, corroborating them with the reader's own experiences.[3] On another it demonstrates how urban spaces are criss-crossed by an infinite number of narratives, which intersect without necessarily ever resolving themselves. While realist fiction has traditionally embraced causality and resolution in a factitious process of 'making sense', a novel such as *Climbers* shows how misleading it is to accept realism at face value, to surrender unthinkingly to its totalizing vision of the world.

A good example of how Harrison uses seemingly mundane material to striking effect is the moment in 'A Young Man's Journey to Viriconium' (1985) when the reader could be forgiven for thinking that they have exchanged the fantastical world of 'all the cities that have ever been' for the more prosaic circumstances of an Alan Bennett play. The narrator is working in The Gate House, a tourist café in York, when a couple come in and sit down 'near one another but at separate tables' (Harrison, 2000b: 546). He describes them carefully, noting the man's pairing of 'green knitted pullover and pink shirt' (Harrison, 2000b: 546), the way in which 'he might have been anywhere between thirty and sixty' (Harrison, 2000b: 547), and their views on the likely availability of fruit cake. The woman scoops the half-melted sugar from the bottom of her coffee cup, and

> glance[s] round at the other customers with a kind of nervous satisfaction, like an Eskimo or an Aborigine in some old TV documentary – the shy, sharp glance which tells you they are getting away, in plain view, with something that is unacceptable in their own culture. It was done in no time, with quick little licks and laps. (Harrison, 2000b: 547)

This scene exemplifies several important aspects of Harrison's writing. First, it is keenly observant, sensitive not simply to physical appearance and accoutrement, but to the non-sequiturs which have often to shoulder the burden of communication in long-established relationships. Second, it notes the ways in which people interact with their environment: the man looks around the room 'as if he had never seen a calendar with a picture of Halifax town centre on it' before, or, more disconcertingly, 'a chair, or a plate ... as if he was continually surprised to find himself where he was' (Harrison, 2000b: 547). Third, there is the command of audacious figurative effects, similes that might seem extravagant if they were not so seamlessly embedded in the fabric of the piece and the characterization of the narrator. His striking reference to the Eskimo or Aborigine is fully in keeping with his observations elsewhere, such as the moment when the narrator of *The Course of the Heart*, an occultist of sorts, likens two young skinheads on a train to 'acolytes in a Buddhist temple' (Harrison, 1992: 44). Finally, and most important perhaps, is the sense that the apparently ordinary is profoundly strange, even miraculous; the man's quiet bewilderment when faced with such quotidian things captures that dislocation or separation which so many of Harrison's protagonists feel and endure.

A page or so later, when the narrator has observed that the 'meaning of what they said to one another was carefully hidden in its own broken, insinuatory rhythms' and that 'their lives were so intricately repressed that every word was like a loose fibre woven back immediately into an old knot' (Harrison, 2000b: 549), the significance of the encounter becomes clearer and the story takes an unpredictable turn. The man is Doctor Petromax, whom we told 'found an entrance to Viriconium in the lavatory of a restaurant in Huddersfield' (Harrison, 2000b: 549).[4] If the previous pages had presented quintessential features of Harrison's style, that sentence encapsulates his weird aesthetic, one he defines as, 'The subtlest possible rupture of the mundane by the uncanny and the subtlest possible rupture of the uncanny by the mundane.'[5] One might ask which is uncanny – Huddersfield or Viriconium? – and which mundane, but it would be misleading, for each city is simultaneously familiar and strange. As the narrator of 'Egnaro' (1980) realizes, the lost domain that at once hides and reveals itself in 'obliquities', is simultaneously 'the substrate of mystery which underlies all daily life' and 'the exact dead point of ordinariness which lies beneath every mystery' (Harrison, 2003a: 115, 125). At such moments, the 'everyday shades into the lyric, which tends to the allegorical, which becomes the surreal, which at last curves round to reveal itself again as an aspect of the heart-breakingly actual' (Macfarlane, 2013: xx).

Sick of the North: Manchester, Huddersfield and 'Making Strange'

This fascination with the everyday runs through Harrison's output, and plays an important role in his ongoing arguments with notions of genre, 'a marketing device that got out of hand, and leaked into the audience' (Lea, 2012: n.p.). Harrison's refusal of generic pigeonholing is exemplified by his depiction of two cities he knows well, Manchester and its surrounding districts, and, across the Pennines, Huddersfield. Both make frequent appearances in his work, though his portrayals of them are unlikely to win the affection of civic authorities. In *Climbers*, Normal works in Manchester's 'High Adventure', an outdoor pursuits shop where 'the rain blowing down Deansgate made white streaks on the windows and his customers argued desultorily over the merits of a hank of fluorescent rope' (Harrison, 2013: 27). Later in the novel, Mike has a job in a bookshop 'which by reason of its own guilt was tucked away in the blackened labyrinth south of Tib Street' (Harrison, 2013: 170). This in itself is not 'weird', yet the shop has obvious affinities with Lucas's in 'Egnaro', which is also situated in a back street behind the city library. Both premises stock second-hand pornographic magazines 'sealed in plastic bags' to prompt misleading expectations of their content (Harrison, 2013: 172). Both have proprietors whose accounting practices are at best free-and-easy. Yet it is the apparently fantastical 'Egnaro' that features some of Harrison's most detailed portrayals of quotidian realities – the office 'with its litter of half-empty plastic cups and plates of congealed food' (Harrison, 2013: 2003a: 106), Lucas's denunciation of Wimpey homes and washing powder – even as it implies the existence of their alternative, the perhaps mythical city (or country) of Egnaro that 'reveals itself in minutiae, in that great and very real part of our lives when we are doing nothing important' (Harrison, 2013: 104). As the narrator observes 'the filthy blue carpets, and the innuendos of the debt-collectors' (Harrison, 2013: 119), the Golden Country's importuning becomes harder and harder to ignore. Iain Banks (1988: ix) observed in 1988 that 'The more bizarre and displaced Viriconium becomes, the more closely it seems to mirror our experience of our own cities, our own focal points of population and culture'. By 'Empty' (1993), a story Harrison described as being in some respects 'an out-take from *Climbers*' (Harrison, 2003e: 441), Hyde has become oddly akin to Viriconium's Tinmarket, with people 'trying to sell each other the most pointless things they could find: second-hand shoes, rusty tools, "Wooden handles, Sop"' (Harrison, 2003b: 346). Annie, the narrator's sometime lover, writes that she is 'sick of the north' as if the region were some sort of incurable disease, a place where ruined people wither away 'among rusty gas stoves and bits of broken furniture' (Harrison, 2003b: 349). The rain is constant, as it is in The Grand Cairo's recollections of life in a northern city where:

The people in their black overcoats seemed to drift along a few
inches above the pavements ... Their faces were white with conspiracy. ... Each one would do anything for you if he believed he had been
let into some secret unknown to the rest. (Harrison, 2000a: 496).

Is this paranoia the same as that afflicting the narrator of 'Egnaro',
or an inevitable reaction to a locale which seems to retain its character no matter in which story it appears? In *The Course of the Heart*,
Lucas writes 'Was the Heart waiting for something? (Nothing, sure-
ly, that could ever happen in Manchester!)' (Harrison, 1992: 153).
Manchester even surfaces in 'The Ash Circus' (1969), where its central library is made the scene of violent insurrection, an anarcho-fas-
cist *putsch* in which Jerry Cornelius leads 'his detachment on a frontal
attack' (Harrison, 1993: 42). Meanwhile, in the bar of Manchester
Piccadilly station, 'A faint, weary smell of disinfectant hung in the
air' as a customer 'juggl[es] small change in a puddle of spilt beer, his
fingers clumsy strips of uncooked sausage' (Harrison, 1993: 40, 41).
Each text catalogues the small details of everyday life that underpin
the potential of radical change, destabilizing generic expectation and
in the process making the city itself mundane and fantastical, a site of
visionary perceptions, subjective or alternative histories.

Huddersfield emerges as similarly bleak, but imbued with the
same transformative power. Its dismal portrayal is not an endorsement of clichés concerning the supposed grimness of northern life,
and neither is it a work of anthropological reclamation or a straightforward political comment about Conservative governments' recurrent tendency to concentrate state investment in the South-East.
Harrison instead deploys Huddersfield as a kind of objective correla-
tive to its inhabitants' emotional states, or connects them to it in symbolic or occult ways. In *The Course of the Heart*, Pam Stuyvesant has
a mastectomy in Huddersfield General. She and her husband, Lucas,
are trapped in its maze, where 'every exit [is] marked "Oncology"'
(Harrison, 1992: 135). Those unfamiliar with the building are 'easily
snared in the web of primary-coloured lines painted on the corridor
floors' (Harrison, 1992: 155). As her condition worsens, she is admitted to Manchester's cancer-hospital where she rides 'an hourly see-saw

of pain and morphine' (Harrison, 1992: 162) watched by Lucas and the narrator. Outside the hospital, life is oblivious to her struggles: an old Bengali woman tries to clear the snow from her doorstep with a 'small red plastic dustpan' (Harrison, 1992: 173); 'The illuminated signs of bed-and-breakfast hotels, electrical dealers and Chinese chippies receded along a wide street brown with slush' (Harrison, 1992: 177). Again, the miraculous intervenes. Years earlier, Pam, Lucas and the narrator took part in an occult ritual, and entities from it continue to manifest themselves. Beneath a street lamp, the narrator finds himself 'looking at neither a child nor a dwarf but something of both, with the eyes, gait and pink face of a large monkey' (Harrison, 1992: 179). It knocks Lucas down and leaves him crying in the slush. There is nothing the narrator can do to bring about restitution: 'I left him to his despair and his vile little familiar,' he says, 'walked back to the city centre, and then, after an hour's wait in the raw cold, boarded a train to Huddersfield' (Harrison, 1992: 180).

As soon as it was published, Harrison praised J. G. Ballard's *The Atrocity Exhibition* (1970) for its 'unshakeable basis in observed reality' and its understanding that '*The fiction must be an aspect of the life of its characters, not the sole reason for it*' (Harrison, 2005a: 87). His brief discussion of the book concludes with a far-reaching statement of aesthetic intent:

> Ballard constructs his fantasies from elements to be found all around us, the architectures and cultures and life-styles of the twentieth century; his end product may be thoroughly alien, but it sends disturbing pseudopods and nerve-fibres back into the world we inhabit. Fantasy is *not* just around the corner. Neither is reality. The one stems from the other, and they are as inextricably woven as the lives of patient and doctor in the psychiatric ward. (Harrison, 2005a: 87)

As when Lucas encounters the 'familiar' in Manchester's dirty snow, or when Jill in 'Gifco' (1991) announces that Tenerife 'looks just like bloody Southend ... Southend will follow you wherever you go' (Harrison, 2003c: 277), Harrison's fiction abounds in moments of what might be termed soiled epiphany, when the experience of vision, in the heightened, quasi-mystical sense of that term, rubs up against the resolutely prosaic and reveals their inseparable conjunction. In a 1989 essay, Harrison spoke of what he termed 'the breach of the familiar', and quoted the Russian formalist, Victor Shklovsky, of whose resistance to 'the steady domestication of all new experience' he approved (Harrison, 2005b: 151). Shklovsky insisted that art should counter 'the automism of perception' through a calculated process of estrangement (*Ostranenie*) or 'the poetic use of devices such as disrupted metrical patterns, long descriptive passages, metaphors and other figures of rhetoric to produce a semantic shift which makes the habitual appear strangely unfamiliar, rather as though it were being perceived for the first time' (Macey, 2000: 284). Harrison regularly deploys such effects, refusing, even in his earliest stories, to offer genre fiction's explanations, clarifications and consolations.

Lost in Soho

Harrison's fondness for found material, 'dialogue you've heard on the bus', dates back to his youthful reading of *The Waste Land*, a poem in which T. S. Eliot fashions 'a whole thing out of fragments and at the same time demonstrates that it is still fragmentary' (Lea, 2012: np). *Climbers*, *The Course of the Heart* and *Signs of Life* – written as Margaret Thatcher gave way first to John Major and then to the 'New' Labour of Tony Blair, and free market capitalism became ever more aggressive and damaging in a Britain more divided than it had been since the nineteenth century – turn this aesthetic on an increasingly atomized country which, hard as it occasionally tried, could no longer begin to make sense of itself.

In an ambivalent review of *Signs of Life*, Liam McIlvanney notes its 'evident flaws': a lack of 'purposive structure', an 'uncoordinated' narrative, the 'static quality of photographs' that mar 'its episodes', the 'small masterpieces of layered description' that '[enrich] the texture' but 'clog the narrative [and] hinder its momentum' (1997: 22). Although his final comment – 'When you write with [such] uncommon brilliance ... you can be forgiven almost anything' – sweetens a bitter pill, McIlvanney fails to recognize how the book's style is integral to its substance. *Signs of Life* is a decadent novel, or rather, a critique of decadence which turns the characteristics of a decadent epoch against itself. The French novelist Paul Bourget argued a century ago that,

> A decadent style is one in which the unity of the book breaks down to make room for the independence of the page, in which the page breaks down to make room for the independence of the sentence, and the sentence to make room for the independence of the word. (Constable et al., 1999: 16)

Harrison does not go as far as this, but the sense in which individual observations resist coalescing into a harmonious whole runs throughout the novel. It is the juxtaposition, rather than conjunction, of sites and places that ultimately joins them; they are linked through acts of imaginative association and intuitive recognition. Hence the Soho of expensive restaurants and designer clothes exists alongside, and is partially built on, places such as the northern quarry where Choe illegally dumps radioactive waste and mutated genetic material. The money Choe earns from these despoilings is funnelled back into London, feeding the capital's insatiable appetite for consumption and display.

Michael Bracewell's *The Nineties: When Surface was Depth* opens with a tableau reminiscent of many of the descriptions in *Signs of Life*:

> Here we were at the tail end of the 1980s, children of the late Fifties and early Sixties, beginning to feel the odd twinge of the thickening process of early middle age, but still young enough to want to carry the fight to the enemy; to emulate the Balzacian hero, staring down on the city of Paris, to declaim, 'And now you and I come to grips!' (Bracewell, 2002: 2)

As Bracewell adds however, things were not quite as they seemed.

> But what, exactly, right now, was there down in the city to come to grips with? The heroism of the war-cry had been replaced by a kind of Mock Heroism, which had declared itself (out of nowhere, too – a sudden hesitancy in the voice, skidding a few tones from manly au-

thority to punctured confidence) only at the moment of announcing the challenge. Or were the vocal cords simply learning the cadences of irony? (Bracewell, 2002: 2)

Pre-millennial England was clearly not somewhere Harrison felt at home; his depictions of it insist on its vapidity, its obsession with surface, the vulgarities of unchecked consumerism and the increasing erosion of 'community' even as an idea. Part of the problem with the Major (and Blair) years is the sense not that there has been a decline from a mythical Golden Age, but that the entropic dissolution that had been such a feature of *New Worlds*'s fiction had become all-pervasive and seemingly irreversible: Fenris had snapped his chain and Asgard was falling in increasingly tatty fragments. Harrison however said little of mere party politics. The malaise Britain suffers in *Signs of Life* is in part the 'reflection on post-imperial melancholy' (Luckhurst, 2005: 1777), but it is also a more urgent criticism of prevailing ideologies, of 'the fierce ease with which capitalism husks humanity' (Macfarlane, 2013: n.p.). Both Choe and Isobel make the mistake of thinking that they can buy their dreams, or in the latter's case, that being able to buy a dream is the same thing as being able to afford it, or to live with its consequences. Neither can accept that the promises made in glossy brochures never come true, for each clings to their particular illusion: a faster car, more powerful stereo speakers, the power of flight.

McIlvanney's (1997: 22) review drew attention to the ways in which Harrison's prose, 'intoxicated with the detail of urban life', was 'almost pathologically precise' in distinguishing whether someone wears 'Levi 501s or 620s'. Arguing that it 'enriches the texture' of the book but slows the pace of the story, he did not consider what motivated the obsession with brand names, marques and technological details. In his first person narrative, China's perceptions are reflexive, informing readers about his surroundings, but also providing insights into his character. Keenly attuned to the nuances of denim, the superiority of one Tom Waits album over another, or the 'faint smell of money ... unleaded fuel and sophisticated catalysers' associated with Audis and BMWs (McIlvanney, 1997: 15), China is indivisible from the culture that supports his business, 'lost in Soho', and often uncomfortable, watching younger women sitting 'under the ads for Jello-shots, Schlitz and Molson's Canadian' drinking Lowenbrau in the company of boys in 'soft three-button shirts and Timberland boots' (McIlvanney, 1997: 23). As Bracewell (2002: 2–3) writes, 'In the lab of semiotics ..., everything was significant, busily signifying something - it was all signage'. Globalized, purposeless, the London of *Signs of Life* fulfils the direst prophecies of Guy Debord or Jean Baudrillard, the representation of the real supplanting the real itself. Far from being some sort of prose cornflour, as McIlvanney suggests, these 'texture-thickening' catalogues are cultural indictments, making the book a dark parody of the 'shopping and fucking' novels that dominated the decade's airport bookstalls, and linking it with the precise military and technological details that serve such ironic purposes in the Cornelius stories. *Signs of Life* hacks at London the way Tom Wolfe's *Bonfire of the Vanities* (1987) hacked at the New York of ten years earlier, though with far less liberal self-righteousness or empty cynicism.

Harrison's use of brand names allows a precise snapshot of his milieu; twenty years on, the novel is, albeit grudgingly, an evocative historical artefact, a time-traveller's Berlitz guide to media London, where 'The women were in PR: the last of the power dressers. The men were in advertising, balding to a pony-tail' (Harrison, 1997: 20). They also serve as an indirect judgement of character. Whereas Stephen King litters his novels of the 1980s with brand names to create a believable place and time that could then be disrupted by horrific events, Harrison opted for a more restrained approach, noting details but not commenting on them, as when Flaubert (1992: 106) presents Homais the pharmacist in 'a frock-coat, yellow nankeen trousers, beaver-skin shoes' and leaves the reader to draw their own conclusions as to his likely worth. In Harrison's words, 'If you showed the kinds of things that people wanted and used the brand names – then you wouldn't need to do any more. It would condemn itself' (Bould, 2005: 331).

The technique is used most insistently, and effectively, in the portrayal of Choe. Although China often dissects his friend's character, it is his preferences that are most revealing of his state of mind, as when he has a fondness for listening to Lou Reed singing 'What's Good' from his *Magic and Loss* album or puts his fish and chips in the microwave and melts half a pound of St Agur cheese over them. Choe's passions for extreme sports, fast cars and attention-seeking behaviour often make him unpopular (and a veritable personification of his epoch), but they serve ultimately to make his revelation about the green girl and Jumble Wood all the more poignant as Harrison once more imbricates the miraculous and the mundane. On China's first visit to the now despoiled place, 'There was a dead sheep in the shallows, bloated and grey. Around it floated literally hundreds of used latex gloves, their whiteish transparent fingers ghostly as live squid in the dim light' (Harrison, 1997: 55). He later reflects on the significance of this violation:

> Something happened to Choe in Jumble Wood when he was young: something that centralised itself in his life so thoroughly that for over twenty years, puzzled, charmed and frustrated, he was compelled to return there yearly on the anniversary of the event. (Harrison, 1997: 252–3)

(Extra)ordinary: trash or treasure?

In 'Ring of Pain' (1971), Harrison's narrator beholds:

> Chainstore spilled onto the pavement, bright gilt bracelets, buttons, o pretty pretty. Bijou teeth of freegift society wrapped in cellophane. Sale of shopsoiled goods – municipal buildings, pissoirs, beauty spots – all slightly marked, prices slashed. Decorated himself with a string of plastic beads ...
> Finally found a Sainsbury's, helped himself to a pink carrier bag. (Harrison, 1975: 131–2)

The story lacks the control of later pieces (is that 'pretty pretty' *really* an allusion to *Barbarella*?), but for all its sub-Joycean compounds, it provides further evidence of Harrison's ability to imbue cultural detritus with visionary possibilities, and to thereby encourage fresh perceptions in line with the teachings of mystics and Russian Formalists alike. There is a sense too that like this story's contemporaries, Elizabeth Beresford's Wombles, Harrison is an inveterate recycler, someone who is always 'making good use of the things that he finds, Things that the everyday folk leave behind'. Discarded, insignificant rubbish is gathered up and transformed into art. A Harrison description always offers some beautifully worked phrase or image, even when the thing described is soiled, broken or cruel. The danger is that the aesthetic will overshadow the political, or that an exquisite metaphor will occlude what it ought to illuminate, but as Harrison's story notes, reviews, essays and frequent blog posts demonstrate, he has long been wary of these temptations and scathing of works which yield to them. Uncompromising, mordant, cynical without being nihilistic, his fiction continues to unsettle and surprise, and his urban excavations to resonate.

Notes

1 In a discussion of his film, *Prospero's Books* (1991), at the Bristol Arnolfini in 1991.

2 Swinburne Sinclair-Pater, 'aesthete extraordinary and Interstellar Anarchist' (Harrison, 1974: 64), appears in *The Centauri Device*.

3 In the toilet of a Blackpool nightclub I saw the graffiti: 'I like beer because I'm from Warrington'.

4 Harrison (2003e: 438) notes that 'Petromax is the brand name of a gaslamp used in Himalayan villages in the 1950s'. 'Petromax's mirror, if anyone wants to know, is in the lavatory of the Merrie England café,' we are told, 'behind the pictogram on the neat gray door, above the sink with its flake of yellow soap' (Harrison, 2000b: 560, 561). However, Harrison later noted, 'Viriconium entradistas will be disappointed to find [the café] is no more' (Harrison, 2003e: 438), raising the intriguing notion of readers seeking it out, as Beatles fans might head for a certain zebra crossing.

5 Harrison made this comment at a reading at The Horse Hospital, London, on 7 November 2013.

Works Cited

Banks, Iain (1988) 'Introduction', in M. John Harrison, *Viriconium*, pp. vii-xii. London: Gollancz.

Bould, Mark (2005) 'Old, Mean and Misanthropic: An Interview with M. John Harrison', in Mark Bould and Michelle Reid (eds) *Parietal Games: Critical Writings by and on M. John Harrison*, pp. 326–41. London: Science Fiction Foundation.

Bracewell, Michael (2002) *The Nineties: When Surface was Depth*. London: Flamingo.

Constable, Liz, Dennis Denisoff and Matthew Potolsky (1999) 'Introduction', in *Perennial Decay: On the Aesthetics and Politics of Decadence*, pp. 1–32. Philadelphia: University of Pennsylvania Press.

Flaubert, Gustave (1992) *Madame Bovary*, trans. Geoffrey Wall. London: Penguin.

Harrison, M. John (1974) *The Centauri Device*. New York: Doubleday.

Harrison, M. John (1975) 'Ring of Pain', *The Machine in Shaft Ten*, pp. 131–7. London: Panther.

Harrison, M. John (1992) *The Course of the Heart*. London: Gollancz.

Harrison, M. John (1993) 'The Ash Circus', Langdon Jones and Michael Moorcock (eds) *The New Nature of the Catastrophe*, pp. 35–48. London: Millennium.

Harrison, M. John (1997) *Signs of Life*. London: Gollancz.

Harrison, M. John (2000a) *In Viriconium*, in *Viriconium*. London: Gollancz. 437–540.

Harrison, M. John (2000b) 'A Young Man's Journey to Viriconium', in *Viriconium*, pp. 541–62. London: Gollancz.

Harrison, M. John (2003a) 'Egnaro', in *Things That Never Happen*, pp. 105–25. San Francisco, CA: Night Shade.

Harrison, M. John (2003b) 'Empty', in *Things That Never Happen*, pp. 329–49. San Francisco: Night Shade.

Harrison, M. John (2003c) 'Gifco', in *Things That Never Happen*, pp. 259–83. San Francisco, CA: Night Shade.

Harrison, M. John (2003d) 'The Horse of Iron and How We Can Know It', in *Things That Never Happen*, pp. 243–57. San Francisco, CA: Night Shade.

Harrison, M. John (2003e) 'Story Notes', in *Things That Never Happen*, pp. 435–43. San Francisco, CA: Night Shade.

Harrison, M. John (2005a) 'A Literature of Comfort', in Mark Bould and Michelle Reid (eds) *Parietal Games: Critical Writings By and On M. John Harrison*, pp. 84–8. London: Science Fiction Foundation.

Harrison, M. John (2005b) 'The Profession of Science Fiction, 40: The Profession of Fiction', Mark Bould and Michelle Reid (eds) *Parietal Games: Critical Writings By and On M. John Harrison*, pp. 144–54. London: Science Fiction Foundation.

Harrison, M. John (2013) *Climbers*. London: Gollancz.

Lea, Richard (2012) 'M. John Harrison: A Life in Writing', *Guardian* (20 July), accessed 1 April 2016, https://www.theguardian.com/culture/2012/jul/20/m-john-harrison-life-in-writing

Luckhurst, Roger (2005) *Science Fiction*. Cambridge: Polity.

McIlvanney, Liam (1997) 'M. John Harrison, *Signs of Life*', *The Times Literary Supplement* (30 May): 22.

Macey, David (2000) *The Penguin Dictionary of Critical Theory*. London: Penguin.

Macfarlane, Robert (2013) 'Introduction', in M. John Harrison, *Climbers*, pp. xi–xx. London: Gollancz.

Pater, Walter (1986) *The Renaissance: Studies in Art and Poetry*. Oxford: Oxford University Press.

Wilde, Oscar (2006) *The Picture of Dorian Gray*, ed. Joseph Bristow. Oxford: World's Classics.

Withnail and I (1987) writer and director Bruce Robinson, Handmade Films.

On Versioning

Ryan Elliott

In nearly all of his stories, M. John Harrison reuses images, descriptions, scenes, characters and narrative structures to bridge texts in a primarily thematic and interpretive manner. He calls this 'versioning'.[1] Its visibility to readers draws attention to the artificial, performed nature of writing, thereby confronting an underlying set of assumptions common to popular fiction – such as the value of and necessity for suspension of disbelief – and encouraging a radical disruption of the ways in which we typically envision authorial process and experience and interconnect stories. While some of the best critical treatments of Harrison's work take note of versioning and what it contributes to the reading of particular stories,[2] the full extent of Harrison's versioning has yet to be addressed.

The reader as author, and a context theory of textual construction

In one of few instances of Harrison speaking about versioning, he grounds the process with ideas on textual construction that will be familiar to the post-structuralist:

> I don't see much difference between a fiction compounded of other fictions which used to be separate, and a lot of fictions which used to

be part of one thing, that have been separated and de-compounded into single fictions. For me the whole process is to do with the flow between those two concepts, with the result that a short story like 'The Quarry' can become briefly a chapter in *The Course of the Heart*, [but] could easily have become a chapter in something else. There is no inherent rightness for any of the things in a novel or a story to be together. They're only together because I write the connective material that makes it seem as if they're together. (Strahan and Wolfe, 2013)

This statement extends Harrison's long-running commentary on the interlinked processes of reading and writing, the densest and most pointed example of which is the blog post 'very afraid', in which he writes:

My feeling is that the reader performs most of the act of writing. A book spends a very short time being written into existence; it spends the rest of its life being read into existence. That's why I find in many current uses of the term 'active reading' such a deeply ironic tautology. Reading was always 'active'; the text itself always demanded the reader's interaction if the fiction was to be brought forth. (Harrison, 2007b: n.p.)

According to this model of textual construction, a story is not a settled object. Rather, it is a set of textual elements the reader assembles into the intuited shape of a story. The writer does not generate it, but rather provides an arrangement of rhetorical constructs that the reader combines in a more or less anticipated fashion. The resulting texts are never exactly the same: Harrison posits that 'even with an apparently plain and simple novel, if it has twelve thousand readers there will be twelve thousand different novels' (Strahan and Wolfe, 2013). Since it is ultimately the reader who makes the fiction, a writer cannot sculpt a Platonic textual object that will be viewed and experienced the same way by everyone, but must rely on a more or less shared cultural backdrop and a mutual understanding of language to guide the reader's inferences. Thus, Harrison leaves clues towards particular ways of reading his stories.

A recent clue is the word 'context' in the novel *Empty Space* (2012). The word appears there thirteen times, a substantial increase from its once-a-book presence in both *Light* (2002) and *Nova Swing* (2006). It is especially helpful when reading Harrison to remember Paul de Man's observation that 'to the extent that all language is conceptual, it always already speaks about language and not about things ... If all language is about language, then the paradigmatic linguistic model is that of an entity that confronts itself' (De Man, 1979: 152–3). Applied to the fiction in which they find themselves, two dialogues about 'context' reveal its centrality to understanding the composition of stories. Here, in the word's first appearance, Brian Tate speaks to Anna Kearney:

> After some minutes he put the bag down, leaned across the table and tapped Anna's hand sharply.
> 'Ow,' said Anna.
> 'Nothing is real,' he said.
> 'I'm sorry?'
> 'Nothing is real. Do you understand? There are only contexts. And what do they context? ... More contexts, of course!' (Harrison, 2012: 5)

A story, then, is a reader-generated context that makes a cohesive shape out of disparate, re-combinatory linguistic elements, in the same way that when using the phrase 'connect the dots', we acknowledge that there is not a line or a shape already there, but that through an act of interpretation we create a line or a shape that will context the dots. Really, there are only dots and possible contexts the dots can be interpreted into and out of, hence constellations.

Later, Aschemann's Assistant expresses another aspect of this burgeoning context theory to George the gene tailor:

> 'Come out of a [twink] tank, you spend your life trying to get back in one.'
> She didn't know about that, she said. 'But you quickly see that every context has another context wrapped around it, and another one round that.' (Harrison, 2012: 209)

After telling us that fictions exist not as self-subsistent objects, but as observer-dependent contexts, *Empty Space* then tells us that these endlessly parse and infinitely stack. So when we compare two fictions, we do not merely place two stories side by side, but rather generate a third thing out of that comparison – a new context comprised of both stories compounded.

Reader-generated contexts are how fictions are constructed and what they ultimately are. 'Intertextuality' occurs when an element in one text references another text, and so generates an additional context involving them both. One text becomes a context for another, and from this new frame of reference the texts change, mutating into different texts together. 'Versioning' is an intertextual process whereby Harrison references his own work by reinserting or otherwise revisiting prior material in new fictions. In nearly all of his work since *A Storm of Wings* (1982), Harrison has reused elements, from images to narrative structures.[3] The fictions in which he first deployed and later redeployed these elements can all be experienced as putative singular stories. One might ordinarily read 'A Young Man's Journey to Viriconium' (1985), for example, in a separate context from *Climbers* (1989), yet since each contains an instance of the same scene, the two stories are made to occupy a context together.

In the short story, a mentor character, Mr. Ambrayses, tells the narrator how 'when [he] was a child [his] grandmother often took [him] about with her' (Harrison, 2003b: 175). He recalls an incident that happened in a café looking out onto some gardens:

> Along the whole length of the room we were in ran a tinted window, through which you could see the gardens in the gathering twilight, paths glazed with drizzle giving back the last bit of light in the sky, the benches and empty flower beds grey and equivocal-looking, the sodium lamps coming on by the railings. Superimposed, on the inside of the glass, was the distant reflection of the café: it was as if someone had dragged all the chairs and tables out into the gardens, where the serving women waited behind the stainless steel counter, wiping their faces with a characteristic gesture in the steam from the *bain marie*, unaware of the wet grass, the puddles, the blackened but energetic pigeons bobbing round their feet. (Harrison, 2003b: 175–6)

In the novel, the narrator, Mike, describes the same incident, though in his version the café looks out onto a car park. The two versions differ in terms of some descriptive elements, but otherwise remain much the same:

> There was a tinted plate-glass window the whole length of the place we were in. Through it you could see the car-park in the Bradford rain – long shallow puddles ruffled by the wind, one or two cars parked at careless angles, the back entrance of Smith's or Menzies'. On the inside of the glass was the reflection of the cafe. By an optical accident they were superimposed. It was as if someone had dragged thirty plastic tables out there, and a hundred plastic chairs. The women behind the stainless steel counter wiped their faces with a characteristic gesture in the steam, unconscious of the puddles under their feet. (Harrison, 2004: 9)

Both versions culminate with one of the waitresses seen in the reflection looking up and 'staring ahead as if she had begun to suspect that she was caught up in two worlds':

> Suddenly she ... looked directly out at me and waved. She beckoned. I could see her mouth open and close to make the words, 'Here! Over here!'
> She's alive! I thought. It was a shock. I felt that I was alive, too. I got up and ran straight into the plate-glass window and was concussed. (Harrison, 2003b: 177; cf. Harrison, 2004: 10)

Sharing this scene makes the stories exist, superimposed, as a third thing. When we read *Climbers* and notice the versioned scene, 'A Young Man's Journey' asserts itself as a constant backdrop; and the same occurs with *Climbers* when we re-tread 'A Young Man's Journey'. One text becomes a context for the other and vice versa, beckoning different readings of each and thereby making new texts out of both.

While this scene meta-textually offers an image of versioning – of creating a new text through superimposition – its shared content addresses a key concern of both texts: people who believe the world offers more than what it initially seems to, and so desire escape into a part of it they imagine as being fuller, more 'alive', than where they are now. In 'A Young Man's Journey', the narrator wanders northern England looking for a way into Viriconium, a city that reputedly lies on the other side of a mirror; in *Climbers*, the narrator leaves London to seek rejuvenation by obsessively climbing around northern England, thereby forming a counterpoint to the short story's escape route. The destination of escape inverts across texts, indicating that what is of note – via what overlaps – is the urge to escape, as well as a complementary sense of the world's potential immanence.

One of versioning's central functions, then, is to fold stories into and across one another around focal points through which they ought to be interpreted. The nature of this linkage is largely thematic, philosophical and abstract rather than literalistic, and asks: Why is this character, image, narrative structure or piece of text being recycled? Working atop the theory that texts and their messages mutate across readings, Harrison leverages this process of contextual (re)building to steer it along particular lines of enquiry. Versioning as a form of intertextuality disrupts the way that we tend to delineate genres, piece together an authorial oeuvre, and interconnect texts in general.

Death at the hands of the text

By re-contextualizing language and literary constructs, versioning not only mutates the meanings of words, names, passages, images and narrative structures but also reconfigures our understanding of writing itself. In a blog post, 'burn other people's stuff', Harrison quotes artist Chris Ofili, who says, 'The studio is a laboratory, not a factory ... An exhibition is the result of your experiments, but the process is never-ending. So an exhibition is not a conclusion.' Harrison adds:

> Neither is a novel. I prefer the way artists & performers describe their practice to the way writers describe theirs. I prefer rehearsals to prod-uct ... I don't mean a draft; that I shouldn't be taken to mean a draft is precisely what I'm trying to get over when I say I prefer the way artists & performers describe their practice. (Harrison, 2010: n.p.)

Drafting and versioning are disanalagous because drafts progress to-wards and culminate in a final product that erases or renders unnecessary prior iterations. For Harrison, on the other hand, a piece can and often does become part of another, which makes every Harrisonian text a 'rehearsal' rather than a 'conclusion'.

Commenting on the post, Aaron White refers to theatrical director Peter Brook's *The Empty Space* (1968), which distinguishes between roles that are 'built' and roles that are 'born':

> A character isn't a static thing and it can't be built like a wall. Rehearsals don't lead progressively to a first night. This is something very hard for some actors to understand ... All through rehearsals [the really creative actor] has been exploring aspects of a character which he senses always be partial, to be less than the truth – so he is compelled, by the honesty of his search, endlessly to shed and start again ... He must destroy and abandon his results even if what he picks up seems almost the same ... And this is the only way that a part, instead of being built, can be born. The role that has been built is the same every night – except that it slowly erodes. For the part that is born to be the same it must always be reborn, which makes it always different. (Brook, 1968: 141–2)

Brook rejects the distinction between rehearsal and production, since repetitions of the former do not 'build' to an instance of the latter; rather, with every iteration, the actor destroys and abandons his work, undercutting the idea that a performance bears any essential difference from a rehearsal.

Any text is provisional; the process is the product. Considering any Harrisonian text – or, indeed, any text – final or stand-alone isolates it from a wider discourse and ignores its role in a more meaningful operation. A more accurate depiction of Harrison's writing – and of writing more generally – has every piece existing in a state of constant flux. Versioning literalizes this process, and not only does away, like Brook, with a rather useless distinction, but also opens the door to more radical ways of understanding the act of writing and the role of the author. By preferring the term 'rehearsal' to 'draft', Harrison gestures towards writing as a kind of performance, and he is not alone. Robert Frost claims that 'I look at a poem as a performance. I look on the poet as ... a performer' (Poirier, 1960: n.p.), and Stanley Kunitz calls poetry 'an art of transformation, that magical performance' (Busa, 1982: n.p.). Kunitz goes on to compare writing to climbing, a 'performance of death' (Busa, 1982: n.p.) in the way a trapeze artist or tightrope walker risks their life in a kind of performance, an image Harrison deploys in *Nova Swing*.

Harrison dedicated *Empty Space* to Forced Entertainment, a theatrical group whose work, with artistic director Tim Etchells, is durational and relies heavily on improvisation involving the continual re-use of prepared text and props. Asked how Forced Entertainment influenced the novel, Harrison explains:

> I had never before seen anything like [their work] in my life, so it was bound to have an impact on everything I did thereafter ... I suddenly began to see my own work in terms of a performed thing that possibly it would only be performed the once between me and the page ... More than that, the whole idea of performance, the whole idea of theatre which questions the nature of theatre and the nature of performance, and by doing that turns itself the other way around and questions the nature of performing reality, performing being a person – it was something that interested me before. But once I began to be involved with Forced Ent and Tim, it became a major thing, and I think that in *Empty Space* ... the definition of identity is that which is performed.[4]

If writing is performance, and identity is 'that which is performed', then writing and identity are linked processes. Versioning presents an interface for interpreting – and so an engine for generating – identity, continuously engendering the authorial self by interpreting and re-contextualising a prior self *qua* piece of writing. Just as there is no final or conclusive 'product' of the writing process, there is no absolute, singular or even fully coherent authorial identity.

In the comments below a blog post, 'sightline', Harrison toys with this notion. He asks, 'So am I saying that the book is a tool too, which I use to write a different me? Do you ever feel anything like that?' (Harrison, 2008: n.p.). The idea also manifests in a passage from *Nova Swing* versioned from 'The Neon Heart Murders' (1997). It depicts the members of a two-piece band, one a young pianist, the other an older saxophonist. The short story's version is longer, and so perhaps more revealing:

> The pianist must always be setting one thing against another. Every piece he played was a turn against – a joke upon – some other piece, some other pianist, some other instrument ... [Y]ou could tell that when he was alone in his room at night ... he would play against himself, and then against the self thus created, and then against the next: until all fixed notion of self had leaked away into this infinite slippage. (Harrison, 2003a: 409–10)

As for the saxophonist, 'the universe now remade itself for him continually,' we are told, 'out of a metaphor, two or three invariable rules, and a musical instrument' (Harrison, 2003a: 410). Together, the descriptions serve as commentary on not only the construction of these two stories, but on Harrison's wider approach. We notice versioning in the tendency of the pianist to 'play against himself'; and from 'the self thus created', see that his identity is entwined with his process. The author interprets a prior self via a prior work, and remakes both of those in same gesture.

Harrison also includes himself in the decomposition and recomposition that occurs with versioning, by repeatedly using Mike and Michael as character names in his fiction. Like many Harrisonian characters, those who share a name with him exhibit characteristics of disorder, dissociation or denial to varying degrees. Mike in *Climbers* obsessively wraps his life around climbing in an escape vector from a failed marriage, while Michael Kearney spends *Light* running from an entity he tries to keep at bay by killing his sexual partners. We recall Ashlyme, the protagonist of *In Viriconium* (1982), who makes his career painting unflattering portraits. Attaching his own name to troubled characters suggests Harrison painting unflattering *self*-portraits, just as the Viriconium stories serve as unflattering portraits of the genre of which they partake, not to mention previous versions of themselves.

While this process of self-investigation and self-critique seems largely conscious or controlled, a repeating component of Harrison's work – and statements from Harrison himself – argue to the contrary:

'there's a huge and welcome unconscious input', he says, 'I never refuse an intuition, the more inexplicable the better' (Mathew, 2007:
n.p.). Representations of the unconscious or otherwise unknowable
pervade Harrison's fiction, often deployed as a setting or an aspect
of the setting: the shifting, eponymous city of the Viriconium stories; the Pleroma of *The Course of the Heart* (2992); the event site
in *Nova Swing*; and the Tract in all three of the *Empty Space* novels.
Unconscious drives also define Harrison's characters, many of whom
are compulsive or obsessed. Determined to self-destruct, they often
lose themselves seeking personal fantasies, escape from wounded circumstances, some kind of transcendence, solutions to insoluble problems, or an intersection of all of these. The nexus of any Harrisonian
text is therefore the friction between his characters and the external-
ized representation of the unconscious, since characters confront the
uncontrolled and unknown in themselves as they confront it in the
world. Moreover, they are nearly all destroyed by it. To read Harrison's
fiction is to witness various ways that controlling people, needy people, and people 'lost in their own lives' collide with what can never be
understood or contained, and wind up irrevocably altered or dead.

Detective Aschemann, the protagonist of 'The Neon Heart
Murders' and a protagonist in *Nova Swing*, provides a case study. Both
stories task him with solving a series of bizarre killings. In 'The Neon
Heart Murders' he visits his estranged wife's house, 'less in a search
for clues,' we are told, 'than a search for himself – for a detective capable of understanding the crime' (Harrison, 2003a: 406). His ex-wife,
Utzie, is an agoraphobic whose compulsion to fill her home with a
maze of objects is outdone only by his own dissociation from his effects on others. While Utzie keeps the world at bay with her maze,
Aschemann hypocritically keeps himself at bay through a constant
denial of responsibility. Like *Light's* Michael Kearney, whose attempts
to escape his anxiety propel him inexorably towards the source of it,
whereupon it kills him, Aschemann's need to evade himself drives him
into the event site that is *Nova Swing's* unconscious. Unsurprisingly,
he dies there, watching his body dissolve from the legs up and wondering if he will be reborn as one of the Café Surf two-piece's 'bebop
golems'.

If the unnamed city of 'The Neon Heart Murders' is its unconscious, a 'surf, of buildings and people and consumer goods', then what, we are asked, 'if crimes are whipped off the crest of events like spray, with no more cause than that?' (Harrison, 2003a: 412). With this in mind, this passage from *Nova Swing* sends a message to the reader ('seek me inside'):

Aschemann had a high turnover in assistants because he was fond of advising them, 'The true detective starts in the centre of the maze: the crimes make their way through to him. Never forget, you uncover your own heart at the heart of it.' Another of his favourites, even more puzzling to young men and women conditioned to seek answers, was, 'Uncertainty is all we have.' (Harrison, 2007a: 27)

Aschemann's professed approach to detective work fulfils both the role of the metaphorical author (interpreting the 'crimes' generated by his own unconscious) and of the metaphorical reader (interpreting the 'crimes' of the text), an uncertainty that tells us the two positions are not distinguishable, but rather entangled or superposed. As Aschemann invites assistants to consider his process and confronts them with unorthodox notions about detective work, so Harrison encourages the reader to think of themselves as an author, and authors to think of themselves as readers, both engaged in a continuous act of self-interpretation with the text – or texts, as it were – as mediator. Harrison turns the textual mirror towards us so that we might find our own hearts at the heart of it, and subsequently experience a kind of death.

Almost all Harrisonian characters die from, or are irrevocably altered by their encounters with the insoluble at the heart of a given work, telling us that the dovetailing processes of reading and writing involve the interrogation and ultimately the destruction of identity at the hands of the unconscious, the inexplicable, the empty space between the components of a metaphor, the ambiguities language can never banish from itself. Death or transformation for his characters is often violent or tragic in proportion to how much they attempt to control, understand or escape the inscrutable workings of the world, themselves and others. Moreover, the process cyclically repeats: in

Empty Space the Assistant takes up Aschemann's position as detective. At the end of her investigation she finds herself at the heart of the maze, but in doing so loses herself – her self – as well. Each text dismantles identities, only for the subsequent text to take those identities apart in turn.

Against 'worldbuilding' and popular fiction

A great deal in Harrison's fiction serves as commentary on the entangled processes of writing and reading. While some characters enact the mode of reading encouraged by Harrison's texts, others function as critiques of different modes of writing and reading; or, to be more precise, against certain psychological drives behind engaging with fiction. *The Course of the Heart* is a particularly vicious example. Much of the novel concerns two versioned characters, Pam Stuyvesant and Lucas Medlar, who respond to their failed marriage by mutually constructing a fantasy with which they attempt to inject meaning into their lives and compensate for unmet desire.

Lucas and Pam's fantasy mimics the construction of fantasy fiction in its popular form. Key to this narrative is their inclusion in it: Lucas, through his authorial insert Michael Ashman, 'discovers' the secrets of a European kingdom called the Coeur, which was lost to history; while Pam is 'revealed' to be the successor to its royal lineage. Both function as parodies of roles and tropes in fantasy, and through them we see the centrality of immersion and consolation to this kind of fiction. Likewise, we witness the consequences of trying to flee the world through fantasy, since their narrative of the Coeur fails to alleviate but rather exacerbates their pain and sense of loss.

The Coeur itself represents the 'secondary worlds' of fantasy fiction, the construction of which is commonly referred to as 'worldbuilding'. Worldbuilding fiction is a subset of popular fiction that focuses on setting as a means of providing immersion. It seeks to replace 'setting' with 'world', and a conception of the former as merely a rhetorical device with the hope that something more substantive can be referenced instead. After prioritizing the secondary world concept, language becomes a tool not merely to convey setting, but to convince the reader that it possesses qualities of an actual place that we might conceivably visit: consistency; completeness; ontological autonomy (it subsists independently of any one reader or act of reading); and epistemic certainty (we can know things about it via the text). This, however, is a goal that language cannot achieve. Harrison advises:

> You cannot replicate the world in some symbols, only imply it or allude to it ... Writing isn't that kind of transaction. Communication isn't that kind of transaction. It's meant to go along with pointing and works best in such forms as, 'Pass me that chair. No, the green one.' (Harrison, 2007b: n.p.)

Antagonistic towards language possessing some degree of irresolvable ambiguity, a primary aim of worldbuilding fiction is to prevent the interpretability that Harrison considers responsible for every act of reading producing a different text, and which versioning leverages for its effects.

As part of preventing interpretability, intertextuality in worldbuilding fiction often reduces to spatio-temporal literalism. Characters, settings and events must retain an air of consistency across texts to convey the sense that the separate fictions are all one continuous fiction – the closer to arrive at their not being a fiction at all. Prequels and sequels form the lifeblood of the modern entertainment industry, with fictions being bolted onto the back and front ends of franchises as fast as possible. Unsatisfied with mere secondary 'worlds', these vast worldbuilding exercises promise entire secondary 'universes'. 'Reboots' are as close as popular fiction comes to versioning's multiplicity, but instead of resonating with or interrogating their previous incarnations, they erase or overwrite works that are considered failures or have exhausted themselves from a commercial standpoint, no longer able to give consumers the escape and consolation they supposedly desire.

Secondary worlds and suspension of disbelief are central to popular fiction because these are often considered necessary for the text to become a portal to a realm where we get what we want but cannot find in the world, such as consistency, comprehensibility and closure

– all things Harrison's characters desperately seek, only to wind up 'batter[ing] themselves to death like huge rawboned moths inside the Japanese lamps of their own neuroses' (Harrison, 2006: 2). Yet these psychological drives also propel texts one would not consider 'exhaustive[ly] surveyed' (Harrison, 2007b: n.p.) and which do not employ fantastic settings. Before taking up Lucas's worldbuilding project of the Coeur, Pam avidly reads romance novels, a genre that does not always employ secondary worlds, yet is nonetheless known for its wish-fulfillment aspect.

Harrison's position extends itself to indict more than just a particular mode of reading and writing fiction. The concept at the heart of 'Egnaro' (1980) – a secret known to everyone but yourself – is the quintessential conspiracy theory: a narrative designed to make sense of random coincidence, and which positions the theorist at the centre of the world. In *The Course of the Heart*, Lucas (who shares his name with the conspiracy theorist in 'Egnaro') and Pam construct an alternate-history Europe, which pivots around an ancient royal lineage that ends with Pam herself. This push towards recognizing acts of fantasy beyond their outlet in fiction evokes the ways political, corporate and social forces manipulate the perceived boundaries between possible and impossible, between reality and fantasy, to fuel our desire for what is unattainable and so keep us in a perpetual state of fix-seeking which their offerings never fully satisfy.

Versioning, considered in terms of the politics of fantasy and desire, then, serves an ideological role, since it prevents not only one text, but all the texts in which versions are recognized, from being read in an escapist fashion. Authorial process made visible to the reader ruptures suspension of disbelief and upends the immersive element central to popular fiction. A story's uniqueness, completeness and self-subsistence disintegrates, and the true nature of fiction is revealed. It is artifice, a performance, an ongoing language game between writer and reader, not a self-subsistent door onto a counterfactual realm of faux-objects and fulfilment. Moreover, since it calls to mind another instance of the same piece of text or literary construct, but from a different context, versioning sparks an analytic faculty that compares the versions and their contexts. After rupturing suspension of disbelief, and inviting readers to approach fictions in a thematic, ideological and psychological mode rather than a literalistic one, the content of Harrison's work then propels them into a confrontation with the politics of desire, escape and consolation. A concept or ideological position is often maintained via the survival of what is deemed its opposite. Versioning, at its core, is merely author-specific intertextuality. When we note that versioning does not require the repetition of large units of language, but includes the merest repetition of names, images or symbols, it seems that the literalistic intertextuality connecting works of popular fiction also counts as versioning. So versioning and worldbuilding's literalistic intertextuality are not opposites; rather, worldbuilding's intertextuality is a subset of versioning that confines itself to an interconnectivity that, instead of enlivening texts, deadens them through an active suppression of interpretive possibility.

Writing on *The Course of the Heart*, Graham Fraser develops Jan Zwicky's ideas on 'resonance' to illuminate the ways in which fragmentation and versioning in Harrison's fiction achieve their effects. Without space between fragments or versions, without 'distinctness', resonance does not occur:

> Resonance is indeed a function of the attunement of various distinct components of a whole. But their distinctness is crucial: resonance involves the carrying-over of an impulse from one component to another. If components are fused, a resonant relation between them is impossible. (Fraser, 2005: 306)

With versioning, each iteration of a name, symbol or piece of text resonates with others owing to the *differences* in their contexts. So while the name 'Lucas' appears in both 'Egnaro' and *The Course of the Heart*, the distinctness of these stories paradoxically encourages a comparative interpretation. Versioning employs language's allusive capacities to encourage interpretive resonance within and between texts. Literalistic intertextuality, on the other hand, fuses the separate components together by methodically eliminating the distinctness of the contexts in which components occur, rendering the connectivity between texts inert.

The intertextuality of worldbuilding fiction is an anxious attempt to seal off interpretability from the reader, and so amounts to a kind of failed writing. Again, we are reminded of Harrison's characters, who, on the run or in hiding from themselves, try to rationalize the irrational, control the uncontrollable, escape the inescapable, or obtain the unobtainable, only to later be mangled by it. And again we ought to recall Paul de Man: 'The paradigmatic linguistic model is that of an entity that confronts itself'. In popular fiction, the relationship between the components of writing is without confrontation. The relationship between the reader and the text, between the author and the text, between the text and itself, and other texts – all of these desperately try to interact in the forever frictionless and amiable fashion that is the dream-portrait corporations paint for us of capitalism and themselves. Versioning, however, through its embrace of the idea of all writing as rehearsal – a performed confrontation with a previous self *qua* piece of writing – provides glimpses of the linguistic model from which all other acts of writing derive. Indeed, if we were to take the author out of versioning, we would be left with intertextuality, and see that all writing is a kind of versioning.

Notes

1 Personal correspondence.

2 See, for example, Fraser (2005) and Kincaid (2013).

3 Kincaid (2013) suggests versioning can be detected in Harrison's fiction as early as 'The Lamia and Lord Cromis' (1971).

4 Q&A session, *Irradiating the Object* conference, 21 August 2014.

Works Cited

Brook, Peter (1968) *The Empty Space*. New York: Atheneum.

Busa, Chris (1982) 'The Art of Poetry No. 29, Stanley Kunitz', *The Paris Review* (Spring), accessed 12 November 2015, https://www.theparisreview.org/interviews/3185/stanley-kunitz-the-art-of-poetry-no-29-stanley-kunitz

De Man, Paul (1979) *Allegories of Reading: Figural Language in Rousseau, Nietzsche, Rilke, and Proust*. New Haven, CT: Yale University Press.

Fraser, Graham (2005) 'Loving the Loss of the World: *Tęsknota* and the Metaphors of the Heart', in Mark Bould and Michelle Reid (eds) *Parietal Games: Critical Writings by and on M. John Harrison*, pp. 299–318. London: SFF.

Harrison, M. John (2003a) 'The Neon Heart Murders', in *Things That Never Happen*, pp. 403–13. San Francisco, CA: Night Shade.

Harrison, M. John (2003b) 'A Young Man's Journey to London'. *Things That Never Happen*, pp. 167–85. San Francisco, CA: Night Shade.

Harrison, M. John (2004) *Climbers: A Novel*. London: Phoenix.

Harrison, M. John (2006) *The Course of the Heart*. San Francisco, CA: Night Shade.

Harrison, M. John (2007a) *Nova Swing*. New York: Random House Kindle Edition.

Harrison, M. John (2007b) 'very afraid', *Uncle Zip's Window* (27 January), accessed 27 April 2014, http://web.archive.org/web/20080410181840/ http://uzwi.wordpress.com/2007/01/27/very-afraid/

Harrison, M. John (2008) 'sightline', *Ambiente Hotel* (19 June), accessed 12 February 2015, https://ambientehotel.wordpress.com/2008/06/19/ sightline/

Harrison, M. John (2010) 'burn other people's stuff', *Ambiente Hotel* (January 16), accessed 12 November 2015, https://ambientehotel.word-press.com/2010/01/16/burn-other-peoples-stuff/

Harrison, M. John (2012) *Empty Space: A Haunting*. London: Gollancz.

Kincaid, Paul (2013) 'Reprint: A Young Man's Journey', *Through the Dark Labyrinth* (5 December), accessed 6 June 2014, https://ttdlabyrinth. wordpress.com/2013/12/05/reprint-a-young-mans-journey

Mathew, David (2007) 'M. John Harrison interviewed', *infinity plus* (6 July), accessed 12 November 2015, http://www.infinityplus.co.uk/nonfiction/ intmjh.htm

Poirier, Richard (1960) 'The Art of Poetry No. 2, Robert Frost', *The Paris Review* (Fall), accessed 12 November 2015, https://www.theparisreview. org/interviews/4678/robert-frost-the-art-of-poetry-no-2-robert-frost

Strahan, Jonathan and Gary K. Wolfe (2013) 'Episode 147: Live with M. John Harrison!', *The Coode Street Podcast* (22 June), accessed 6 August 2015, http://jonathanstrahan.podbean.com/2013/06/22/episode-147-live-with-m-john-harrison/

'LIGHT TRANSFORMS ALL THINGS'
THE SUPERPOSED MUNDANE-SUBLIME IN
M. JOHN HARRISON AND ANDREI TARKOVSKY

Christina Scholz

The *Empty Space* trilogy is hard to classify. *Light* (2002), which won the James Tiptree, Jr. Award, *Nova Swing* (2006), which won the Arthur C. Clarke and Philip K. Dick Awards, and *Empty Space: A Haunting* (2012) seem 'only loosely connected to one another':

> each is a Space Opera whose central focus is shared – the Kefahuchi Tract, a kind of light-years-wide interstellar honeypot, whose episte-mological and ontological mysteries have created rifts/riffs in reality that have haunted Alien species for aeons, and humans more recently – but which are otherwise dissimilar. (Clute, 2011: n.p.)

Stylistically and thematically, they transgress genre boundaries. They share imagistic, highly metaphoric storylines, often relating more to psychology and the 'soft sciences' than to ('hard') sf. Ostensibly concerned with the near and far future, and with potential future technologies, they are also turned inward, treating outer space as a literary manifestation of inner (psychological) space.

This essay will establish and explore a series of parallels between the trilogy and the work of Soviet filmmaker Andrei Tarkovsky, to which Harrison explicitly and implicitly alludes, especially in *Nova Swing* and most notably when referring to the interconnectedness of nostalgia and *saudade*. Nostalgia is an 'acute longing for familiar surroundings', 'a desperate attempt to achieve an imagined topographic wholeness' (Skakov, 2011: 167, 168). *Saudade*, 'a Portuguese word that has no immediate translation in English',

> refers to a deep emotional state of nostalgic longing for an absent something or someone ... It often carries a repressed knowledge that the object of longing might never return ... It is a constant feeling of absence and ... a wishful longing for completeness or wholeness. (Bell cited in Emmons and Watkins Lewis, 2006: 402).

Its untranslatability means there is no direct correspondence, no single expression that transports the same meaning. In English, there is 'longing', 'desire', 'nostalgia', 'homesickness', and so on, but every one of those words represents a more or less discrete concept, while *saudade* is more diffuse, can cover every one of those feelings and something more, something that might be difficult or impossible to put into words – a missing something that is not necessarily known, or a missing out on something, a feeling that the world (or oneself) is not complete. *Saudade* is both a condition and a place name in Harrison's trilogy.

Attempts to escape *saudade* can be found throughout Tarkovsky's work, most notably in *Stalker* (1979), which is adapted from Arkady and Boris Strugatsky's *Roadside Picnic* (1972) and frequently alluded to in *Nova Swing*. Each iteration of the story revolves around a wishing machine, a mundane object rendered sublime through an overload of potential meaning, which is treated as a vector for an escape. Redemption seems to be the *telos* in both Tarkovsky and Harrison, but their treatment differs markedly.

Light

The first poem in Tarkovsky's *Mirror* (1975), 'First Meetings', written and read by his father Arseni, contains the following lines:

> In the world everything was transfigured, even
> Simple things – the basin, the jug – when

Between us stood, as if on watch,
The stratified and solid water. (Skakov, 2011: 110)

Visually, these lines open up an associative portal to a scene in *Stalker* that shows mundane objects – dinner plates, coins, iron springs, calendar pages, guns, icons – submerged under water and thus transformed; their everyday connotations stripped away, they are charged with new sublime meaning. *Nova Swing* echoes and re-contextualizes this scene in a description of the alien event site, itself an echo of *Stalker*'s 'zone':

> Shallow water over chequerboard tiles and cast-off domestic objects, books, plates, magazines, empty tunnels smelling of chemicals, a black dog trotting aimlessly round him in his sleep on some dirty waterlogged ground neither in nor out of anything you could think of as the world. (Harrison, 2009: 189)

Thematically, these descriptions connect to a passage in *Light*:

> Light will transform anything: a plastic drinking glass full of mineral water, the hairs on the back of your hand, the wing of an airliner thirty thousand feet above the Atlantic. All these things can be redeemed and become for a time essentially themselves. (Harrison, 2007: 124)

This in turn is the echo of an earlier iteration, in 'A Young Man's Journey to Viriconium' (1984), that ends with the assertion that these objects' 'visual distinctness becomes metonymic of the reality we perceive both in them and in ourselves' (Harrison, 2000: 546).

There are several direct references to Tarkovsky in *Empty Space* and many indirect ones in *Nova Swing*: the novelist and the filmmaker are both concerned with 'light writing' (as a repeated theme and, literally, as in 'photography'). They both also create what the subtitle of Nariman Skakov's book on Tarkovsky calls 'labyrinths of space and time', treating 'reality as a subjective layering of inextricable snippets of various times and spaces' (Skakov, 2011: 14) as their narratives deal with dreams, uncertain and alternative realities, memory and nostalgia.

Interior journeys: time, memory, dream

In *Empty Space,* many characters (and the reader) experience spatio-temporal discontinuity. We are transported through time and space, and in the process we mix up and re-edit times and spaces. This is how memory works: a gathering of objects, people and experiences, already devoured by time, in a mental space. When revisited, when we recall phantoms of the real past, our memory changes in and through the process of remembering. Memory is therefore situated somewhere between the realms of reality and dream.

Both Harrison and Tarkovsky transform the mundane into the sublime, then on into the newly charged (quantum-entangled, superposed) mundane-sublime. Their characters, searching for symbols, meaning and language, and for a resolution of *saudade,* stumble through opaque, incomprehensible alien event sites, through unsolvable labyrinths where space, time and dream become one. Their stories take place in interstitial spaces – waiting rooms, street corners and bars, cars or spaceships on their way to somewhere else. Character's homes never really feel like homes – they are more like memory storage facilities – and the past is a cosed system. *Nova Swing*'s Edith keeps all her old costumes and accordions, the long since outgrown and ruined mementoes of her musical career, in her room, where they gather dust and 'now [make] her cry'. (Harrison, 2009: 71). She cannot escape from a past she hoards around her. Similarly, *Empty Space*'s Anna Waterman uses her summerhouse primarily as a storage space for old keepsakes; decontextualized from personal history and specific memories, their subjective meanings collapse and their value is lost. In these kinds of narrative universe, outer space turns out to be inner (psychological) space; finding patterns in the noise is revealed to be nothing more than humanity's own Rorschach test, at best providing insights into ourselves.

Many of Tarkovsky's characters 'inhabit hallucinatory landscapes, completely lose the sense of spatial orientation, and consequently, dwell in the "chronic non-chronological time"' (Skakov, 2011: 4). Something similar befalls *Light*'s Michael Kearney who, in his escapist childhood fantasies, inhabits a phantasmatic place he calls

Gorselands, where he hides to watch his cousins masturbate. In Tarkovsky's *Nostalghia* (1983), Domenico (Erland Josephson) asks, 'Where am I when I'm not in reality or in my imagination?' In *Solaris* (1972), journeys into space are simultaneously journeys into the human psyche or, as *Stalker's* melancholy Writer (Anatoli Solonitsyn) would have it, into 'psychological abysses'. According to the Stalker (Alexander Kaidanovsky), the 'trap', the real danger of the wishroom, is that only 'your innermost wish, born of suffering', the wish you do not even know you are harbouring, will come true. The corresponding element in *Empty Space* is 'the unthought known' (Harrison, 2012: 25, 151, 213, 283), which refers to a mystery at the heart of things, possibly Anna's repressed memory of the moment when she briefly saw into the real nature of the universe in *Light*, possibly Anna's earlier suicide attempt (or the memory of it).

As the Stalker explains, 'everything that's going on here depends not on the Zone but on us. ... one doesn't return here the way one comes'. In fact, according to Harrison, returns are impossible:

> The hero ... sees that she was conned all along, as much by ideas of 'return' as by the idea of a goal: the journey, like the self, is both meaningless and unavoidable, but more important it is endless. The journey is without telos and what happens on the journey is the mechanics of the journey. Anything else is a wish fulfilment of the 1940s or, to be more precise, of Joseph insanely boring bloody Campbell. (Harrison, 2013: n.p.)

Both Harrison and Tarkovsky explore the relation of dreams and fiction, deliberately leaving events unexplained and ends untied. Anna's dream landscape in *Empty Space*, in which horses are transformed into satyrs, and Tarkovsky's dream sequences in *Mirror*, *Solaris* and *Andrei Rublev* (1966), suggest that outward journeys are inward journeys into the psyche (and/or memory); indeed, this is true of all the characters' stories and journeys – the 'tractates kefahuchii' – in Harrison's trilogy. In it, we encounter characters whose names and their spelling seem to shift with every new iteration – most notably in *Empty Space's* Pearlant/Pearlent – and characters who seem to be alternative iterations of characters from earlier books (for example,

Light's Valentine Sprake, Yaxley in *The Course of the Heart* (1991) and Ansel Verdigris in the Viriconium sequence). Moreover, *Empty Space* seems to have several different outcomes, and the connections picked up from *Light* do not quite make sense. (Did Michael Kearney drown, drown himself, just walk away from the story, or actually disappear from the contemporary plot and emerge in the far-future plot? Did the data from Tate and Kearney's experiments ever make it to the future so the space drives could be based on the 'Tate-Kearney transformations'?) The Kefahuchi tract, the central mystery connecting the novels, functions like an interior (dream) landscape, constantly spitting out objects (or illusions of objects) associated with the characters' pasts. For this quantum fiction, there is no 'ideal' reader and no 'ideal' way to read it. Every new act of reading, every new interpretation, every act of mentally writing 'ghost chapters' (Eco, 1984: 212) in order to causally or temporally connect unconnected events in the books, establishes one possible storyline.

The Zone

Both Tarkovsky's Zone and the Saudade event site are described as the result of an alien event 20 years in the past, both are cordoned off with barbed wire and military guards, and both are characterized by inexplicable phenomena and strange physics. They are filled with decontextualized objects from someone else's past. We struggle to make sense of them. Sometimes the only meaning we can attach to them is deeply personal. Sometimes we cannot assign any meaning at all. Over time, *Nova Swing*'s recurring phrase 'neon heart', tattooed (in various iterations) on the victims of the 'neon heart murders' but never described as an actual existing object, takes on the mystery of Tarkovsky's wishing room. As long as it remains unsolved, the Neon Heart turns into some sort of Holy Grail, an artefact which is the key to the world and which will provide explanation, perhaps even an instrument of salvation (like *Stalker*'s never-seen, wish-fulfilling device). This holds true throughout *Empty Space*: Anna Waterman's daughter, for example, finds a small plastic heart among the summerhouse bric-a-brac. In only one iteration, one possible interpretation – if it turns out to be just this: a Valentine heart which lights up – does the sublime collapse back into the mundane. After all, if it *is* anything else, it is *Anna*'s key to her world, to herself: 'Send me a neon heart/ Send it with love/*Seek me inside*' (Harrison, 2007: 193, emphasis added). In Tarkovsky's Zone and in Harrison's event site, maps do not work, and all we can find is ourselves, our desires, our memories and dreams, our past. All journeys are one and the same journey (but not Campbell's monomyth).

Thus, we can never leave the Kefahuchi Tract (which is described as a singularity without an event horizon [Harrison, 2007: 309]), Saudade City or the Zone. There is no way out, and a system can only be fully understood and explained from the outside. Harrison tells us as much describing a Budapest courtyard in *Signs of Life* (1996):

> The arch framed a well of grey light into which snow fell as slowly as the snow in a Tarkovsky film, every flake intensely visible, making the courtyard seem at once depthless and too deep, a lighted space the revelatory nature of which could only be experienced from outside. (Harrison, 2005: 317)

This echoes the ending of Tarkovsky's *Nostalghia*, yet reverses it. Tarkovsky's protagonist is immersed in the miracle, which from inside cannot be understood, only experienced. Harrison is rather more sceptical. Returns and salvation are impossible, and we remain outside the sublime space, looking in, only ever offered brief glimpses. If we entered the mirage, it would transform back into a mundane courtyard.

In Tarkovsky, the combination of mundane images and a soundtrack that features either a contrasting musical score, silence or poetry renders the mundane sublime. As a result, the men depicted in *Mirror*'s Lake Sivash archive footage 'are not just overcoming a concrete obstacle by crossing the lake – they are entering and moving within metaphysical grounds' (Skakov, 2011: 124). Thus, the mundane is supercharged with possible meanings and rendered sublime.

In *Empty Space* we learn that 'When the Kefahuchi Tract expanded, in what came to be known as "the event", parts of it fell to earth on

129

planets all along the Beach' (Harrison, 2012: 155). This is redolent of the notion from Lurianic Cabalism that the Godhead is too massive for this world and only little sparks of it can be found, spread all through our reality. Each of them, being godly, would necessarily contain the totality of the deity. The Saudade event site, a fractal part of the Tract, works exactly like the Tract itself,[1] and 'sparks' can be found throughout the trilogy.

Alienation

Nostalghia's protagonist, Gorchakov (Oleg Yamkovsky) 'overcomes the unbearable fact that he is located in an alien land by undermining the stability of his own location in space and time' (Skakov, 2011: 180), when, in the film's final scene, he experiences being inside a vision of superposed realities that combines Italy and Russia. This is mirrored in Harrison's trilogy. Part of the connection of *Light* to *Empty Space* revolves around Anna Waterman's alienation – from life, from her daughter, from her middle-class environment, and ultimately from reality – culminating in her becoming the composite entity Pearlant (or Pearlent) and thus, in a sense, becoming the Kefahuchi Tract. (She is the Weird phenomenon – she is her own Other.) Harrison's descriptions of Pearl/Pearlant/Pearlent and Anna's memory of her suicide attempt recall the woman in *Stalker* who, when her husband leaves for the Zone, lets herself slip from the chair to the floor, then lies there, crying convulsively. She says that if her husband ends up in prison, she will die, which means that as long as he is in the Zone, she is – like Pearlant – suspended between life and death.

Anna, a largely absent mother, repeatedly enters the narrative as the disembodied voice of Pearlant, recalling the disembodied voice of the absent father in *Mirror*, a film in which a 'woman meets her own old self' and Ignat (Ignat Daniltsev, who also plays the young Andrei) 'realises that he has lived through the very moment he is experiencing once before' (Skakov, 2011: 115, 120). Similar hauntings and breaks in both conventional storytelling and in the perception of time recur in *Empty Space*. Pearlent,[2] presented as a haunting from the future, sometimes 'just for a moment ... looks like a much older woman' (Harrison, 2012: 173), and the nameless Assistant', who ultimately also forms a part of the composite entity Pearlant, appears to her earlier self to issue a warning.

Both *Empty Space* and *Solaris* are critical of anthropocentrism. In the latter, Snaut (Jüri Järvet) dismisses the exploration of other worlds as 'futile' because 'anthropocentric attitudes cancel out the very possibility of meaningful contact with the ultimate Other' (Skakov, 2011: 91). At the same time, the human facsimiles created by the eponymous sentient ocean world that visit the space station crew represent suppressed human memories and desires. These material(ized) hauntings turn outer space into inner space. We can learn nothing about the Other, only ever about ourselves.

In *Light*, Michael Kearney says, 'I was thinking that sunlight will transform anything':

> Actually he'd been thinking how fear transformed things. A glass of mineral water, the hairs on the back of a hand, faces on a downtown street. Fear had caused these things to become so real to him that, temporarily, there was no way of describing them. (Harrison, 2007: 86)

Again, through a shift in perspective, the mundane is rendered sublime. According to Hegel, the sublime is 'the attempt to express the infinite without finding in the sphere of phenomena an object which proves adequate for this representation' (cited in Skakov, 2011: 132). Kearney loses the ability to describe concrete objects, moving him beyond signification into the realm of the infinite, of the Other, of the Shrander – into the realm of cosmic horror.

The Shrander's head – in the manifestation so feared by Kearney – is the skull of a horse. In *Solaris*, the 'dark horse' motif likewise symbolizes an encounter with the unknown.

The first scenes that feature a horse take place on Earth. In the shots establishing the dacha, a bridled horse trots past the lake, just before disgraced spaceship pilot Berton (Vladislav Dvorzhetsky) arrives, with his young son (Vitalik Kerdimum), to visit the protagonist, Kelvin (Donatas Banionis). Later, the unnamed boy flees in terror from an outhouse, in which a loudly whinnying unbridled horse stands imposing. The boy asks, 'What is it down there, standing in the garage and looking at me?' Kelvin's aunt, Anna (Tamara Ogorodnikova), soothes the boy, explaining that the horse is gentle and beautiful, but somehow it continues to exceed such containment, remaining, as in Freud's (2002: 113) case study of 'Little Hans', a 'symbol of sublime terror' and of life irreducible.[3] Later, on the space station, in the room of Dr Gibarian (Sos Sargsyan), there is a picture of a similar dark horse. Immediately before we see it, Gibarian's video message to Kelvin says, 'It's your only chance to establish contact with this monster', referring to the uncanny oceanic lifeform inhabiting Solaris. In Kearney's final encounter with the Shrander, this Other is depicted as alien, but not evil, not a menace: 'Why did you run so hard?', it asks, 'All I wanted to do was show you something' (Harrison, 2007: 387). As in quantum physics, reality is determined by perspective.

Nostalgia/*saudade*

Tarkovsky and Harrison establish and explore the interconnectedness of nostalgia and *saudade*. The nameless yearning of the latter is captured in the words of *Stalker*'s Writer:

> How would I know the right word for what I want? How would I know that actually I don't want what I want? Or that I actually don't want what I don't want? They are elusive things: the moment we name them, their meaning disappears, melts, dissolves like a jellyfish in the sun.

Just as the past or family history or a personal memory exert a hold upon on Tarkovsky's characters so, throughout the *Empty Space* trilogy, Harrison's characters are stuck, held back, unable to leave the liminal topos of Saudade city because they cling to their pasts or to objects representing their pasts. While the filmmaker experiments with the nature and unreliability of memory and the inaccessibility of the past, Harrison treats nostalgia as inherently dangerous, prone to the kind of commodification in which photographs usurp actual memories. And as long as characters clutch their misremembered and romanticized pasts, they cannot move on. In a 2008 blog post, Harrison wrote:

> Nostalgia came of age as an unacceptable sentiment with the invention of cheap, easy data storage – photography, tape recorders, analogue film cameras. At that point, memory started to die because its direct relationship with the felt began to die. Before the age of storage a memory arrived as an emotion. Now, memory is conceived of as something separate that can be guaranteed by a piece of equipment.
>
> & there's another rhetorical move since the 80s: nostalgia is part of your life come back to burn your fingers, so you piss on not just this fire but the whole idea of fire, as quick as you can. (Harrison, 2008: n.p.)

Empty Space turns the idea of fire around, and again draws directly on Tarkovsky. In the first description of Anna Waterman's garden, Harrison explicitly mentions 'a leaning summerhouse which looked like something from a 1970s Russian film' (Harrison, 2012: 1). When, in a hallucinatory scene, it catches fire, Anna observes but lets it burn: 'The flames roared silently up, amid showers of gold sparks' (Harrison, 2012: 29). This fire is turned sublime by its 'sparks', and by the revelation that the flames do not destroy the burning summerhouse. They are either symbolic or only occur in some of all possible realities. In personal correspondence, Harrison explained:

> When I wrote the burning summer house I was thinking of all Tarkovsky's fires, but, yes, especially the one in *Mirror*. Anna's is a bonfire of memories, which seems a Tarkovskian thing; but it's also a reference to the bonfire of Audsley King's paintings in my novel *In Viriconium*.

The images of the fire in *Mirror* are heralded by cat and dog noises and accompanied by voices from the past. They also seem to quote and foreshadow other Tarkovsky films – a vase falling off a table by itself recalls the ending of *Stalker*; the blaze that destroys the house in *Mirror* prefigures the conflagration that consumes the house in *The Sacrifice* (1986), itself a standing-in for the narrowly-averted nuclear holocaust. The bonfire of memories also offers us a possible way out of *saudade*: it consigns the past to the past. As Harrison writes,

It is not the responsibility of the living to redress – or even facilitate the redressing – of wrongs in the past. The past is only the past: we do not owe it any guilt, we cannot even recognise anymore what constitutes it. The past is just some decaying, meaningless echoes. When we 'learn' from it, all we are doing is rewriting it according to what we need at the time.
As soon as A understands this, she gets well. The hauntings stop. She has laid the past to rest not by understanding it but by consigning it to the past where it belongs. (Harrison, 2015: n.p.)

But can this be realized? Can *saudade* be resolved? Can the universe, the individual, the story ever be complete?

Slavoj Žižek's attempt at a purely materialistic, object-oriented approach to Tarkovsky's films focuses on the Lacanian object-Thing – the unattainable object of desire – 'rendered as part of ourselves that we eject into reality' in order to 'bring relief' by 'cancelling the horror vacui of staring at the infinite void of the universe' (Žižek, 1999: n.p.). Žižek singles out one version of this Thing: 'the Thing as the Space (the sacred/forbidden Zone) in which the gap between the Symbolic and the Real is closed' and thus 'in which ... our desires are directly materialized' (Žižek, 1999: n.p.). He identifies two major occurrences of such Things in Tarkovsky: the planet Solaris, 'the blind libido embodied', and the Zone, 'the void which sustains desire' (Žižek, 1999: n.p.). These locations are elaborated upon in *Nova Swing* as the Saudade event site and the Kefahuchi Tract itself. In *Solaris*, this 'Other Thing' returns Kelvin's 'deepest dreams ... to him' as a 'message in its true form that the subject is not ready to acknowledge' (Žižek, 1999: n.p.). Always-already present, without explanation or decipherable intention, such 'decentered opaque Id-Machine[s]', whether in Tarkovsky or Harrison, are Weird phenomena *par excellence*. The hauntings they generate are derived not just from some psychic ideal of the 'ultimate fantasmatic objectal supplement/partner that [one] would never be ready to accept in reality' (Žižek, 1999: n.p.) but also from memory. The paranoia, fear and aggression with which characters greet Tarkovksy's 'visitors' and Harrison's K-culture 'artefacts' and sentient 'daughter code' (named after the Stalker's mutant daughter in Tarkovsky's film) point to an inherent horror of the non-human. Just as Berton's son recoils from the unprecedented horse, so other characters recoil from the uncanny Other, the incomplete or misremembered, the not-quite-human.

Žižek describes the Zone in *Stalker* as 'the material presence, the Real of an absolute Otherness incompatible with the rules and laws of our universe' (Žižek, 1999: n.p.). Like the Saudade event site, it exists because it is cordoned off, forbidden; and, like the Kefahuchi Tract, it is mysterious because it can never be understood: 'The point, of course, is that the question "so which is the true meaning of the Zone?" is false and misleading: the very indeterminacy of what lies beyond the Limit is primary, and different positive contents fill in this preceding gap' (Žižek, 1999: n.p.). From outside the Limit, the Zone and Harrison's analogues are perfect black boxes, filled with quantum possibility; once inside the Limit, one possible reality is established by the questions one asks and the things one expects to find. This is reiterated by the wish room at the centre of the Zone, which can never be entered – and thus the wave function never collapses, and the mystery remains.

The opposition between the two Things identified by Žižek, between *Stalker* and *Solaris*, is the opposition between our inability to formulate our wish and an oversaturation of wish-fulfilment, and in Harrison between *saudade* and K-tech, body-modification and consumerism. Is it possible to break free of this suspension between – and indeed by – these extremes? *Stalker*, as well as *Nostalghia* and *Sacrifice*, seems to suggest that redemption – a 'longed-for spiritual reconciliation found not in elevation from the gravitational force of the Earth but in a full surrender to its inertia' (Žižek, 1999: n.p.) – might be possible through (very personal) sacrifice. However, the conclusion of *Solaris*, in which Kelvin is reunited at the dacha with his father, the 'object of [his] innermost longing' (Žižek, 1999: n.p.), implies that salvation is only an illusion: 'the camera ... slowly pulls back to divulge the properly fantasmatic setting', that the dacha is another of the mysterious alien ocean's (re)constructions.

Consequently, in contrast to Harrison, Žižek concludes that nostalgia is 'safe', and that the idea of attaining salvation through sacrifice is only a means to reconcile us to the inevitable realization that we can never achieve it (because it is impossible). In respect to Tarkovsky and the sense of wonder at the end of many of his films, Žižek's purely materialistic perspective does not suffice, does not explain Tarkovsky or do him justice. The wish, the longing, to be made whole, to be saved, is central also to Harrison's fiction. In 'Egnaro' (1980), the eponymous realm is described, like something from Arthur Machen, as a hidden, elusive, sublime phenomenon, a place 'behind the surface of things', 'at once inside and outside you' (Harrison, 2003: 98, 102). It reveals itself in glimpses, allusions, associations, similarities, Freudian slips and mondegreens. As a place that cannot be directly accessed, it offers itself as a consolatory utopia.

> 'You felt,' Lucas said, 'that if you asked them why they'd come here the answer would be: "My dog spoke to me of Egnaro, the queer old thing, and I came"; or, "I heard we would all be cured there." I felt that very strongly.' (Harrison, 2003: 104)

The narrator's epiphany, his glimpse of the sublime, is induced by a quality in the light:

> I went to the window but the view was blocked by a tree. All I could see through its long dark branches was a blur of sunlight. Where a ray of light penetrated the curious leafage, it filled the room with a dusty glow the color of geranium petals. ... Standing in that room, soothed by its proportions, I know I was in some country so foreign I could not imagine it. ... I felt assuaged and expectant, as if by some glimpse of happiness to come. I heard someone begin to say,
> 'Comfort us now & in the hour of our deaths.' (Harrison, 2003: 112)

In addition to the Tarkovskyian religious framing of the protagonist's yearning for redemption, there is again a superposition of realities, an interconnection of the mundane and the sublime. The story concludes:

> No one, I suspect, can have any clear understanding of [Egnaro]. All events are its signature: none are. It does not exist: yet it is quite real. The secret is meaningless before you know it: and, judging by what has happened to Lucas, worthless when you do. If Egnaro is the substrate of mystery which underlies all daily life, then the reciprocal of this is also true, and it is the exact dead point of ordinariness which lies beneath every mystery. (Harrison, 2003: 114–15)

The wave function never collapses. The mystery's pull before quantum decoherence sets in, before any 'solution', any 'reality' is established, is undiminished. As in the Kefahuchi Tract, as inside the event site, 'old maps are useless' (Harrison, 2003: 114). As in Tarkovsky, unreal, sublime spaces and phenomena emphasize that insolubility of the mystery: we can only experience it. What remains is the inaccessible goal: the wish-room that nobody enters, the Neon Heart, Sigma End at the heart of the Kefahuchi Tract, the impossible wish to resolve *saudade*.

In *Light*, Dr Haends, an iteration of the Shrander, tells Seria Mau in a hallucinatory scene that may or may not be a dream, 'You must forgive yourself for everything' (Harrison, 2007: 338). Her brother Ed's dream while he is falling into the wormhole echoes this – 'Time to forgive yourself these things' (Harrison, 2007: 379) – and the Shrander also ultimately tells Michael Kearney that 'You can forgive yourself now' (Harrison, 2007: 388). The past should be consigned to the past.

In *Instant Light: Tarkovsky Polaroids* (2004), Giovanni Chiaramonte and Andrey A. Tarkovsky, the filmmaker's son, juxtapose polaroid pictures taken by Andrei Tarkovsky with passages from his diaries. Line breaks, added retrospectively, turn these quotations into poetry about Tarkovsky's relationship to photography, and about the relationship between a picture and the world – the one depicted and the one outside the picture, subject to the passage of time:

> The image is not a certain meaning,
> expressed by the director,
> but the entire world

reflected as in a drop of water. (Chiaramonte and Tarkovsky, 2004: 13)

An artistic image
is one that ensures its own development,
its historical viability.
An image is a grain,
a self-evolving retroactive organism.
It is a symbol of actual life,
as opposed to life itself.
Life contains death.
An image of life, by contrast,
excludes it, or else sees in it
a unique potential
for the affirmation of life. (Chiaramonte and Tarkovsky, 2004: 57)

In contrast to Roland Barthes, Tarkovsky sees the photograph not as the thing being replaced by the reference, not as a reference to an absence and thus always a reference to death, but as an image of life and as life-affirming. Similarly, Tarkovsky's endings give us hope and wonder, a vision of home in a foreign country, the possibility of being reunited with loved ones, even in a dream or semblance of reality, of being forgiven. Harrison, however, refuses to give us closure, to resolve his storylines, to connect all the threads. Where Tarkovsky maps interior landscapes and manifestations of the deepest wish, and where Steven Soderbergh's remake of *Solaris* (2002) instead concludes by re-establishing the bland bourgeois purgatory of a middle-class kitchen (presented as wish-fulfillment), the sceptical Harrison suggests a synthesis of the two. Rejecting and negating the hero's journey, he asks: what if we are already trapped in that purgatory and we don't even know what we want?

Notes

1 It produces hallucinatory images (and people), and it is surrounded by an aureole of its own, where its effects are lessened.

2 This alternate spelling is deliberate: throughout *Empty Space*, Harrison uses 'Pearlant' and 'Pearlent' interchangeably.

3 Discussing *Andrei Rublev*, Tarkovsky said 'the horse symbolizes life ... when I see a horse, it seems to me that I have life itself before me' (Ciment et al., 2006: 25). Bould (2014: 41–6) draws out the connection between the horse and Kelvin's absent mother.

Works Cited

Bould, Mark (2014) *Solaris*. London: BFI/Palgrave Macmillan.

Clute, John (2011) 'Harrison, M. John'. *The Encyclopedia of Science Fiction*, http://www.sf-encyclopedia.com/entry/harrison_m_john

Chiaramonte, G. and Andrey A. Tarkovsky (eds) (2004) *Instant Light: Tarkovsky Polaroids*. London: Thames & Hudson.

Ciment, Michael, Luda Schnitzer and Jean Schnitzer (2006) 'The Artist in Ancient Russia and the New USSR', trans. Susana Rossberg, in John Gianvito (ed.) *Andrei Tarkovsky: Interviews*, pp. 16–31. Jackson: University Press of Mississippi.

Eco, Umberto (1984) *The Role of the Reader: Explorations in the Semiotics of Texts*. Bloomington: Indiana University Press.

Emmons, Shirlee and Lewis, Wilbur Watkins (2006) *Researching the Song: A Lexicon*. Oxford: Oxford University Press.

Freud, Sigmund (2002) 'Analysis of a Phobia in a Five-year-old Boy ["Little Hans"]', trans. Louise Adey Huish, in *'The Wolfman' and Other Cases*. London: Penguin.

Harrison, M. John (2000) 'A Young Man's Journey to Viriconium', in *Viriconium*, pp. 541–62. London: Gollancz.

Harrison, M. John (2003) 'Egnaro', in *Things That Never Happen*, pp. 93–115. London: Gollancz.

Harrison, M. John (2005) *Signs of Life*, in *Anima*, pp. 227–473. London: Gollancz.

Harrison, M. John (2007) *Light*. New York: Bantam.

Harrison, M. John (2008) 'written abroad', *Ambiente Hotel*, accessed 27 June 2018, https://ambientehotel.wordpress.com/2008/09/28/written-abroad/

Harrison, M. John (2009) *Nova Swing*. New York: Bantam.

Harrison, M. John (2012) *Empty Space. A Haunting*. London: Gollancz.

Harrison, M. John (2013) 'same old story', *Ambiente Hotel*, accessed 27 June 2018, https://ambientehotel.wordpress.com/2013/02/02/same-old-story/

Harrison, M. John (2015) 'speaking of ghosts...', accessed 27 June 2018, *Ambiente Hotel*, https://ambientehotel.wordpress.com/2015/10/21/speaking-of-ghosts/

Skakov, Nariman (2011) *The Cinema of Tarkovsky: Labyrinths of Space and Time*. London: I. B. Tauris.

Žižek, Slavoj (1999) 'The Thing from Inner Space', *Artmargins*, accessed 27 June 2018, http://www.artmargins.com/index.php/2-articles/457-the-thing-from-inner-space

M. JOHN HARRISON AND ARTHUR MACHEN'S 'WEIRD URBAN MAGIC'

James Machin

In September 2009, a recommendation for M. John Harrison's *The Course of the Heart* (1992) was posted on the user-generated book review website *Goodreads*: 'Perhaps this is my new favourite book; although not because it made me feel good. Hope and helplessness intermingle with transcendence' ('John', 2009/2010: n.p.). The novel expands a narrative first explored by Harrison in 'The Great God Pan' (1988), the title of which was borrowed from Arthur Machen's 1894 novella. *The Course of the Heart* concerns the ruinous effect of a failed occult ritual (never directly represented) on the lives of its participants: Yaxley, the abrasive and barely socialized 'magician', or at least coordinator of the ritual; the unnamed narrator; and the narrator's fellow students Lucas and Pam, who later marry. There are various hints that the ritual was an attempt to rend the veil or breach the divide between the material world and the ideal world of the 'Pleroma', a Gnostic term which can loosely be translated as 'fullness' or the complete unity of the divine, or 'the spiritual universe regarded as the totality of God's powers and manifestations' (*OED Online*: n.p.). The ritual fails, and the narrator, Lucas and Pam are subsequently plagued by misfortunes and hauntings, occasionally in the form of 'pornographic obtrusions' (Luckhurst, 2005: 179). Pam and Lucas's response to this baleful influence is to seek refuge in the creation of the imaginary, medieval realm they designate 'the Coeur' – the recovery of a secret European heritage that occasionally still reveals itself, bestowing spiritual enrichment and uplift in its wake. The narrator is exasperated by their wilful naïveté in clinging to what he sees as an impotent fantasy: Pam develops aggressive, terminal cancer and Lucas is beset by poltergeist-like phenomena. Yaxley dies in an appropriately sordid and mysterious manner, and the 'accidental' death of the narrator's wife in a car accident only confirms that whatever metaphysical trespass they made all those years before is irreparable.

In March 2010, the same Goodreads user, now less enthusiastic, updated his review, reducing the number of stars he awarded the novel to three:

> I have seriously downgraded my opinion of this book after reading *The Green Round* and a few other stories by Arthur Machen. I knew that *Course of the Heart* originally started out as a short story called 'The Great God Pan', which presumably carried a large Machen influence since he had written a story of the same title around the turn of the 20th century [sic]. However, *Course* obviously takes quite a large number of elements from *The Green Round*, etc. and adds very few ideas that seem to originate with Harrison. ('John', 2009/2010: n.p.)

The reviewer not only misunderstands the difference between plagiarism and intertextuality, but his assertion that the novel 'adds very few ideas' to its alleged inspiration misses the profound philosophical schism between the two authors – between Machen's unwavering belief in the potential for spiritual uplift resulting from contemplation of an ecstatic immanence in the universe, and Harrison's repeated gestures of resignation to 'that vacancy which is the source of everything' (Harrison, 1988: 56). Harrison's response to Machen in this respect is analogous to the broader sense of loss immanent in modernity, with Harrison's acknowledgement of this contrasting sharply with Machen's apparent imperviousness to the wider disillusionments of his age.

The *Goodreads* review implies that Harrison simply and superficially retools aspects of Machen's work before presenting them to the reader – an accusation that stops just shy of one of outright plagiarism. Rather, Harrison strips away the numinous, redemptive metaphysical underpinnings of Machen's fiction, ultimately presenting the reader with a very different vision of the world, albeit one that remains in dialogue with its source material. Although working in the same British tradition of Gnostic fantasy of 'writers that struggle at truth that is immanent, that is inexpressible but embedded in everything, in the everyday' (Miéville, 2003: 5), I will argue that ultimately Harrison's 'weird urban magic' is of a far darker and bleaker variety than Machen's.

In 2002, asked about the impact of Machen's work on his own fiction, Harrison confessed to being 'chary' of any un-interrogated, *a priori* definitions of 'influence'. He conceded, however, that:

> I expect I'll always hear his voice, even though I haven't read him for twenty years. My swerve against him and all those other ecstatics and mystic Christians was to poison his reveries with the quotidian. Thus the weird urban magic of 'The Incalling' or *The Course of the Heart*. (Mathew, 2002: n.p.)

Less reticent, Roger Luckhurst (2005: 179) argues that the 'central idea' of *The Course of the Heart* 'owes much to the occult fictions of … Arthur Machen', specifically the 'retreat' of two of the central characters into 'constructing an elaborate fiction about the last earthly appearance of an ideal state lost in the Middle Ages, to which they are the last heirs'. He cites Machen's *A Fragment of Life* (1906) as a possible inspiration. However, rather than valorize this 'counter-modern myth of lost purity', *The Course of the Heart*'s narrator is 'irritated by entrapment in fantasy' (Luckhurst, 2005: 179), demonstrated most starkly by Lucas's dissembling attempt to protect Pam from the truth of her imminent death:

> 'What have you promised her Lucas?'
> 'At least try to understand. It isn't just a book. She's the Heir. She's the Empress.'
> 'Jesus Christ.'
> 'She is the Coeur. She won't die. I've told her she won't die.'
> (Harrison, 1993: 171)

The 'Coeur' is ultimately an impotent fiction offering only transitory relief from the inevitability of entropic reality, and is further evidence that for Harrison 'escapism is ... bondage' (Clute, 1997a: 453).

Machen's writing practice is comparable to Harrison's 'versioning',[1] his unapologetic and strategic 'redeployment' and 'reformulation' of ideas and texts. For example, the 'embryonic idea' for *A Fragment of Life* 'appeared in about 1890 with the title "Resurrectio Mortuorum" or "The Resurrection of the Dead"', before a version appeared in *Horlick's Magazine* in 1904, with chapter four being 'entirely rewritten for book publication' in 1906 (Goldstone and Sweetser, 1965: 29). The first chapter of 'The Great God Pan' originally appeared as a short story in *The Whirlwind* in 1890 before the complete story was published in *The Great God Pan and the Inmost Light* (1894). As well as versioning specific texts, Machen revisited certain tropes with something approaching monomania, although he considerably refined his treatment of the same material, moving away from pure horror towards something far more ambiguous and oblique.

Rather than recapitulating the style of his most famous works, which oscillated between the 'jaunty Stevenson manner' and the Decadent preciosity typical of the 1890s (Lovecraft, 1985: 498), *The Green Round*, like much of Machen's later writing, approaches *faux* reportage.[2] Its protagonist, Hillyer, a reclusive scholar, has developed a nervous condition ascribed by his doctor to his prolonged isolation from general society. He leaves London to recuperate in the 'picturesque little watering-place of Porth, in the west of Wales' (Machen, 1968: 7), a seaside town in which reality seems to be malfunctioning. He is baffled when the hotel's other residents take against him, and rumours spread of his complicity in a local murder because of his association with an evil-looking dwarf. However, having no knowledge of such a companion, Hillyer further questions his sanity. He returns to London but is beset by troubling disruptions – mirrors are smashed, greenhouse glass shatters, scaffolding collapses, a jeweller's shop window implodes just after he walks past – for which he is sometimes blamed. Machen writes:

The dwarfish child of his terror was seen by no eye but his own; so far as we know, at least [this is directly contradicted earlier in the novel]. At other times, the power that troubled him converted him into an involuntary poltergeist: destruction was about all his ways. Here, however, the proceedings followed the established order, and we may even grasp at least the tail of a theory. For it is certain that the poltergeist – when it is not a naughty child, playing mischievous tricks – is always involuntary and unconscious of its own work. (Machen, 1968: 206)

The maleficent dwarf only becomes visible to Hillyer towards the end of the novel, by which time he is so shattered by his experiences that only a doctor's independent verification can convince him of their reality.[3]

The Course of the Heart reworks this haunting by a troublesome dwarf, which attaches itself to Lucas and plagues him with poltergeist phenomena: broken furniture, paintings and mirrors falling from walls, papers destroyed, windows smashed, and so on. The narrator accuses Lucas of comprehensively 'wrecking' his flat and he wonders 'how can you protect someone from a grief which causes him to throw his furniture about in the middle of the night?' (Harrison, 1993: 166–7). The narrator eventually witnesses the entity that is persecuting Lucas with these disturbances, another Weird irruption or obtrusion:

Lucas hadn't got far when a small figure slipped out from between two parked cars and began to follow him closely along the pavement ... I thought at first it was a boy or girl about six or seven years old ... But when I called 'Lucas!' ... it paused under a streetlamp and looked back at me. In the sodium light I found myself looking at neither a child nor a dwarf but something of both. (Harrison, 1993: 179)

This is a 'versioning' of an episode in *The Green Round*:

And as he was hesitating, he saw a very ugly little boy standing by a lamp-post on the other side of the road, and grinning at him: 'Something twisted and deformed about the creature; he had the old face of a dwarf.' (Machen, 1968: 196)

Harrison's 'The Incalling' (1983) had already rehearsed the motif, although the equivalent figure, the son of clairvoyant Mrs Sprake, at first merely puzzles the protagonist Austin with his 'peculiarly mature' voice (Harrison, 1988: 35). By the end of the story, the Sprake 'boy' is stalking the terminally ill Clerk (at one point again positioning himself under a streetlamp) and Austin is moved to violence by the precociously gnomic monologues the 'child' subjects him to when he attempts to intervene:

> I went across to him and kicked the table over. The mirror broke: the bottle fell on to the floor and came uncorked: the candles tumbled end over end through the brown and stinking air. I bent down and hit him while he sat there, as hard as I could on the left cheek.
> 'Speak like a child,' I said. (Harrison, 1988: 54)

Machen's maleficent dwarf has its origins in fairy lore. Over the course of his output, Machen's little people shift from being our pre-human troglodyte ancestors burrowing in the unvisited mountains of Wales, heavily influenced by the 'euhemerist' theories of Scottish folklorist and antiquarian David Macritchie (Fergus, 2015), to more ontologically ambiguous entities.[4] In *The Green Round* and *A Fragment of Life*, as well as *The Course of the Heart*, such beings figure 'the loss of ontological purity' (Harrison, 1993: 69). Machen uses Hillyer's ruminations on the nature of reality, and his attempts at reconciling his strange experiences, to create a sense of unsettling disorientation for the reader, but they are ultimately pressed into critiquing what he regarded as science's wilful myopia with regard to phenomena that contradict or fall outside the purview of 'acceptable and reasoned theory' (Machen, 1968: 202–3). Harrison likewise disorients the reader, but ups the ante by having the narrator insist repeatedly, and in the face of other clearly contradictory textual evidence, that the 'obtrusions' *are* hallucinations: 'Lucas, there are two completely hallucinatory figures in that passage outside her kitchen' (Harrison, 1993: 39); 'Lucas said you had hallucinations for weeks afterwards' (Harrison, 1993: 41); '[William Blake] hallucinated (what else can we think?) a tree full of angels' (Harrison, 1993: 96). The parenthetical 'what else can we think?' is ambiguous, casting further uncertainty over whether the narrator is dismissing the possibility of the obtrusions having any 're-ality' because of a straightforward scepticism, or through an anxious resistance to, or avoidance of, questioning accepted notions of real-ity. A further complicating factor is the repeated suggestion that the narrator is more of a proactive exponent of ritual magic than his ac-count ostensibly admits: co-opted by Yaxley as an able and apparently informed participant in at least three rituals over the course of the novel, he is referred to by Lucas as 'a priest' (Harrison, 1993: 180). His unreliability and inconsistency as a narrator make it difficult not only to establish the veracity of his apparent scepticism, but also to approach this aspect of the novel with anything other than a queasy uncertainty.

Underpinning the question of the reality of the obtrusions is the metaphysical apparatus of the Pleroma itself, and the ritual that serves as the inciting incident of the narrative, described vaguely as some attempt to access the Pleroma. Machen's Hillyer is particularly preoc-cupied with the (fictional) Reverend Thomas Hampole's 1853 work *A London Walk: Meditations in the Streets of the Metropolis,*[5] in which Hampole, in part explanation of certain scenes and perspectives to which he has been privy, alludes to:

[a] method, or art, or science, or whatever we choose to call it (sup-posing that it really exists) ... concerned to restore the delights of the primal Paradise; to enable men, if they will, to inhabit a world of joy and of splendour. I have no authority either to affirm or to deny that there is such an experiment, and that some have made it. (Machen, 1968: 94–5).

The Course of the Heart is also preoccupied with the subjective experi-ence of the numinous, or how 'in special circumstances, the Pleroma breaks into ordinary existence' (Harrison, 1993: 61), but it is also concerned with the question of literary fantasy itself. Another refer-ence point is Elizabeth Bowen's 'Mysterious Kôr' (1944), in which a young woman, Pepita, imbues her rather mundane encounters in wartime London with meaning through the imaginative transforma-tion of the blacked-out capital into Kôr, 'her comfort, her safe place, her charm against life' (Bayley, 1989: 169), itself a reference to the ancient African realm of H. Rider Haggard's *She* (1887). The near homophony of 'Kôr' and 'Coeur' is not coincidental,[6] and it reinforces the notion that the Coeur is a proxy for escapist romance itself, or quest narratives that 'all involve a penetration into the imagined centre of an exotic civilization, the core, Kor [sic], *coeur*, or heart of darkness which is a blank place on the map, a realm of the unexplored and the unknown' (Showalter, 1991: 81).[7] Harrison's explicitly theological language, drawn specifically from Gnostic and Neoplatonic mysticism, implicitly conflates the literary fantastic with metaphysics: fantasy in fiction and religion are interrelated delusions, and the comparison is not flattering to religion. Harrison's attempt to 'poison' Christianity's visionary tradition is equally a critique of literary fantasy.

In Machen's *A Fragment of Life*, Mr and Mrs Darnell's drab suburban lives are transformed by the former's discovery of a secret inheritance: his descent from a line of Welsh mystics strongly hinted to be protectors of the true grail or 'Graal'. The effect is spiritually transformative. The Edwardian clerk and his wife are inspired by the story of the Graal to abandon the dull, endless streets of suburban villas and evenings spent discussing whether or not to redecorate the spare bedroom, and to move west (an idealized, visionary 'West'). The end of the narrative leaves them in a nebulous status somewhere between relocating to the countryside and dematerialising altogether into myth. The narrator concedes that 'from such documents as these it is clearly impossible to gather any very definite information' (Machen, 2011: 222), but the story concludes with the last page of Mr Darnell's own notebook:

> So I awoke from a dream of a London suburb, of daily labour, of weary, useless little things; and as my eyes were opened I saw that I was in an ancient wood, where a clear well rose into grey film and vapour beneath a misty, glimmering heat. And a form came towards me from the hidden places of the wood, and my love and I were united by the well. (Machen, 2011: 222)

This is a near perfect example of what John Clute (1997b: 942) means when he argues that many fantasies are 'fables of recovery', attempts to redress a diminishment or shore up our lives against the reductive materiality of the 'deracinating modern world'. Clute (1997b: 942) describes this process of loss as 'Thinning', citing as a basic example Tolkien's positioning of *The Lord of The Rings* (1954–5) 'at the end of aeons of slow loss', but also applies the term to all the 'Panworship engaged upon by the many Edwardian fantasists – including J.M. Barrie, E.M. Forster, Kenneth Grahame, Arthur Machen, Barry Pain and Saki – who bemoaned the loss of childhood and the rise of suburbia' (Clute, 1997b: 942). The 'spoiling of the suburbs' was the 'process by which established and largely green middle-class suburbs were engulfed by new development, with rows of houses being fitted on to adjacent meadow land, and the gardens of old mansions being bought by speculative builders' (Carey, 1992: 47). Consequently, 'the ruined childhood paradise becomes a familiar refrain in writers' biographies and autobiographies' (Carey, 1992: 47) from the period. Machen (1923a: 126) claimed that the sudden 'irruption of red ranks of brand-new villas' in a previously rural area of Harlesden left an impression of 'wholly new and unforeseen horror, something as strange and terrible as the apparition of a rattlesnake or a boa-constrictor might be to an English child, wandering a little away into the orchard or the wood near the house'. The Darnells experience precisely such a suburban Thinning, the 'lost dreams of an enchanted land' (Machen, 2011: 209), and retrieve lost meaning through the transformative power of the story of the Graal as much as its possible reality.

In 'The Incalling', Austin too is – even in the late twentieth century – keen to avoid the 'brick wastes' (Harrison, 1988: 44) east of Camden towards Islington. In fact, Harrison's London is replete with the detritus, both physical and psychic, of the lost nineteenth and early twentieth centuries. The former grandeur of a Victorian cemetery has long since been lost through its conversion into a dilapidated children's playground populated only by 'sleepy alcoholics' (Harrison, 1988: 44). Alice Sprake's shabby ritual outfit is the 'decayed echo of *fin-de-siècle* water sprites and eurhythmical entertainments' (Harrison, 1988: 40); she is momentarily a 'village hall *danseuse* from some vanished Edwardian summer-twilight rehearsal' (Harrison, 1988: 40) and, later, when glimpsed on the Victoria Embankment, 'the ghost of a Victorian afternoon' (Harrison, 1988: 43). This is not a simple nostalgia for a vanished pastoralism, however, but just one valence of a much wider anxiety immanent in modernity.

While Machen, especially after 1900, produced fables of recovery, Harrison, in dialogue with them, produces fables of resignation and despair. Luckhurst (2005: 177–9), paying particular attention to 'Running Down' (1975), situates Harrison's writing within the wider entropic turn of the British sf new wave, an expression of the 1970s hangover of sixties idealism and increasing post-imperial malaise. However, this malaise can also be located in Machen's work at least half a century earlier. One of the numerous texts mentioned by name in *The Course of the Heart* is W. B. Yeats's *The Trembling of the Veil* (1922).[8] In this gossipy memoir of the 1890s, Yeats repeatedly rails against 'Darwin's Bulldog' T. H. Huxley and John Tyndall, the Irish physicist and mountaineer in whose *Contributions to Molecular Physics in the Domain of Radiant Heat* (1872) 'the blue of the firmament and the polarization of sky light ... were shown to be due to excessively fine particles floating in the atmosphere' (Brock, 2006: n.p.). To Yeats, Machen, and many other writers of their generation, this was a cataclysmic desecration: what job was there left for poetry in the world when the very blueness of the sky itself could be accounted for in such quotidian material terms?

This was just the latest outrage after decades of the old certainties being stripped away – not only by Darwin and Wallace and the advances in geology made by Lyell and others, but also through increasingly sophisticated Biblical criticism. David Strauss's *Das Leben Jesu, kritisch bearbeitet* (1835–6) (*The Life of Jesus, Critically Examined*) and Ludwig Feuerbach's *Das Wesen des Christenthums* (1841) were translated into English by Mary Ann Evans, who would become better known as George Eliot, as *The Life of Christ, Critically Examined* (1846) and *The Essence of Christianity* (1854), respectively: 'Both books saw religion as a purely human construct and the Christian religion as an exercise in mythology' (Wilson, 2003: 167). The coeval confidence of the scientific worldview was articulated unambiguously by Tyndall in his Belfast address of 1874: 'The impregnable position of science may be described in a few words. We claim, and we shall wrest from theology, the entire domain of cosmological theory' (Lester, 1968: 23). By the 1890s, however, even the consolations offered by the Enlightenment vision of a knowable, mechanical universe had been dispensed with by quantum theory and a whole raft of new scientific developments which 'with the full authority of scientific method found flexibility and uncertainty lurking in the Victorian's [sic] concepts of time and space, motion and matter' (Lester, 1968: 29; emphasis added). In 1907, Henry Adams complained that scholars had to adjust to putting up with 'a fraction of the universe, and a very small fraction at that – the circle reached by the senses, where sequence could be taken for granted – much as the deep sea fish takes for granted the circle of light which he generates' (Lester, 1968: 29–30). As John Lester (1968: 21) puts it, 'Man's environment seemed less and less to reflect man's humanity and to grow more and more hostile to it, while at the same time man's ability to comprehend his environment seemed to decrease'.

Machen's response to this newly hostile universe was one of reciprocal 'furious hostility' (Joshi, 2011: xxiv): 'It is monstrous that science, shown to be mad in the abstract, should presume to dictate to us in the concrete' (Machen, 1924: 146). He regarded science as a 'great bully', which 'for the last sixty or seventy years ... has been bragging and blustering and pretending to know everything ... and committing the most tremendous howlers on every possible subject' (Machen, 1924: 148–9). Machen's blithe denial of such a thing as scientific authority enabled him to continue practising his religion unperturbed. Yeats, however, by acknowledging its authority was forced to improvise in order to accommodate that authority within a personal poetic or spiritual worldview:

> I am very religious, and deprived by Huxley and Tyndall, whom I detested, of the simple-minded religion of my childhood, I had made a new religion, almost an infallible church out of poetic tradition: a fardel of stories, and of personages, and of emotions, inseparable from their first expression, passed on from generation to generation by poets and painters with some help from philosophers and theologians. I wished for a world, where I could discover this tradition perpetually. (Yeats, 1922: 6)

This imaginary, created by Yeats through psychological necessity, resonates with and delineates Lucas's and Pam's attempt to shore up the world against its Thinning in *The Course of the Heart* through the creation of the Coeur. But whereas Machen's Mr and Mrs Darnell succeed in their comparable endeavour, and the reader therefore finds solace, Harrison's narrative only suggests failure, and Yaxley finds total failure, writing in his notebook of:

> two distinct and irreconcilable worlds, *pleroma* or fullness – which has come down to us as the muddled Christian promise of 'Heaven'; and *hysterema* or *kenoma*, pain, illusion, emptiness – the life we must actually live. Between them, it used to be said, lies the paradox of boundary-state *horos*. But the great discovery of this century has been to knock at the door of *horos* and find no one at home. *Horos* is the wish-fulfilment dream, the treachery of the mirror. (Harrison, 1993: 121)

And what is ritual when it has no referent? When the door to the Pleroma is revealed to be firmly closed and the spiritual quest to be nothing but an echo-chamber? It becomes a dumb show, empty of referent, a quotidian psychological disorder – a futile pursuit of the wish-fulfilment dream. 'The Incalling' presents us with a magic ritual voided of content and meaning, only existing as a rehearsal of its futile outward gestures:

> She began to trudge along the chalk line, round and round, compliant and bovine, Clerk not far behind ... Her degradation, it seemed to me, was complete: as was that of everybody else in the room. Her feet scraped interminably, and Clerk's scraped after. Round and round they went.
> 'Fucking hell, Clerk,' I said, 'You must be mad.' (Harrison, 1988: 40–1)

The narrator sees only insanity, irrationality and degradation rather than access to the numinous. This ritual is as hollowed of its meaning and as lacking in spiritual uplift as the 'cheap religious pictures' hung on the wall, including a 'lurid' Gethsemane whose tackiness mocks the supposed profundity of Christ's agony in the garden (Harrison,

1988: 37). *The Course of the Heart* develops this futility and bathos through an emphasis on the paraphernalia employed by Yaxley, which are invariably cheap, ephemeral, kitsch, sordid – a bricolage of Machen's (2011: 205) 'weary, useless little things' from that 'rubbish heap that had been accumulating for some centuries', of the chintzy and sordid 'burden of futile or malign objects' (Harrison, 1993: 123).

In Gnostic doctrine, the 'sacrament of the bridal chamber is ... a perfect delineation of the Pleroma conception of unity of separated elements' (Rudolph, 2001: 246). Similarly, 'the real clue to the Heart' found by the alleged author of the Coeur's history, Michael Ashman, is 'the record of a marriage' (Harrison, 1993: 143). Despite Pam's and Lucas's desperate grasping after this vision, Machen's (2011: 216) divine sacrament – 'the consummation of all things, the Bridal of all Bridals' – is ultimately so corrupted by Harrison (1993: 121) that we are left with the unedifying image of a naked middle-aged man standing alone in a filthy flat between a 'burned-out electric kettle' and 'a split PVC bucket' (Harrison, 1993: 121), ineffectually masturbating while listening to the forgotten song of 'some chirpy pre-war entertainer' (Harrison, 1993: 123) on a Dansette record player. This is a long way from Machen's (2011: 215) vision of the entire world as 'but a great ceremony or sacrament, which teaches under visible forms a hidden and transcendent doctrine'. Harrison retains the ceremony but dispenses with the transcendent doctrine which, through faith, we believe makes sense of it.

Machen, described by his son as 'never anything but a High Church Tory' (Machen, 1988: 14), was certainly one of those whom Lester disparages for seizing 'avidly on the loopholes of the materialistic system [and regarding] each loophole found as an affirmation of man's spiritual life' (Machen, 1968: 37). However, the apparent inviolability of Machen's religious convictions, which he set out in 'polemics ... attacking a ridiculously caricatured version of science and rationalism' (Joshi, 2003: 14–15), is frequently betrayed in his own fictions. Along with the spiritual uplift and awe which permeates the visionary cast of his writing, his texts regularly reveal a sublimated fear or anxiety regarding the quiddity of things: a negative, adumbral shadow of the 'Holy' numinous reality that formed the basis of his mysticism. And occasionally Machen (1907: 223), like Harrison, poisons his own reveries: 'All London was one grey temple of an awful rite, ring within ring of wizard stones circled about some central place, every circle was an initiation, every initiation eternal loss'. If Machen's anxiety in this regard is subconscious, and one which he, like Lucas and Pam, tried to write himself free of, Harrison's anxiety is writ large on the page, and is also an explicit and honest response to Machen. Whereas much of Machen's fiction is directly engaged with the ecstatic, either in the form of religion or the poetics of the religious visionary,[9] Harrison uses its deflected light to limn a less comfortable but nonetheless hard true world of poetic vision.[10]

Notes

1 See Ryan Elliott's essay elsewhere in this volume.

2 He had completed a long stint as a Fleet Street journalist, an occupation he bitterly resented and regarded as confirmation of his failure as a novelist (Gawsworth, 2013: 361).

3 This plot summary is accurate but a misleading description of the novel, which Machen frequently interrupts with essayistic digressions on various matters, including alchemy, religion, and the nature of reality, sanity and insanity.

4 The 'Turanian' little people of The Three Impostors (1895) and 'The Shining Pyramid' (1895) become the cruel children in 'Out of the Earth' (1915), who have wizened, repulsive faces, and the 'Bright Boy' (1936), who turns out to be an aged dwarf. The malignant dwarf initially taken to be a child is also found in Daphne du Maurier's 'Don't Look Now' (1971) and Robert Aickman's 'Bind Your Hair' (1964). In an irreverent reference to a presumably genuine preoccupation, the back cover of the first edition of The Committed Men (1971) lists 'dwarfs' as one of Harrison's 'hobbies'. In both Machen and Harrison, the conceit achieves its sinister affect through category pollution between infant and adult, and through uncanny doubling, the dwarfish children shadowing and molesting like troublesome ids.

5 This fictional book later featured in Machen's 'N' (1936).

6 Harrison holds Bowen in high regard, and The Course of the Heart contains a reference to Bowen's similarly titled The Death of the Heart (1938) (see Harrison, 2009).

7 John Bayley (1989: 177) argues that Pepita does not treat Kôr with unambiguous reverence, and neither should the reader: 'Rider Haggard is not, to put it mildly, an entirely serious figure, and [Bowen] is well aware of that'.

8 See Harrison (1993: 29).

9 For Machen's thesis on 'ecstasy' as the key differential between good and bad literature, see Machen (1923b).

10 This closing phrase comes from Bayley's (1989: 175) discussion of 'Mysterious Kôr', which contrasts Rider Haggard's 'self-indulgent world of fantasy' and 'the hard true world of poetic vision' that Bowen's story creates.

Works Cited

Bayley, John (1989) *The Short Story: Henry James to Elizabeth Bowen*. London: Harvester Wheatsheaf.

Brock, W. H. (2006) 'Tyndall, John', *Oxford Dictionary of National Biography*, accessed 8 August 2015, http://www.oxforddnb.com/view/article/27948?docPos=1

Carey, John (1992) *The Intellectuals and the Masses*. London: Faber.

Clute, John (1997a) 'M(ichael) John Harrison', in John Clute and John Grant(eds) *The Encyclopedia of Fantasy*, pp. 453–4. London: Orbit.

Clute, John (1997b) 'Thinning', in John Clute and John Grant(eds) *The Encyclopedia of Fantasy*, pp. 942–3. London: Orbit.

Fergus, Emily (2015) '"A Wilder Reality": Euhemerism and Arthur Machen's "Little People"', *Faunus: The Journal of the Friends of Arthur Machen* (Autumn): 3–17.

Gawsworth, John (2013) *The Life of Arthur Machen*. Leyburn: Tartarus.

Goldstone, Adrian and Sweetser, Wesley (1965) *A Bibliography of Arthur Machen*. Austin: University of Texas Press.

Harrison, M. John (1988). 'The Incalling'. *The Ice Monkey*, pp. 34–58. London: Unwin.

Harrison, M. John (1993) *The Course of the Heart*. London: Flamingo.

Harrison, M. John (2009) 'Dead Lives', *AmbienteHotel*, 5 August 2015, https://ambientehotel.wordpress.com/2009/08/29/dead-lives/

Joshi, S. T. (2003) *The Weird Tale*. Rockville, MD: Wildside.

Joshi, S. T. (2011) 'Introduction', S. T. Joshi (ed.) *The White People and Other Weird Stories*, pp. xi–xxiv. London: Penguin.

Lester, John A. (1968) *Journey Through Despair 1880–1914: Transformations in British Literary Culture*. Princeton, NJ: Princeton University Press.

Lovecraft, H. P. (1985) 'Supernatural Horror in Literature', in *Dagon and Other Macabre Tales*, pp. 421–512. London: Panther.

Luckhurst, Roger (2005) *Science Fiction*. Cambridge: Polity.

Machen, Arthur (1907) *The Hill of Dreams*. London: Grant Richards.

Machen, Arthur (1923a) *Far Off Things*. London: Martin Secker.

Machen, Arthur (1923b) *Hieroglyphics*. London: Martin Secker.

Machen, Arthur (1924) *Dog and Duck*. London: Jonathan Cape.

Machen, Arthur (1968) *The Green Round*. Sauk City: Arkham House.

Machen, Arthur (1988) *Selected Letters*, ed. Roger Dobson, Godfrey Brangham and R. A. Gilbert. Wellingborough: Aquarian.

Machen, Arthur (2011) 'A Fragment of Life', in *The White People and Other Weird Stories*, ed. S. T. Joshi, pp. 148–222. London: Penguin.

Mathew, David (2002) 'M John Harrison Interviewed', *infinity plus*, accessed 14 July 2015, http://www.infinityplus.co.uk/nonfiction/intmjh.htm

Miéville, China (2003) 'The Limits of Vision(aries): or M. John Harrison Returns to London and it is Spring', accessed 12 August 2015, *Things That Never Happen: Stories by M. John Harrison*, pp. 1–9. San Francisco, CA: Night Shade.

OED Online (2017) 'pleroma, *n.*', accessed 12 August 2015, http://www.oed.com/view/Entry/145726?redirectedFrom=pleroma&

'John' (2009/2010) 'A Review of *The Course of the Heart*', Goodreads, accessed 29 July 2015, accessed 29 July 2015, https://www.goodreads.com/review/show?id=70870332

Rudolph, Kurt (2001) *Gnosis: The Nature and History of Gnosticism*. London: A&C Black.

Showalter, Elaine (1991) *Sexual Anarchy: Gender and Culture at the Fin de Siècle*. London: Bloomsbury.

Wilson, A. N. (2003) *The Victorians*. London: Arrow.

Yeats, W. B. (1922) *The Trembling of the Veil*. London: T. Werner Laurie.

THE MISANTHROPIC PRINCIPLE

Vassili Christodoulou

M. John Harrison is a writers' writer. As George Martin, Brandon Sanderson and others toil in Tolkien's shadow on doorstopper volumes of feudal adventure, so a generation of more literary-minded fantasists imitate Harrison's exacting imagery, philosophical dexterity and talent for uncovering the numinous in the quotidian of everyday life. His provocative assault upon the staid conventions of science fiction and fantasy (SFF) liberated a generation of younger novelists to give full flight to their imaginative talents. For Iain Banks (1988: xii), Harrison is 'one of the English language's greatest writers'; for Neil Gaiman, an intimidating, revelatory figure, whose prose is unforgettable – as clear 'as mountain-water and as cold'; for China Miéville, a Nobel worthy figure without whom *Perdido Street Station* (2000) would not have been possible.

Critics read Harrison's own fiction almost exclusively in light of this pervasive influence upon the development of SFF. Literary theorists and commentators are delighted by his refusal of traditional escapist comforts and celebrate his ability to collide naturalism with the heady dream-stuff genre readers expect: the *Guardian*'s Stuart Kelly (2012: n.p.) notes, for example, that in *Empty Space* (2012) 'there are space ships, but they have pigeon shit on them'. Yet to celebrate Harrison solely for his subversion of and impact upon other genre fiction is to miss most of what is vital and exhilarating about his oeuvre – namely, that he is first and foremost engaged with our own world's mysteries and only secondarily with destabilizing SFF tropes. Whether critiquing the act of world-building to the fury of Reddit trufans or inflicting postmodernity on the residents of a swords-and-sorcery metropolis, Harrison also dares us to entertain new notions of life, not simply of art.[1] This essay seeks to map a little of this critically neglected terrain by charting parallels between Harrison's *Empty Space* trilogy (2002–12) and the work of an outspoken contemporary thinker with whom he shares a set of philosophical concerns that rub against the received wisdom of the age: the political philosopher John Gray.

Free to live as we choose

A generation after the political scientist Francis Fukayama (1992: xi) famously announced *The End of History and the Last Man*, his claim that capitalist democracy will be the 'final form of human government' seems less premature than dangerously naive. A litany of global challenges and catastrophes, from the 2008 financial crisis to the resurgence of nationalism and religious fundamentalism, have come to suggest to the rest of us that the ultimate victory of liberal democratic values is very far from assured. But though other commentators might now gloat at their twenty-twenty hindsight, Fukayama was never a lone voice in the wilderness. Rather, he was simply the loudest advocate of a neo-conservative claim that dominated Anglo-American intellectual life. In the aftermath of the Cold War, a singular worldview prevailed, valuing the freedom of the individual above all else, and holding liberal capitalist constitutional democracy to be the only system of social organization under which human beings can flourish. John Gray was a rare sceptical voice, arguing that liberal ideologues would never be capable of justifying their conclusions against the tide of contrary historical evidence. For Gray (2009), Fukayama's vision of perpetual peace and prosperity owes more to Hegel's teleological philosophy of history than any rational account of why liberal democratic institutions are uniquely necessary.

By the turn of the millennium, Gray's (2002: xi, xi–xii) attack on this orthodoxy had germinated into an iconoclastic new vision of human nature, intended to rebuke the 'central article of faith of liberal societies': the Enlightenment humanist belief that 'unlike any other animal, ... we are free to live as we choose'. It was a stance at odds with almost the entire canon of Western philosophy, from Socrates to the postmodernists. In *Straw Dogs*, the first and most essential of Gray's volumes rejecting the notion that humans might become masters of their own destinies, only David Hume, Paul Feyerabend, Bertrand Russell and Arthur Schopenhauer are singled out for praise; even Friedrich Nietzsche and Martin Heidegger, who considered themselves hostile to the framework of Enlightenment humanism, are shown to ultimately depend upon its conceits. The opprobrium which greeted Gray from within his own academic community, then, was utterly predictable. Terry Eagleton's (2002: n.p.) assessment of *Straw Dogs* as a collection of 'half-truths, plain falsehoods, lurid hyperbole, [and] dyspeptic middle-aged grousing' indicates the extent to which he alienated mainstream Anglo-American philosophers.

The seeds of Gray's ideas are found outside his own academic tradition. He regards Darwinism, Gaia theory, Taoism and New Wave SF to be untainted by the mythologies of liberal humanism, and in *Straw Dogs*, quotations from their key practitioners form a patchwork of illustrations to his 'unfamiliar way of thinking' (Gray, 2002: ix). Within SF, Gray (2010: n.p.) reserves special praise for J. G. Ballard, whom he credits with being the first novelist to abandon the belief that humans and their creations could 'shape the future', instead employing the genre's conceits to demonstrate how the psyche might be liberated following the collapse of civic order. Gray acknowledges that Ballard helped to distil his thoughts on humans and other animals into a coherent philosophy, but understates the degree to which the edifice of *Straw Dogs* is built on Ballardian terrain. An earlier description of Ballard's 'particular view of the world' summarizes a perspective he would soon present as his own:

> It is a view of things that goes flatly against the pieties of the age. It takes a certain nihilism as given. Ballard regards with suspicion all

schemes – liberal, environmentalist – that aim to make the world over. Such schemes repose a faith in human society that Ballard plainly lacks. (Gray, 1999: n.p.)

It is a testament to the strength of their mutual sympathy that Ballard himself was an enthusiastic public champion of *Straw Dogs* – as were younger novelists influenced by Ballard's oeuvre, such as Will Self and M. John Harrison. Harrison's *Ambiente Hotel* blog evidences excitement at the prospect of forthcoming Gray titles, and *Nova Swing* (2006) takes one of *Straw Dogs'* aphorisms as an epigram.

Ballard's influence on Harrison is most pronounced during SF's New Wave:

> Those of us who cut our teeth on Ballard in the mid-to-late 1960s, like puppies gnawing on a chair leg, understood very little but nevertheless elected him as father, map, compass. Later, perhaps, we understood more, but had already gone on to do something different. (Harrison, 2014: n.p.)

The Committed Men (1971), Harrison's odyssey across the motorways of post-nuclear England, siphons the essence of Ballard's cataclysm quartet,[2] contrasting those who attempt to continue the now meaningless rituals of civilization with an *avant garde* celebrating the psychic fulfilment possible in their new world. *The Centauri Device* (1974) merges space opera with Ballard's aesthetic of the unconscious, or 'Inner Space', as surreal junk-filled landscapes and a grotesque supporting cast flesh out a universe as incomprehensible to humans as our own minds. It climaxes in the nihilistic, entropic spirit characteristic of Ballardian fiction from *The Drowned World* onwards, as the space tramp John Truck initiates the destruction of the galaxy.

At the same moment as Gray's *Straw Dogs* revealed his new philosophy, Harrison's *Light* (2002) marked his return to Ballardian themes. Although neither Harrison nor Gray publicly expressed admiration for the other before 2002, these works are uncannily similar, implying a unique, nihilistic conception of nature and our place within it. Given the anarchist politics of Harrison's early work and Gray's political meandering – from 1970s Burkean conservative to Hayekian

liberal in Thatcher's Britain to disillusioned Blairite and radical plural-
ist, changing schemes by a belief in the necessity of pragmatic political action and a Ballardian fear of world-changing schemes – it seems
an unlikely convergence, but it has only grown more apparent in their
public dialogue. Harrison's *Empty Space* novels use science-fictional
metaphor to conjure a reality close to that which Gray imagines us
already to inhabit, in which the Enlightenment models of selfhood,
moral agency and free will are simply placebos in a universe neither
intelligible to human minds nor sympathetic to human concerns. No
longer able or willing to endorse anthropocentric myths, Gray and
Harrison imply that meaning might instead be found in the 'passive
nihilist' philosophy described and witheringly rejected by Friedrich
Nietzsche, and in so doing, share a startlingly similar vision of how
human beings might live.

The boys from Earth

I call this vision the 'Misanthropic Principle'. The original 'Anthropic
Principle', a contentious but influential idea in astrophysics, implies
in its 'strong' form that the purpose of the universe is to give rise to
intelligent life. According to cosmologists John Barrow and Frank
Tipler (1988), the probability of the universe's fundamental con-
stants falling within a range capable of supporting conscious life is
too narrow adequately to be accounted for by chance. In seeking to
restore humanity to a privileged position after the displacements of
the Copernican and Darwinian revolutions, they share with humanists the goal of reconciling a naturalistic worldview with one in which
human life is the arbiter of meaning.

The creation of a self-confessed 'equal opportunities misanthro-
pist' (Lea, 2012: n.p.), M. John Harrison's *Empty Space* universe is
antagonistic to humanity through its very lack of any such benevolent
governing principles. All grand unifying theories work, even as they
rule out 'one another's basic assumptions':

> If your theory gave you a foamy space to work with – if you had to
> catch a wave – that didn't preclude some other engine, running on a

perfectly smooth Einsteinian surface, from surfing the same tranche of empty space. It was even possible to build drives on the basis of superstring-style theories, which, despite their promise four hundred years ago, had never really worked at all. (Harrison, 2002: 139)

By suggesting in a space opera that the laws of nature might be closed to the rational mind – or, indeed, that such ultimate laws might not exist at all – Harrison upturns one of the prime conventions of a genre that, from Robert Heinlein to *Star Trek*, might be deservedly caricatured as celebrating the triumph of human reason over the perils of the cosmos. In its ineffability, the *Empty Space* universe more closely resembles the misanthropic milieu of H. P. Lovecraft's cosmic horror stories, or of the weird fiction of Arthur Machen, whom Harrison read exhaustively in his formative years.

The physics of the *Empty Space* universe owe an equal debt to Paul Feyerabend. In his *History of Science Fiction*, Adam Roberts celebrates Feyerabend's anarchist approach to the scientific method – which encourages scientists to take every theory seriously, no matter how contradictory or irrelevant to current science – and suggests that SF writers do just that, using fiction as a laboratory for investigating new and outlandish ideas off limits to real scientists (Roberts, 2006: 7–9). Harrison adapts Feyerabend's ideas more radically. While the authors Roberts cites explore the implications of a single new scientific theory, implying that their fictional universes still have tangible rules even if they are different to our own, Harrison's reality is so pliable that every speculative physics is apparently useful, and none ultimately true.

This has bleak consequences for humanity's sense of self-worth. John Gray (2002: 23) explains that our common view of science as the disinterested pursuit of truth 'works to entrench anthropocentrism' and 'encourages us to believe that, unlike any other animal, we can understand the natural world, and thereby bend it to our will'. This is a manifestation of the Socratic belief that truth will set us free, passed to modern day liberal humanists from Plato via Christianity to August de Compte and John Stuart Mill. But Feyerabend's insight is that irrational processes – 'prejudice, conceit, passion' (Gray, 2002: 23) – contribute greatly to the advancement of scientific knowledge.

Theories are chosen for political reasons, or for their utility, and not because we have learned to read the language of the book of nature. In Lovecraft's fiction, protagonists confronting the universe's ineffability are driven to bombastic, theatrical madness. For Harrison's 'boys from Earth', the discovery is less melodramatic. They are afflicted by an 'insecurity magnificent in scope', a loss of stature for which they attempt to compensate by pursuing an agenda of rapine and warmongering across the galaxy:

> They dived right in. They started wars. They stunned into passivity five of the alien races they found in possession of the galaxy and fought the sixth – which they called 'the Nastic' out of a mistranslation of the Nastic's word for 'space' – to a wary truce. After that they fought one another. (Harrison, 2002: 139)

In so doing, they meet Gray's expectations for what humanity will always be: a species best characterized as 'Homo rapiens' (Gray, 2002: 152). In stark contrast to humanists such as psychologist Steven Pinker, who argues that Enlightenment values have helped bring about a gradual and continuing decline in global levels of violence, Gray claims that,

> Genocide is as human as art or prayer. ... From the stone axe onwards, humans have used their tools to slaughter one another. Humans are weapon-making animals with an unquenchable fondness for killing. (Gray, 2002: 91–2)

Raging across the Beach with a fleet of warships capable of operating in thirteen dimensions, Harrison's future humanity bears out Gray's prophecy.

Although Gray rejects the notions that scientific progress is either benevolent or entirely rational, he concedes that the expansion of knowledge through science is irreversible: the only form of progress, in fact, which can be said to truly exist. By manifesting visibly in our daily lives through technological innovation (Gray, 2002: 18), progress in science worsens the delusion that human history is also a progression. We assume technology to be a force within our control, leaving us largely blind to the chaotic nature of its influence on our development. Borrowing without direct acknowledgement from Ballard's *Crash* (1973), Gray (2002: 15) offers the motorcar as the prime example of a modern technology with unforeseen consequences: 'Which is more important today: the use of cars as means of transportation, or their use as expressions of our unconscious yearnings for personal freedom, sexual release and the final liberation of sudden death?'.

In *Light's* opening scene, Harrison's misanthropic protagonist, physicist Michael Kearney, employs a puerile version of this insight to disrupt an optimistic after-dinner game. In an 'enclave of mild academic and political self-satisfaction', Kearney's companions celebrate the promises of the future, answering the question 'how do you see yourself spending the first minute of the new millennium?' with evocations of the comforts of prosperity and technology: 'They would drink until they fell down, have sex, watch fireworks or the endless sunrise from a moving jet' (Harrison, 2002: 1). Kearney's own answer – 'driving someone else's car between two cities [he] doesn't know' – is a hostile expression of his disillusionment with the humanist narrative of scientific and social progress implicit in the answers of his dinner companions:

> The freedoms represented – the warmth and emptiness of the car, its smell of plastic and cigarettes, the sound of a radio playing softly in the night, the green glow of dials, the sense of it as an instrument or a series of instrumental decisions, aimed and made use of at every turn in the road – were as puerile as they were satisfying. They were a description of his life to that date. (Harrison, 2002: 2)

His corrosive, deliberately provocative tone is better suited to a teenage iconoclast than a middle-aged scientist, as Kearney's girlfriend Clara notes: '"Well, that wasn't very grown-up."' (Harrison, 2002: 2)

This desire to antagonize is one of Kearney's strongest impulses. Following an animal rights arson attack aimed at the previous occupants of his lab, he makes it known in the scientific community that 'he subscribed to the A[nimal] L[iberation] F[ront]' (Harrison, 2002: 4), with the express purpose of stoking their moral outrage. If the evidence of Harrison's work can be said to give us any insight into his character, then it would appear that Michael Kearney shares this drive with his creator and namesake. For example, in its deliberate denial of the escapist pleasures of swords-and-sorcery, his *Viriconium* sequence constitutes 'barefaced trolling of the sff reader' (Harrison cited in Franklin, 2015: n.p.). Considering Eagleton's assessment of him as a dyspeptic grouch, we might reasonably conclude that Gray has similar motives. The Misanthropic Principle may owe its existence, in part, to a desire to troll the humanist intelligentsia.

Liberated from historical truth by SF's futuristic, metaphoric nature, Harrison is able to deny myths of scientific progress to the inhabitants of the *Empty Space* universe. Partly functional 'found' technologies have studded his deep futures since *The Pastel City* (1971), where they reinforce a classical cyclical model of civilization's rise and fall and contribute to a collage effect reminiscent of T. S. Eliot's 'The Waste Land' (1922). The ancient alien salvage of the *Empty Space* trilogy retains these significances while adding a new dimension: the savage undercutting of the humanist image of scientific research as a heroic endeavour, pursued with rationalist objectivity unaffected by human fallibility or the socio-economics of the age. Harrison's (2002: 28) twenty-fifth-century 'thieves, speculators [and] intellectual cowboys' adopt the symbols of scientific practice to dignify their excavation of preceding civilizations with the humanist conception of science as the search for truth, and this move illustrates the hollowness of their enterprise to the reader. Seria Mau's prospectors, more interested in 'profit-sharing deals, art events they had seen, [and] holidays at the core' (Harrison, 2002: 97) than the exogeology that ostensibly motivates their investigation of the Kefahuchi culture, are Michael Kearney's direct inheritors.

Fragmentary dreams

Harrison's Beach-combers are less committed to liberal humanism than we are – or at least, less committed than the intelligentsia attacked in *Straw Dogs*. Rather, their experience of science contributes to the impression that all humans lack control over the direction of their lives. The metamorphoses made possible by genetic engineering are sold with the luminous promises of consumer freedom, but the most commonly adopted vat-grown bodies (or 'cultivars', in the novel's vernacular) serve only to advertise the bondage of their owners, whether as prize fighters, prostitutes or rickshaw girls resembling indentured oxen. Gray (2002: 6) imagines our remodelling as a species will be performed 'as an upshot of struggles in the murky realm where big business, organised crime, and the hidden parts of government vie for control', and so it is along Harrison's Beach, where the privatized military government and the criminal franchise of Uncle Zip – who 'didn't care what he cut, or who he cut for as long as they could pay' (Harrison, 2002: 47) – dominate the marketplace for gene-splicing. Perhaps luckily, their net effect on individual freedom and servitude is precious little. Like the ethical consumer choices derided by Slavoj Žižek – coffee without caffeine, beer without alcohol – the cultivars provide symbolic meaning for their recipients but soften attendant risk and consequence, ironically reinforcing the impotence of their lives (Kul-Want, 2012: 115). The full absurdity of this idea is revealed in a throwaway moment featuring some of Harrison's most affecting prose:

> As soon as [Seria Mau] was gone, two of the shadow boys turned on the third and cut his throat for cheating, then, overcome by the pure existential moment, cradled his head in the warm golden light as he smiled softly up at nothing, bubbling his life out all over them like a benediction. 'Hey you,' they comforted him, 'you can do it all again. Tonight you'll do it all again.' (Harrison, 2006: 63)

Of all the tailored protagonists we encounter, only Irene the Mona takes Uncle Zip's philosophy of choice seriously. She emphasizes the importance of 'personal development and aspirational goals' (Harrison, 2012: 241) to Liv Hula and Fat Antoyne with aphorisms resembling those of self-help culture, attempting to convince her friends of the reality of the unified, free and autonomous self popularized by Descartes. Ultimately, though, she is a bathetic figure, for the divide between the language of the popular humanist conception of the self and the reality of personal experience in Harrison's universe is too great to wilfully ignore. In his review of the *Empty Space* trilogy, Gray identifies this gulf as the unifying theme of Harrison's career. It is exhibited most clearly in the central activity of his mimetic novel *Climbers* (1989), which Gray (2013: n.p.) takes to be an 'expression of a fantasy of control that aims to escape human vulnerability and limitation' – a fantasy for which Gray and Harrison share an abiding mistrust. In *Empty Space*, the catastrophe of war exposes Irene's life as a fragile stage set, much as the Second World War did for Ballard and his fictional manqué Jim in *Empire of the Sun* (1984). She realizes the errors in her understanding of human nature: 'Change your game, you change your luck ... that's everything I used to believe in life ... Now I recognise each change of heart is just another scam performed upon yourself!' (Harrison, 2012: 190). Shortly afterward, Irene's cruel, unexpected and meaningless death provides the reader with further evidence for her argument against the reality of personal autonomy.

Daunted by the overwhelming complexity of their existence, most of *Light*'s protagonists believe the nature of the self impossible to determine. Seria Mau's dreams give 'her a sense of herself as a kind of bad natured origami, a space accordion folded to contain more than seemed possible, or advisable, as full of invisible matter as the halo itself' (Harrison, 2002: 75), Invoking a passage from Harrison's earlier novel *A Storm of Wings*, she considers the unintelligibility of the alien Nastic:

> 'Motives,' she thought, staring at the collection of legs and eyes in front of her, 'are a sensorium thing. They are an *Umwelt* thing. The cat has a hard job to imagine the motives of the housefly in its mouth.'
> (Harrison, 2002: 12)

Ironically, Seria Mau is equally short in fellow feeling for human beings, and by degrees the same might be said of almost everyone in the trilogy. As the detective Lens Aschemann tells his beleaguered Assistant in *Nova Swing*: 'no one ever understands anyone' (Harrison, 2006: 152). Written under the conscious influence of *Straw Dogs*, that novel interrogates Gray's claims concerning selfhood by reconfiguring the Kefahuchi Tract into the Saudade event site, shifting its metaphorical emphasis as an invocation of the ineffable away from the metaphysical and toward a representation of that 'which cannot be understood' (Harrison, 2006: 74) within the human mind. The site is a piece of the Kefahuchi tract that fell to earth: an 'elastic' environment in a constant state of flux, thick with imagery dredged up from the unconscious (Harrison, 2006: 64). *Nova Swing's* epigram from *Straw Dogs* says 'Our lives are more like fragmentary dreams than the enactment of conscious selves', a simile literalized by the Saudade event site. It is abundant in 'people, memes and artifacts no one can quite describe' (Harrison, 2006: 74) – concretized dream fragments obeying their own ineffable laws:

> The air was perfectly still but full of old shoes, floating around one another as if they'd been lifted up on a strong wind. As if shoes had a gravity of their own. He said they exhibited something that looked like flocking behaviour. (Harrison, 2006: 65)

For Gray, although we believe 'our actions express our decisions', in fact,

> They arise from a structure of habits that is almost infinitely complicated. Most of our life is enacted without conscious awareness. Nor can it be made conscious. No degree of self-awareness can make us self-transparent. (Gray, 2002: 69)

As a site guide, Vic Serotonin is a 'corrupt tour operator of the soul' (Harrison, 2006: 261), and his customers desire to become self-transparent in both a conventional psychological sense and by demonstrating mastery over the site: 'They had sex with you in open view of the thing out there – as if that was how they understood it; not as a state of affairs but as a live thing, perhaps even a conscious thing, they wanted it to be watching when they came' (Harrison, 2006: 211). They are simultaneously repulsed by the little they can discern of the Site and their own selves, and urgently motivated to uncover more. Elizabeth Kielar articulates this paradox in her journal, encapsulating the tension between the epistemic guilt and growing self-awareness that forms the crux of her sexual and commercial relationship with Vic: 'The known is slicked onto everything like a kind of grease. You would do anything to avoid the things you already know ... I don't want to go in [to the event site] but I must' (Harrison, 2006: 85). It is a conflict suffused with the character of the Promethean and prelapsarian myths. The science-fictional conceit of a forbidden place where the laws of nature do not apply is borrowed from the Strugatsky brothers' *Roadside Picnic* (1972). 'The further into the Zone' of their novel, we learn in another of *Nova Swing's* epigrams, 'the nearer to Heaven'. Harrison's site is less a form of Heaven and more an alternative Eden, where transgressive knowledge of the true nature of the human animal is not sexual and moral awareness but an understanding of the illusory nature of the self and the place of the pre- and un-conscious in determining our actions. It is a concern that reverberates throughout his fiction, and is made explicit in his essay 'What it Might Be Like to Live in Viriconium'. Harrison warns the reader that they 'can't hope to control things':

> The conscious mind operates at forty or fifty bits a second, and disorder is infinitely deep. Better admit that. Better lie back and enjoy it—especially since, without the processes implied by it, no one could write (or read) books anyway. (Harrison, 2001: n.p.)

For Harrison, as for Gray, the ultimate inability of humans to be self-transparent and in control is both inevitable and essential to all that is worthwhile in human life.

The Kefahuchi boogie

Science presents no fixed view of reality, history has no discernible trajectory, and humans are unknowable even to themselves: in such a world, how do the proponents of the Misanthropic Principle believe we might tolerably live? Sharing their concerns a century earlier when faced with the decline of Christianity in the face of Darwinism, Nietzsche categorizes possible answers as 'active' and 'passive' forms of nihilism (see Critchley, 2008).

The former encompasses all attempts to make the world anew according to a single will, and is the stance Nietzsche adopts through the infamous fantasy of the ubermensch. Alienated, chaotic and often psychopathic, the archetypal Ballardian anti-hero is an active nihilist for the twentieth century, and Ballard himself occasionally personally endorses the importance of being true to oneself in a Nietzschean fashion. In an *Interview with Rolling Stone*, he says:

> The challenge is for each of us to respond, to remake as much as we can of the world around us, because no one else will do it for us. We have to find a core within us and get to work ... Just get on with it! (Cott, 1987: n.p.)

From Travers in *The Atrocity Exhibition* (1970) to *Crash*'s Vaughan, Ballard's psychopathological menagerie take this attitude to a horrifying satirical conclusion. For Ballard, active nihilism is the probable outcome of the bourgeoisification of life in the west: an answer to the insipid boredom of post-industrial middle class life, in equal parts toxic and alluring.

Although his novels may ultimately serve to warn 'readers against the possibilities of the future' (Ballard, 2014: 61), the sheer *joie de vivre* of Ballard's anti-heroes tempers the degree to which one could consider their author a misanthrope. One might condemn his protagonists for their transgressive behaviour, but we also revel in their freedom, power and charisma. Such exuberance is largely absent in Gray and Harrison; in their criticism of active nihilism, they decline to address why it has such appeal. Their greatest concern is with wilful attempts to create more rational societies. While world-builders of generic fantasy literature may risk only limp and unpoetic fiction, Gray believes that the political application of this drive results in failed states, brutalized lives and genocides. In a 2007 blog post indicative of their increasing philosophical synchronicity, Harrison appropriates many of Gray's arguments to summarize his own aesthetic principle:

> The whole idea of worldbuilding is a bad idea about the world as much as it is a bad idea about fiction. It's a secularised, narcissised version of the fundamentalist Christian view that the world's a watch & God's the watchmaker. It reveals the bad old underpinnings of the humanist stance ... [and] flatters everyone further into the illusions

of anthropocentric demiurgy which have already brought the real world to the edge of ecological disaster.[3]

Harrison is not in the business of creating singular meanings, let alone an instruction manual for how his readers should live their lives. Yet *Light* does imply an alternative to active nihilism. Its climax is a triumphant, inflationary release from its misanthropic universe:

> Years passed. Centuries passed. Then the sky began to change colour, subtly and slowly at first, then faster and wilder than anyone could dream.
>
> THE BEGINNING (Harrison, 2002: 320)

For the first time in his career as a writer – and, judging from the far bleaker denouements of the subsequent *Empty Space* books, perhaps the last – Harrison appears to forgive his core characters their frailties, providing each with an unexpected redemptive arc as they learn to embrace the ineffable rather than run from it. For Kearney, slipping away into the 'raging glory of the light' of the Kefahuchi Tract, tranquillity occurs once he abandons his solipsistic attempt to derive rational meaning from the universe and learns simply to observe it: 'I've been here and seen this', he announces with his dying breath, 'I've *seen* it' (Harrison, 2002: 300). Ed Chianese's subsequent exchange with the Shrander clarifies this position:

> 'Kearney was the brains,' Ed pointed out. 'Not me.'
> 'I don't want you to understand it, Ed. I want you to *surf* it.'
> (Harrison, 2002: 318)

For residents of the Beach worthwhile lives can be best made, as Gray's (2013: n.p.) review suggests, when human beings '[fall] away from the meanings to which they cling'. In place of meaning, readers of *Straw Dogs* are encouraged like Kearney and Ed to cultivate a skilful aesthetic or playful sensibility:

> Other animals do not need a purpose in life. A contradiction to itself, the human animal cannot do without one. Can we not think of the aim of life as being simply to see? (Gray, 2002: 199)

Expressing the attitude Nietzsche characterized as 'passive nihilism' or 'Western Buddhism', Gray's hero Arthur Schopenhauer sought to sever will and desire from one's sense of self to lessen suffering. Gray might better be considered a 'Western Taoist', for, in seeking to modernize Schopenhauer's philosophical strategy, he adapts the mystical *Chuang-Tzu* to offer a way of being less pessimistic than his mentor and less destructive than Nietzsche. For Taoists,

> The good life is only the natural life lived skilfully. It has no particular purpose. It has nothing to do with the will, and it does not consist in trying to realise any ideal ... Western moralists will ask what is the purpose of such action, but for Taoists the good life has no purpose. It is like swimming in a whirlpool, responding to the currents as they come and go. (Gray, 2002: 112)

Harrison's metaphor of surfing is exactly this kind of playful activity: reliant on unconscious skill, aesthetically exhilarating and intervening minimally in the world, to an effect beyond our understanding. As a purpose without a purpose in a universe without value, it is a paradoxical, makeshift ideal: not a way of definitively understanding the universe but of managing and living with its contradictions. The alternative – that the human condition is a puzzle with a possible solution – is the very delusion that, as committed misanthropists, Gray and Harrison are dedicated to rooting out.

Notes

1 Harrison's thoughts on worldbuilding prompted an outcry after they were shared on Reddit's 'writing' thread (Biomancer, 2014), with comments ranging from impassioned defences of 'generic' fantasy to more puerile muck throwing ('what a fucking windbag'). Harrison (2001) discusses at length the postmodern component of his *Viriconium* sequence.

2 *The Wind from Nowhere* (1961), *The Drowned World* (1962), *The Drought* and *The Crystal World* (1966).

3 The original posting by Harrison no longer exists, but it is quoted in the Reddit thread cited in the first footnote.

Works Cited

Banks, Iain (1988) 'Introduction', in *Viriconium*, pp. vii–xii. London: Unwin Hyman.

Biomancer (2014) 'A short essay by the great sci-fi author M. John Harrison about why storytelling must take precedence over worldbuilding', *Reddit* (14 September), accessed 30 June 2014, https://www.reddit.com/r/writing/comments/2p80gc/a_short_essay_by_the_great_scifi_author_m_john/

Barrow, John and Tipler, Frank (1988) *The Anthropic Cosmological Principle*. Oxford: Oxford University Press.

Cott, Jonathan (1987) 'The Strange Visions of J.G. Ballard', *Rolling Stone* (19 November), accessed 30 June 2014, http://www.rollingstone.com/culture/features/the-strange-visions-of-jg-ballard-19871119

Critchley, Simon (2008) 'Truth or Dare', *The Philosophers' Magazine* 40: 74–7.

Eagleton, Terry (2002) 'Humanity and Other Animals', *Guardian* (7 September), accessed 30 June 2014, https://www.theguardian.com/books/2002/sep/07/highereducation.news2

Franklin, Tim (2015) 'M. John Harrison Interviewed by Tim Franklin', *Twisted Tales* (11 November), accessed 30 June 2014, http://twistedtalesevents.blogspot.co.uk/2015/11/m-john-harrison-interviewed-by-tim.html

Fukuyama, Francis (1992) *The End of History and the Last Man*. London: Penguin.

Gray, John (1999) 'Modernity and its Discontents', *New Statesman* (10 May), accessed 30 June 2014, http://www.newstatesman.com/node/149127

Gray, John (2002) *Straw Dogs: Thoughts on Humans and Other Animals*. London: Granta.

Gray, John (2009) 'The End of History, Again?', *Gray's Anatomy: Selected Writings*, pp. 217–23. London: Allen Lane.

Gray, John (2010) 'War of the Words', *New Statesman* (14 June), accessed 30 June 2014, http://www.newstatesman.com/fiction/2010/06/human-life-world-science-city

Gray, John (2013) 'The Kefahuchi Tract Trilogy: A Future Without Nostalgia', *New Statesman* (17 Ocober), accessed 30 June 2014, http://www.newstatesman.com/2013/10/future-without-nostalgia

Harrison, M. John (2001) 'What It Might Be Like to Live in Viriconium'. *Fantastic Metropolis* (15 October), accessed 30 June 2014, http://www.fantasticmetropolis.com/i/viriconium/

Harrison, M. John (2002) *Light*. London: Gollancz.

Harrison, M. John (2006) *Nova Swing*. London: Gollancz.

Harrison, M. John (2012) *Empty Space: A Haunting*. London: Gollancz.

Harrison, M. John (2014) 'Unused Notes for an Introduction', *Ambiente Hotel* (11 July), accessed 30 June 2014, https://ambientehotel.wordpress.com/2014/07/11/unused-notes-for-an-introduction/

Kelly, Stuart (2012) 'Empty Space: A Haunting by M. John Harrison', *Guardian* (2 August), accessed 30 June 2014, https://www.theguardian.com/books/2012/aug/02/empty-space-m-john-harrison-review

Kul-Want, Christopher (2012) *Slavoj Žižek: A Graphic Guide*. London: Icon.

Lea, Richard (2012) 'M. John Harrison: A Life in Writing', *Guardian* (12 July), accessed 30 June 2014, https://www.theguardian.com/culture/2012/jul/20/m-john-harrison-life-in-writing

Roberts, Adam (2006) *The History of Science Fiction*. Basingstoke: Palgrave Macmillan.

'Sparks in Everything' or 'A Tearful Overnight Understanding'
Posthuman Becoming in the *Empty Space* Trilogy

Timothy Jarvis

Towards the end of *Nova Swing* (2006), the second volume of M. John Harrison's *Empty Space* trilogy (2002–12), Lens Aschemann, a site crime detective who has been 'Uncle Zipped', that is genetically modified so as to resemble the older Einstein, finds that while wandering lost in the Saudade event site, a part of the mysterious Kefahuchi Tract that has fallen to the ground, he is dissolving painlessly from the feet up into 'thousands of bright, energetic white sparks' (Harrison, 2012c: 276). This transformation resembles what Gilles Deleuze and Félix Guattari term a *becoming*. They argue that the world is in a state of constant flux and characterized by transformation. A becoming is a transformation from one state to another. But a becoming is always a *becoming-other*. It does not proceed by resemblance, is not part of a rational order. It is not teleological, it does not tend towards apotheosis or ultimate realization. As they explain in *A Thousand Plateaus* (1980): 'becoming is not an evolution, a least not an evolution by descent and filiation' (Deleuze and Guattari, 2004b: 263). Uncle Zipping transforms, but its transformations do not give rise to becoming, as they are structured by resemblance – to Einstein, to Marilyn Monroe, to twentieth-century pulp sf tropes

– but Aschemann's decomposition does resemble a becoming, what Deleuze and Guattari term a *becoming-molecular*.

Deleuze and Guattari conceive of the cosmos as consisting of *chaosmos*, an originary chaos made up of flows of difference, which exists on the *plane of immanence*, of points of intensity that arise from this plane, and of forms that are temporary alliances of these intensities. A becoming-molecular is the return of a provisional form to intensities and flows. As the establishment of form and order is termed *territorialization*, a becoming-molecular is an example of *deterritorialization* – the process by which the energies making up the cosmos mutate. Deterritorialization also has a political aspect, since the static structures that make up territorialized forms impede and restrict the flows of energy essential to life. All forms of political state territorialize their subjects. Deterritorialization is resistance, or a *line of flight*, a way of provoking change.

But energies can never truly return to chaosmos, and deterritorialization will be followed by *reterritorialization*, a return to stability and order. Aschemann thinks to himself, as he nears total dissolution:

> What if there was no new species after all, only the same old one trapped in its same old circularity of reinvention? Would some fresher version of himself soon be staggering down the Corniche away from the Café Surf, singing, full of appetites, ready to be amazed? Or had that already happened? (Harrison, 2012c: 276–7)

This is suggestive of reterritorialization, as is the question Aschemann asks himself next: 'What if we're all code?' (Harrison, 2012c: 277).[1] For Deleuze and Guattari, *code* defines structures and territories, the norms and laws that act as grounds for thinking and acting, and *overcoding* is a method of despotism and control. But this question could also be interpreted as an allusion to the Weird materiality of computer code. As Anna Kearney/Waterman recalls, towards the end of *Light* (2002), Michael Kearney told 'her with a kind of urgent wonder' that 'Information might be a *substance*' (Harrison, 2012b: 357). Consequently, Aschemann's question can also be read as indicative of what Deleuze and Guattari might call a *becoming-code*, a becoming that can be mapped onto a transformation Harrison's trilogy explores:

the shift from human to posthuman.[2] The moment of Aschemann's dissolution therefore holds two obverse concepts and trajectories in tension. In this it is a version, in miniature, of the entire trilogy,[3] which explores what a *becoming-posthuman* might look like, examining what might be at stake and what might be lost, by plotting opposing narrative lines against one another.

Key to the idea of becoming is the notion that subjects are either fixed or possess various degrees of freedom. The trapped subject is stratified by all the attractions of capital, plugged, through its desire, into *desiring-machines* that connect the subject to the machinic assemblage of capital, a network which prevents the subject from realising its potential to become. All its energies are expended on being a productive node in the assemblage. The freed subject is a *Body without Organs* (BwO), an image Deleuze and Guattari (2004a: 9) borrow from Antonin Artaud to describe 'the unproductive, the sterile, the unengendered, the unconsumable', the subject freed from the strata of capital. The BwO is the subject deterritorializing, returning to the plane of immanence.

Deleuze and Guattari explain that the ideal is to free the BwO warily, to experience intensities that relieve the subject of stultifying capitalist hegemony while remaining safely fixed to a stratum:

> This is how it should be done: Lodge yourself on a stratum, experiment with the opportunities it offers, find an advantageous place on it, find potential movements of deterritorialization, possible lines of flight, experience them, produce flow conjunctions here and there, try out continuums of intensities segment by segment, have a small plot of new land at all times. (Deleuze and Guattari, 2004b: 178)

But they also state that there are 'several ways of botching the BwO' (Deleuze and Guattari, 2004b: 178). It is difficult to resist being incautious, going too far, for the BwO is in conflict with the desiring-machines that torment it:

> Every coupling of machines, every production of a machine, every sound of a machine running, becomes unbearable to the body without organs. Beneath its organs it senses there are larvae and loath-

some worms, and a God at work messing it all up or strangling it by organizing it. (Deleuze and Guattari, 2004a: 9)

To go too far is dangerous: 'If you free [the BwO] with too violent an action, if you blow apart the strata without taking precautions, then instead of drawing the plane you will be killed, plunged into a black hole, or even dragged toward catastrophe' (Deleuze and Guattari, 2004b: 178). You end up with a body entirely emptied of organs, a catatonic BwO; this is death or dissolution.

Deleuze and Guattari also describe cancerous BwOs, which are produced not by a precipitous deterritorialization, but by fostering partial, totalitarian and fascist deterritorializations. These BwOs arise from the strata themselves and, through their partial deterritorializations, are able to spread fascism and stifling subjectification; they are 'ready to gnaw, proliferate, cover, and invade the entire social field, entering into relations of violence and rivalry as well as alliance and complicity' (Deleuze and Guattari, 2004b: 180).

Images of both catatonic and cancerous BwOs recur in the trilogy. In *Light*, Seria Mau Gentlicher, captain of the K-ship, the *White Cat*, utterly helpless in her tank, floating in proteome and violated by the connections that plug her into the ship, is the very image of a body that has begun to empty itself of its organs and free itself, but is still tortured by the probes of the desiring-machine. She is also cancerous, violent, a mercenary undertaking missions for the alien Nastic in the ongoing galactic war. At the end of the novel, she allows the entity known as Dr Haends, or Sandra Shen, or the Shrander, to remake her. She undergoes a radical deterritorialization, and is made into some new kind of lifeform. At first she cannot control what she has become, and does not understand how it works, but reassured by Dr Haends she grows used to it, apparently gains mastery:

> Suddenly she laughed. Her laughter filled the vacuum. It was the laughter of particles. She was laughing in every regime. She tried out the different things she could be: there were always more; there were always more after that. (Harrison, 2012b: 404)

But the new form of life Seria Mau has become is really a form of death; she has become an empty or catatonic BwO, dragged towards catastrophe, and her limitless mutability is in fact just another form of stasis. As she says to Imps van Sant, 'I can be anything I want, but I don't want that. I want to be the one thing I am' (Harrison, 2012a: 288). Other characters follow a similar trajectory. In *Light*, Ed Chianese takes control of the K-ship Seria Mau has abandoned, piloting it, or so *Empty Space* suggests, into the heart of the Kefahuchi Tract. At the end of *Nova Swing*, Aschemann dissolves in the Saudade event site; his Assistant, a cyborg who voluntarily infects herself with computer code, becomes less and less human over the course of *Nova Swing* and *Empty Space*.

And the trilogy as a whole also moves towards deterritorialization, acts as a radical line of flight. By the end, the interpenetration of human beings and rogue 'daughter-code' – bizarre and contagious mathematics which walks out of event sites as inchoate simulacra, or are brought out as unfathomable artefacts – has given rise to a new species, a new kind of virulent vitalism, seen as dangerous and banished to derelict space hulks. This vitalism is a kind of posthuman becoming, the becoming-code. The deterritorializing trajectory of the trilogy builds to a moment in *Empty Space* when Ed Chianese, partially reterritorialized, returned from the Tract as a mangled revenant, leads the quarantine hulks, Pied Piper-like, back in.

This narrative line departs from the themes of exhausted materiality at play in some of Harrison's earlier fiction: the zone afflicted by a nebulous plague in *In Viriconium* (1982), the entropic curse of 'Running Down' (1975). It can be read as a culmination of the failed transformations in Harrison's earlier work, such as that of Isobel Avens in *Signs of Life* (1997) who, obsessed with beauty and flight, wants to become a bird. Weighed down by material things, however, she cannot achieve a deterritorializing line of flight:

> she looked so beautiful and eerie in her plumage. But despite all that
> she was a thinnish woman of the Thatcher middle classes who liked
> to have an income of between fifty and a hundred thousands pounds
> a year. Alexander had made her resemble a bird. But underneath the

cosmetic flourish, the DNA treatments, the Miami cut-and-splice, she was still Isobel Avens. ... Eventually she would shop again at Harvey Nichols. (Harrison, 1998: 230)

Too attached to the desiring-machines of capital, Isobel cannot achieve transformation. Like Ed, she is a mangled revenant, come back out of the singularity, but unlike Ed she will never deterritorialize. Even if she could give herself over to the surgery, she would still be trapped; her transformation, rational and engineered, has more in common with the process by which Seria Mau is made into a K-ship captain than with her later transformation from K-captain into a bird. Isobel remains, in effect, a cancerous BwO plugged into the Harvey Nichols desiring-machine.

Unlike Harrison's earlier work, the trilogy depicts exuberant becomings. The Kefahuchi Tract itself is the engine of these deterritorializations. What features give the Tract this transformative potential?

Empty Space is clearly an ironic title. Space in the trilogy is never empty, as the novel's epigraph from John A. Wheeler makes clear: 'No point is more central than this, that empty space is not empty'. Space teems, filled with strange and mutable stuff, antic and of unfathomable purpose. *Light* describes the Tract as:

> A singularity without an event horizon. A place where all the broken rules of the universe spill out, like cheap conjuror's stuff, magic that might work or it might not, undependable stuff in a retro-shop window. (Harrison, 2012b: 412)

It is the way it spews out tat that gives it its power. The Saudade event site is full of potent artefacts, but also detritus, or potent artefacts that look like detritus, such as the 'filthy old shoes, cracked and wrinkled, soles hanging off' that fill the air (Harrison, 2012c: 65). The sometimes powerful, unpredictable K-tech vomited from the Tract, driving change, is perhaps just the junk stored in Anna Waterman's summerhouse:

> ancient maps and charts, curtains Anna couldn't be persuaded to throw out. Christmas tree decorations. A Hornby trainset still in its box. A cannon. Coloured plastic crockery too small for a picnic, too

large for a toy ... joke liquorice, 'X-Ray Specs', handcuffs you couldn't take off ... a japanned box in which you placed a billiard ball you would never find again, though you could hear it rattling about in there forever ... a cup with a reflected face in the bottom that turned out not to be your own; the valentine heart which lit itself up by means of loving diodes within. (Harrison, 2012a: 292–3)

This is the stuff of the Kefahuchi Tract, and sets out the principles on which the physics of its universe works: dissembling, faith, trickery, the shock of recognition. As *Light* puts it, 'In the end, the bottom line was this: *everything* worked' (Harrison, 2012b: 12).

The Shrander, in its Dr Haends guise, uses the trick items and the heart with loving diodes to tempt Seria Mau to her becoming. When he shows them to her, telling her to choose anything she wants, she refuses: 'All these things are fake'; laughing, he replies, 'They're all real too ... That's the amazing thing' (Harrison, 2012b: 395). In the trilogy, the Weird and the abject, the draff and the dross, can be transformative, can do anything you want. But why? Why are the K-Tract from which it all spills and the Shrander, as an emissary of the Tract, sources of transmutative energies?

There are many possible answers. One is the strange transmutative energy of the pack, of the *multiplicity* that allows for the arising of the *anomalous*, something that is essential to transmutation. The anomalous is both part of and outside the multiplicity. It has an allure that tempts across boundaries, it is a 'phenomenon of bordering' (Deleuze and Guattari, 2004b: 270). The anomalous is a member of the pack, but outside the pack, as leader, loner, or banished. Being both within and outside the multiplicity, it shifts the composition of the multiplicity through an alliance with what is outside, and, therefore, brings about a becoming Other: 'not only is [the anomalous] the precondition for the alliance necessary to becoming, but it also carries the transformations of becoming or crossings of multiplicities always farther down the line of flight' (Deleuze and Guattari, 2004b: 275).

So the not quite random collection of junk in Anna's summerhouse, that is, on one level, the 'cheap conjuror's stuff' that spills from the Tract, becomes an engine of transformation because, though these things make sense as a collection of unwanted objects stored in a summerhouse, when they are taken out of that context, and spewed out into the event sites of the tract as bizarre artefacts, they become strange and unfathomable, bundles of qualities and potentials that cannot be known directly. Both multiplicity and anomalous, they become catalysts of change.

Becoming requires us to think of things not as inert lumps, but as bundles of shifting qualities or 'molecular collectivities' (Deleuze and Guattari, 2004b: 303), which Deleuze and Guattari term *haecceities*. Haecceities 'consist entirely of relations of movement and rest between molecules or particles, capacities to affect and be affected' (Deleuze and Guattari, 2004b: 288); they rise from the inert plane of immanence to take off on lines of flight; they allow for a kind of relation other than evolution and filiation. The junk in the summerhouse, the things that come out of the Tract, are alterior haecceities; coming from elsewhere, they have potent effects on those with whom they come into contact.

Multiplicities 'proliferate by contagion, epidemics, battlefields, and catastrophes' (Deleuze and Guattari, 2004b: 266), just like the daughter-code that comes out of the event site artefacts. Those infected by the daughter-code are put into the quarantine hulks, where they become a substance that is 'as beautiful as water in strong sunlight, yet ... stinks like rendered fat, and can absorb an adult human being in forty seconds' (Harrison, 2012a: 36), a substance that resembles Deleuze and Guattari's glittering yet virulently transmutative haecceities, and that recalls the trilogy's refrain: 'Sparks in everything'.

These sparks are part of the trilogy's constellation of allusions to Gnostic doctrines in which, as in Deleuzian thought, the notion of immanence is key. The heart with its loving diodes and the name of *Light*'s sleazy magician, Valentine Sprake, point to a particular version of Gnosticism, that of second-century theologian Valentinus. Harrison's 'The Horse of Iron and How We Can Know It' (1989), the source story for Kearney's Tarot-card train journeys in *Light*, notes that the Hanged Man card represents 'the descent of light into darkness in order to redeem it; in its female aspect, the Sophia of

Valentinus' (Harrison, 2000: 64). Gnostic cosmogony also informs the structure of Harrison's *The Course of the Heart* (1992): its prologue 'Pleroma', the Greek for fullness, is Valentinus's term for the Monad, the Platonic realm of ideal forms; its epilogue, 'Kenoma', the Greek for emptiness or void, Valentinus's term for the lower world, and in Platonic thought, the fleeting, illusory realm of phenomena. That is to say, the novel begins in fullness, and ends in void, with, in between, the cosmos of things, arising from fullness, and perceived by consciousness, if inaccessible to it.

Esoteric traditions, however, are not only aimed at bringing about transformation, becoming, but also at seeking enlightenment, revelation. Although focused on immanence, followers of these traditions have always sought transcendence. Harrison's trilogy can be read in terms of versions of the Hermetic idea of the 'rending of the veil': a metaphysical rending, an approach to the truth of things; a quantum rending, a look round the back of the decoherence that makes things appear as they do to us, rather than as they actually are; and a psychological rending, the breakdown of self and an approach to a posthuman consciousness.[4]

The veil is rent over and over again in the trilogy. A key instance occurs in a childhood memory that comes back to Kearney in a dream. Sitting on a beach, sorting pebbles, he looks away and back, and notices repeated shapes in the arrangement of the pebbles:

> Suddenly he understood this as a condition of things – if you could see the patterns the waves made, or remember the shapes of a million small white clouds, there it would be, a boiling, inexplicable, vertiginous similarity in all the processes of the world, roaring silently away from you in ever-shifting repetitions, always the same, never the same thing twice. (Harrison, 2012b: 29)

The 'boiling, inexplicable, vertiginous similarity' of this Weird epiphany can be read as the rising of haecceities from the plane of immanence. Through their composition, they initiate a deterritorialization through repetition and difference, and then becoming: 'Out of the sand, the sky, the pebbles – out of what [Kearney] would later think of as the willed fractality of things' (Harrison, 2012b: 29), the Shrander emerges, just as it will also later emerge from a minute of decoherence-free space that Tate has rendered. This 'willed fractality' is the only revelation the Shrander, the terrifying entity that Kearney has been running from all his life, ever grants. When it finally catches up with him, and takes him out to the Tract, it does not reveal the fundamental truth we expect, but merely tells him: 'Everywhere you look it unpacks to infinity ... There will always be more in the universe. There will always be more after that' (Harrison, 2012b: 390). The veil has been rent, but nothing profound has been revealed; there is just more and more stuff.

And what lies beyond the veil is not just gross materiality. It is also haphazard. In *Empty Space*, Irene the Mona tells of her dream of three old men in white caps who, like the Norns of Norse mythology, play games to decide the fate of the universe. Subsequently, she sees these very men, throwing their dice in the Starlight Room of the Deleuze Motel, and is terrified. This strand of the story recalls Einstein's well-known rebuttal of quantum randomness in a letter of 1926 to Max Born:

> Quantum mechanics is certainly imposing. But an inner voice tells me that it is not yet the real thing. The theory says a lot, but does not really bring us any closer to the secret of the 'old one'. I, at any rate, am convinced that He does not throw dice. (Einstein et al., 1971: 91)

In the Kefahuchi cosmos, however, God *does* play dice; behind the numinous lies only randomness, the play of difference and repetition, haphazard materiality, indiscriminate stuff. In 'a kind of infinite palimpsest, each page peel[s] away only to expose another' (Gray, 2013: n.p.), leaving Self, narrative, cosmos, everything in shreds.

The recent, loose philosophical school of speculative realism is, in part, an attempt to think through the fragmentation to which the trilogy incessantly returns again and again: the fragmentation that heralds the posthuman. Speculative realism is a post-phenomenological tradition that continues the Deleuzian project of addressing philosophy's post-Kantian anthropocentric bias by collapsing the phenomenological and the noumenal, the sensory and the world of objects (rather than embracing relativism, as many poststructuralists did). A number of speculative realists do this by positing a real, but unthinkable, receding, inaccessible material realm underlying our experience of the world. Graham Harman (2010: 51), for example, models a cosmos in which objects retreat from each other, retaining an inexhaustible, 'dark primal integrity',[5] while Eugene Thacker describes an utterly indifferent world-without-us:

> To say that the world-without-us is antagonistic to the human is to attempt to put things in human terms, in the terms of the world-for-us. To say that the world-without-us is neutral with respect to the human, is to attempt to put things in the terms of the world-in-itself. The world-without-us lies somewhere in between, in a nebulous zone that is at once impersonal and horrific. (Thacker, 2011: 5)

Things in the *Empty Space* trilogy can be sources of horror, despite an essential lack of malice. The Shrander, the Tract, and the things that spill out of it have their own strange and implacable purposes, and a 'mad old algorithm' (Harrison, 2012b: 296) turns Billy Anker and the Mona to feathers. Various becoming-code things are described in terms of visceral disgust, such as the mobster, Paulie de Raad, and the member of a violent child gang, a Point kid, who, infected, become grotesque amalgams of flesh and mathematics:

> the two of them were embracing awkwardly, as if it was new to them despite all the practice they had. They were breathing gently into one another's eyes. Neither of them had much on, and their china-white bodies were covered in a thin, slick, resinous film which, though it looked liquid when you first saw it, was constantly hardening and cracking off, like something they exuded to protect them from the air. (Harrison, 2012c: 217–8)

Quentin Meillassoux (2008: 5), like other speculative realists, dismantles the phenomenological/noumenal binary, which he terms correlationism, as it arises from the idea that 'we only ever have access to the correlation between thinking and being, and never to either term considered apart from the other'. Beyond correlationism, Meillassoux find Weird materiality, or 'hyperchaos', which he describes in terms reminiscent of Harrison's depictions of the Kefahuchi Tract:

> If we look through the aperture which we have opened up onto the absolute, what we see there is a rather menacing power – something insensible, and capable of destroying both things and worlds, of bringing forth monstrous absurdities, yet also of never doing anything, of realizing every dream, but also every nightmare, of engendering random and frenetic transformations, or conversely, of producing a universe that remains motionless down to its ultimate recesses, like a cloud bearing the fiercest storms, then the eeriest bright spells, if only for an interval of disquieting calm. (Meillassoux, 2008: 64)

However, while Harman and Thacker merely observe this inaccessible, chaotic foundation, and see it as fundamental to things, Meillassoux suggests a solution to the terrifying abyss. He proposes moving thought from this chaotic absolute to an absolute founded on mathematical principles, which for him have a truth outside the human mind and, therefore, allow for thought and the absolute, the phenomenological and the noumenal, to be reconciled. The trilogy's human/code amalgam could, on one level, be seen as a cognate response to the problem of the primordial chaos arising as we move from anthropocentric to posthuman understandings.

And there *is* an exuberance in the trilogy about becoming posthuman, particularly if we read the flight into the K-Tract of the hulks filled with the infected, the becoming-code posthumanity, in Gnostic terms as the escape of the divine spark into the Pleroma. But there is also a melancholy. Saudade, the name of the city in which *Nova Swing* is set, is a Portuguese word meaning à sad longing for something absent. This makes clear something implicit in the retro-fashions of Harrison's future: it is haunted by nostalgia for an imagined past, the loss of illusory wholes. And underlying this melancholy is a horror. Not the virulent but indifferent cosmic horror of speculative realism, it is a gruesome, intimate horror of bodies, exemplified by the brutal description of the process of being remade as a K-ship captain, which ends on a note of terrible regret: 'You will never walk again. You will never touch someone or be touched, fuck or be fucked. You will never do anything for yourself again. You will never even shit for yourself' (Harrison, 2012a: 188).[6] K-captains are no longer human. Fused with the ships they pilot, they are posthuman BwOs that have reterritorialized. Floating in tanks of proteome, controlled by their ships and the ships, mathematics, with only the illusion of agency, they are trapped by the desiring-machines into which they are plugged. They are cancerous, fascistic and warmongering. But the other kind of becoming-posthuman depicted in the trilogy, that which results in a flight from restrictive structures, is also coloured by regret. It is related to destructive deterritorialization, to the catatonic BwO; remember Seria Mau's sorrow over not being able to be the one thing she is.

So what is at stake in the trilogy's depictions of becoming posthuman? Deleuze argues that works of art 'produce disruptive affect [that] allows us to think intensities, to think the powers of becoming from which our ordered and composed world emerges' (Colebrook, 2002: 39). Central to the trilogy's affectual terrain is the way in which it deals with transmutations into something other than human. Rather than giving rise to existential horror or terrifying transcendental ecstasy, as in earlier Weird fiction, it presents transmutation as a source of bodily violations and regret. In a world of posthuman diversification, when there is no longer a fully constituted, coherent Enlightenment human to be transformed by an encounter with otherness, then Lovecraftian cosmic terror no longer has teeth: 'the horror in question is not cosmic – indeed, it is more intimate than the traditional sources of horror' (Stableford, 2007: 91). The posthuman is already here, and there is no going back, but maps of the affectual terrain, such as the *Empty Space* trilogy, are needed.

There are two moment, first in *Light*, then again in *Empty Space*, in which punning forces the word 'tear' to oscillate between its two heteronyms. In the first, New Man, Tig Vesicle, wakes weeping from a dream of gangsters collecting their rents, and 'somewhere between waking and sleeping, "rents" had become "tears", and this, he felt, summed up the life of his whole race' (Harrison, 2012b: 19–20). In the second, when the Assistant is allowed a vision of the Aleph by R. I. Gaines, the Aleph has the shape of a 'tear' and the image constantly repeats: 'By the third or fourth repetition, "tear" had somehow translated in her mind to "rip": at that everything stopped, as if such understanding could be, in itself, a switch' (Harrison, 2012a: 80).

This figure is literalized, in a crucial scene in *Light*, when the bad physics and fractality of the Shrander and the K-Tract first escape into the world. Michael and Anna find Brian Tate in a room in his suburban mock-Tudor house that he has made into a Faraday cage, frightened something will get out. He is crying, 'tears pouring in a silvery stream' from the inner corners of his eyes:

> There were too many of them for Tate's grief. Every tear was made up of exactly similar tears, and those tears too were made from tears. In every tear there was a tiny image. However far back you went, Kearney knew, it would always be there. At first he supposed it was his own reflection. When he saw what it really was he grabbed Anna by the upper arm and started dragging her out of the room. (Harrison, 2012b: 282)

Tate and his white cat, also crying, melt, dissolve into 'a slow glittering liquid' (Harrison, 2012b: 283), which foreshadows the becoming-code things of the later books. Tate's tears are simultaneously grief for a lost humanity and the haecceities of a radical deterritorialization.

This all suggests a rending of the veil, a fragmentation of self, narrative and cosmos, and a sadness and nostalgia. Fragmentation and longing for wholeness are held in quantum flux, a non-collapsing wave front between the sublime and the mundane. On the one hand there is radical deterritorialization, which can also be read as the Gnostic return of the divine spark to Pleroma; on the other, yearning for what must be lost, what is already lost. This yearning represents attempts to reterritorialize, to remain a healthy, rather than a catatonic, BwO; it is a movement from Pleroma to Kenoma, from the upper realm of the divine to the flawed Earth. That is, of course, the trajectory suggested by trilogy's titles. Like *The Course of the Heart*, it begins in Pleroma and ends in Kenoma, moving from *Light* to *Empty Space*, from inaccessible substance to humanity.

This human path, one that proceeds in a trajectory opposed to that of exuberant dissolution, is best represented by two characters: Anna, who wants only to find herself but never manages it, who falls through the floor of her summerhouse and ends up suspended in the Aleph, like the Hanged Man;[7] and the Assistant, made over as a posthuman entity, who desperately seeks a name and an identity, seeks to regain her lost humanity by, among other things, frequenting a virtual reality in which she role-plays as a twentieth-century housewife. But the Assistant also seems to want to give it all up, and jumps into the Aleph with Anna. Together they become the entity Pearl – a grain of grit trapped in layers of unreality, in the gross things of the world – and her coming into being brings about a transformation, the blooming of the Aleph, which seems to give rise to the quarantine hulks' dash, led by Ed Chianese, into the Kefahuchi Tract. Pearl seems to be both the Sophia of Valentinus and Christ the Avatar of Light, both trapped divine spark and the agent of its freeing. Or Deleuze and Guattari's anomalous, changing the composition of the pack through an alliance with what is outside, leading the multiplicity into a becoming, a becoming that arises from a desire to move beyond the human, to transform.[8]

But neither Anna nor the Assistant want the becoming. They both go back through time, against the flow. Anna returns to warn herself not to enter the summerhouse. The Assistant, angry and murderous, stalks through her life in reverse. They just want to be human, though it seems they have no choice but to become posthuman. This central tension is emphasized at the end of *Empty Space*. The penultimate chapter, 'The Medium is Not the Message', depicts the turbulent posthuman becomings and transgressions of limits initiated by the events of the trilogy from a fragmented, almost incoherent, point of view. The final chapter, 'Lay Down Your Weary Tune', returns to the trilogy's near future strand and to a more stable, more human perspective, seeing the aftermath of Anna's death through the eyes of first her daughter, Marnie, and then her psychiatrist, Helen Alpert. This does not imply that the human has won out, since, even in this near future, the self is seen as a quaint relic; Marnie, comes across Anna's collection of books: 'Anna still owned books. In them, the self figured largely: self-help books of thirty years ago, novels about women finding themselves, a book of photographs entitled *Events of the Self*; even books by a man calling himself Self' (Harrison, 2012a: 297).

This melancholy acceptance of the dissipation of the self makes some sense of the last thing that happens in the trilogy – Helen separating cocksure pharm, Dominic, from his friends, taking him upstairs, and fucking him carefully 'to a tearful overnight understanding of the life they all led now' (Harrison, 2012a: 302).

Notes

1 The concluding chapter of *A Thousand Plateaus* contains a parallel to this moment, opening with an image of the older Einstein, eyelids drawn down, cheeks pouchy, rendered by a computer, in now primitive graphics.

2 This is not to claim that Deleuze's thought can offer anything like an complete explanation of the trilogy's manifold enigmas (such an idea would be antithetical to Deleuze's distrust of totalizing explanations and solid foundations for knowledge), but to argue that Deleuze's notion of becoming can elucidate some of its complexities. The invocation is not entirely arbitrary, either; a key location is revealed, in *Empty Space*, to be called the Deleuze Motel.

3 Not inappropriately, given the importance of fractality to the novels.

4 According to Joshua Ramey (2012), Deleuze can be read as an engagement with and extension of Hermetic thought.

5 It is also significant that in Harman's cosmology, as in the tradition of hermetic doubt that Gray (2013) describes in relation to Harrison's works, 'nothing ever becomes unveiled' (Harmon, 2010: 62): no one object can ever exhaust all the characteristics of another.

6 The hardware bridge that plugs the brain of the K-ship captain into the ship's mathematics is called 'the Einstein Cross', an allusion to to Einstein's naïve faith in an ultimate meaning and to the Gnostic Christ.

7 Interestingly though, she is merging, blurring with her cat, which suggests a *becoming-animal*, an early stage of a Deleuzian deterritorialization. Both Sophia and the Demiurge (who has a leonine face) of Gnosticism, she is trapped between becoming and reterritorialization.

8 This moving beyond the human has something in common with all Deleuzian becomings: 'Becoming begins as a desire to escape bodily limitation' (Massumi, 1992: 94).

Works Cited

Colebrook, Claire (2002) *Gilles Deleuze*. Oxford: Routledge.

Deleuze, Gilles and Guattari, Félix (2004a) *Anti-Oedipus: Capitalism and Schizophrenia*, trans Robert Hurley, Mark Seem and Helen Lane. London: Continuum.

Deleuze, Gilles and Guattari, Félix (2004b) *A Thousand Plateaus*, trans. Brian Massumi. London: Continuum.

Einstein, Albert, Born, Max and Born, Hedwig (1971) *The Born-Einstein Letters*, trans. Irene Born. London: Macmillan.

Gray, John (2013) 'The Kefahuchi Tract Trilogy: A Future Without Nostalgia', *New Statesman* (17 October), accessed 9 February 2017, http://www.newstatesman.com/2013/10/future-without-nostalgia

Harman, Graham (2010) *Towards Speculative Realism: Essays and Lectures*. Winchester: Zero Books.

Harrison, M. John (1992) *The Course of the Heart*. London: Gollancz.

Harrison, M. John (1998) *Signs of Life*. London: Flamingo.

Harrison, M. John (2000b) 'The Horse of Iron and How We Can Know It', in *Travel Arrangements*, pp. 59–76. London: Gollancz.

Harrison, M. John (2012a) *Empty Space*. London: Gollancz.

Harrison, M. John (2012b). *Light*. London: Gollancz.

Harrison, M. John (2012c) *Nova Swing*. London: Gollancz.

Massumi, Brian (1992) *A User's Guide to Capitalism and Schizophrenia*. Cambridge, MA: MIT Press.

Meillassoux, Quentin (2008). *After Finitude: An Essay on the Necessity of Contingency*, trans. Ray Brassier. London: Continuum.

Ramey, Joshua (2012) *The Hermetic Deleuze: Philosophy and Spiritual Ordeal*. Durham, NC: Duke University Press.

Stableford, Brian (2007) 'The Cosmic Horror', in S. T. Joshi (ed.) *Icons of Horror and the Supernatural: An Encyclopedia of Our Worst Nightmares, Volume 1*, pp. 65–96. London: Greenwood Press.

Thacker, Eugene (2011) *In the Dust of this Planet: Horror of Philosophy, vol 1*. Winchester: Zero Books.

'Something That Looked Partly Like a Woman Partly Like a Cat'
Deliquescence, Hybridity and the Animal in the *Empty Space* Trilogy

Chris Pak

The purposefully ambiguous *Empty Space* trilogy (2002–12) develops a grotesque–sublime aesthetic to challenge the ontological categories into which we divide up the world. Metaphorical images of animals and instances of boundary-defying animals play a key role in destabilizing the borders between categories.[1] Animal motifs, especially cats and dogs, appear and reappear throughout the novels, helping to stitch the trilogy together while disturbing traditional ontologies and encouraging us to think through what it means to create new concepts that do not enclose the external world with bounded explanations. Representations of human–animal relationships and the specific ways that the human is represented as animal provide vectors for the trilogy's interrogation of human nature in a confused landscape where the markers of identity continually shift. They provide narrative cohesion by connecting spatially- and temporally-disparate characters and settings. They trouble the boundary between humans, other animals and the monstrous hybrid, and recalibrate the relationships and conceptual distinctions between these categories.

Building on human–animal studies' engagements with narrative disruption, companion species and hybridity, this essay links the figure of the 'amborg' to the Bakhtinian grotesque, and ultimately demonstrates how Harrison mobilizes the animal and the grotesque–sublime to build ambivalent worlds that resist containment and closure.

Animal motifs and the sensual

Intriguingly, the trilogy often refers not to the presence of specific animals, but to absences made explicit by a smell or sound. In *Nova Swing* (2006), when Fat Antoyne presents the eponymous spaceship to Liv Hula, she calls it a 'dog,' and we learn that it 'smelled of refugees, contraband, animal shows' (Harrison, 2009: 289), thus establishing resonances between the spaceship, Sandra Shen's circus in *Light* (2002) and the canines of *Empty Space* (2012).[2] In the latter novel, when the Assistant wraps Liv Hula in a blanket aboard the ship, we learn that it 'smelled as if someone had wrapped an animal in it' (Harrison, 2012: 53). At the event site, an oneiric landscape where physics itself is uncertain, Vic registers 'the usual smells, as rank as rendered fat; the usual distant animal noises' (Harrison, 2009: 168). Aschemann takes the Assistant to Pellici's in Neutrino, where you can 'hear the food smoking in the animal fat' (Harrison, 2009: 119). Anna, falling through the summerhouse and into the mysterious object known as the Aleph, notices that it 'stinks of cat in here, some filthy animal' (Harrison, 2012: 274). Absent animals convey the ghost of a presence – a haunting – through olfactory responses associated with filth and degradation.

The sensory references – especially to smell, the sense that most closely interacts with memory – keep the notion of the 'animal' firmly in mind, even in scenes where non-human animals or animal-like entities do not appear. Their absence indexes the lack of a potentially hybridizing response between the human and non-human, what Joan Gordon (2008: 195) describes as an 'amborg gaze': an interspecies exchange of glances in which recognition and response are brought together in a feedback loop that is 'unstable, unpredictable, dynamic, teeming with implications political, social, and ethical about our place(s) in the world'. Harrison's persistent references to felt absences

and the sensuous relationship between the human and animal anticipate an ontological landscape of hybridizations and transformations
to come.[3] The amborg gaze draws on Laura Mulvey's (1975) discussion
of the male gaze in classical Hollywood cinema, and on Jakob von
Uexküll's notion of the *umwelt* to draw attention to the way in which
our perspective, our gaze, carries with it a series of epistemic assumptions that make an individual's worldview situated, contingent and finite. The human *umwelt* refers to the image of the external world built
up through our sensory impressions and our actions in it. This cognitive reconstruction of the world is, of necessity, limited; there will
always be something 'out there' that escapes the capacity for embodied beings to recognize and to respond; and our epistemic complexes
can and do preclude other competing conceptions of the world. The
failure to recognize other humans as active subjects who can return
the gaze levelled at them makes possible the domination of humans
and non-human others. Likewise, the failure to recognize in the active animal subject the capacity to return the human gaze is a failure
to recognize the relatedness of humans and other animals living together and engaging in reciprocal exchanges. The view of the animal
as passive, as an instinctual reflex machine, and as a discrete object
for manipulation, represents an episteme that prevents the individual
from recognizing alternative conceptions of the animal as agentic and
involved in experiences independent of humankind.

The *Empty Space* trilogy teems with instances of failed responses
between amborg subjects: between human characters, various transhumans and aliens, and between them and the mysterious forms
that emerge from the Saudade event site. A continually shifting zone
from which emerge entities that cannot be explained, the event site
is named after the Portuguese *saudade*, often translated as 'nostalgia'
or 'malaise'; it is a term 'suitable for expressing the relationship of the
human condition to temporality, finitude, and the infinite', and it 'proceeds from a memory that wants to renew the present by means of
the past in a loving soul that is restrained by the limits of its condition'
(Santoro, 2013: 929). The hybridity of the transhumans, their irreality and their captivation by the presentness of the world, closes off

the possibility for the return of a desired past condition, while many characters attempt to renew aspects of their past within the space of a future that simultaneously invites and resists this activity. Memory is reactivated by the absent presence of animals summoned into the living present through the olfactory senses. The mysteries of the event site, the Aleph, the Tate-Kearney transformations and the Assistant herself are overlaid with a sense of *saudade,* inviting reflection on what it means to be human in a universe that exceeds – seemingly paradoxically – temporality, finitude, and the infinite. The question of the relationship between humans and other animals is thus an important aspect of the trilogy because it invites us to interrogate the place and the limits of the human in relation to the universe.

There is a connection between the references to the smell of an animal and Harrison's representation of the various trans- and post-humans. The Assistant, after a violent encounter with Alice Nylon and Paulie DeRaad in *Nova Swing,* 'smelled as sharp and sour as an animal cage' to Vic (Harrison, 2009: 230). In *Empty Space,* the Assistant exudes an odour that tells anyone in the know that she is deadly: 'you could smell the animal smell of the fights, the chemicals in her tears' (Harrison, 2012: 75). This recalls the fighters that Vic takes Edith to see in *Nova Swing*: 'despite their vitality – which streamed out into the air like the life force you would expect of a horse or other large animal – the fighters were less than real' (Harrison, 2009: 124). The animal and the vital are connected, but this does not necessarily equate to a sense of something 'real'; the fighters' bodies and their lives are unreal because – to Vic's eyes – they are fashioned to conform to limits imposed by their role within the specific cultural context of violent spectacle. They are grotesque parodies or caricatures whose existence and *raison d'être* are circumscribed, but they are also individuals who live entirely in the moment of the fight, and in the associated lifestyles that attend to their status.[4] Given the myriad ways of manipulating the body, such limits do not absolutely circumscribe the fighters' lives, but they do lend to this sense of irreality a further disjuncture between the body as a site for the accumulation of lived experience (which entails some sort of memory) and the body as a site for complete involvement in the present.

This sense of complete involvement in the immediate experience of the fight recalls Giorgio Agamben's discussion of the *umwelt*, the Heideggerian world and *Dasein*.[5] The fighters are held by their bodies within the 'world', which is constituted by their sensory experience of and bodily relation to what is external to them. Agamben explains that the construction of the concept of the human is predicated on a philosophical splitting off of animal characteristics from the human, a historical ontology that has profoundly influenced conceptualizations of the human and the non-human animal in Western philosophical and scientific discourses. The transhumanism of the *Empty Space* trilogy – in which the animal and human approach convergence and, in some cases, meet in the bodies of individuals – bridges this split, and thus challenges this species ontology. In the moment of violence, the fighters and the Assistant are captivated by their immediate experience of the world and act accordingly.[6] The world is open to them in the sense that their circumscribed place in relation to other bodies calls forth responses that are automatic; they do not interpret the objects that are present to their awareness, but react to them according to their nature. This is especially clear in the case of the Assistant's failure to recognize and interpret her own status in relation to herself: her body is the site for a splitting between the human, the animal and, indeed, the machine.[7] The trilogy stages a reconciliation between these divided identities.

Transformation

Anna's dreams in *Empty Space* bring the trilogy's concern with transformations and blending between categories into focus:

> She was not turning from a woman into an animal or from an animal into a woman. If she was not in transit, neither was she in any sense 'caught' between those two states: she was busily occupying them both at once. (Harrison, 2012: 220)

This is distinctly not a transformation between states that confine or determine an identity, not a passive being, but an active occupation of both at once, a becoming, a continuous unfolding in the present. It is tempting to read this image in terms of the dynamics of figurative language which, in this case, involves no metaphorical 'transport' or transfer of meaning from one category to another, but operates more like a symbolon in which multiple categories are thrown together and simultaneously exert a force that constitutes the figure's meaning. In this sense, the metaphorical and literal references to animals throughout the trilogy work to create symbolons that encapsulate multiple aspects of becoming and an orientation towards what Agamben, following Heidegger, describes as the open, a caesura in which the categories of the human and animal are suspended. This boundary-space fosters the potential for a responsiveness to other lives that recognizes such others as irreducible to a systematizing project (taxonomy) and a definition of the animal as radically separated from the human.

Anna's dream of transformation, which combines a human and a non-human animal (a cat), is anticipated in *Nova Swing* by a recording in Emil's journal that describes:

> something that looked partly like a woman partly like a cat. Though it seemed immobile at first, H. said it was slowly changing from one shape to the other. H. said he was 'struck silent' by the potential of this. He was 'full of a tranquil sense of his own possibilities.' Cat a kind of ivory-white colour. (Harrison, 2009: 268)

This image recalls Seria Mau and her K-ship, the White Cat, and, in contrast to the symbolon of the Aleph, it harbours an unspecified potential alluded to at the conclusion of *Light*, in which the Shrander/ Magician instigates a metamorphosis that transforms Seria Mau into a sublime entity, thus freeing her from her ambivalent failure to occupy both her humanity and her technological second-life. Such potential calls for a response which the viewer of the image – the mysterious H. – reciprocates.

This image of slow transformation between the human and non-human animal also recalls the Assistant, described in *Empty Space* as 'now look[ing] partly like a woman in a ruched metallic gown around five hundred years old, and partly like a cat' (Harrison, 2012: 205). Again, she combines humanity, non-human animality and the machine into a single image, resonating strongly with Anna's experience when falling into the Aleph. These three women, then, are related through the undecidability of the transformations they undergo. Anna, however, is somehow able to transcend the vacillation between states to which the other two are subject.

The Aleph alludes to Jorge Luis Borges's short story, 'The Aleph' (1945), in which a narrator by the name of Borges is shown the eponymous structure, 'the only place on earth where all places are — seen from every angle, each standing clear, without any confusion or blending'. Echoing the individual in that story who likewise discovers the Aleph while falling, Anna's interaction with the object occurs while her senses of balance and orientation are overturned. The Aleph is a point that collapses all of spacetime, ultimately forming connections between everything in the universe. In the trilogy, it is a manufactured object of immense age, 'the purpose of which was to contain a piece of the Kefahuchi Tract itself' (Harrison, 2012: 80), as one character claims. The research team studying the artefact hopes it will allow them a measure of control over the mystery of the Tract, the event site in Saudade and, ultimately, over the cosmos itself. The Aleph represents the possibility of ordering and maintaining inertia over the physical world and of shoring up the boundaries between categories and bodies. That Anna's disappearance into the Aleph is coupled with her death highlights how such complete, godlike access to and control of the universe is itself a termination. When Anna steps through the summerhouse and out of this world, she takes with her a machine, the drive containing the Tate-Kearney data, and is joined by an animal, her black and white cat James: 'all three of them ... fell out of this world together' (Harrison, 2012: 223) and, subsumed by the Aleph, blend within its no-space. This formation recalls Donna Haraway's examination of the interface between the human, the machine and the animal, and of the 'infolding' between multiple species. She now prefers the latter term, since '*infolding* better ... suggest[s] the dance of world-making encounters' (Haraway, 2008: 249), a dance that does not determine relationships but describes an ever-shifting set that creates the potential for responses between entities undergoing different modes of becoming. Harrison's metaphors and the resonances he establishes between entities figure this dance.

Deliquescence

The recurring motif of black and white cats, sometimes combined into one body (as in Anna's James), stitches together Seria Mau's narrative and the narratives involving Kearney and Anna, and they resonate throughout the trilogy in other less prominent ways. References to Kearney's laboratory, set 'fire [to] repeatedly by extreme animal rights factions' (Harrison, 2007: 4), connects Seria Mau's transformation into the White Cat to the history of vivisection, animal experimentation and the broader industrialization and commodification of the animal. Sherryl Vint (2010: 12) notes that sf arose alongside these phenomena, and thus it is unsurprising that animals haunt 'sf, always there in the shadows behind the alien or the android with whom we fantasise exchange'. At the same time, the potential that animals offer for the 'embodiment of ideas and relations conceived by speculative thought on the basis of empirical observations' (Lévi-Strauss, 1964: 89) suggests that one strategy that sf adopts to categorize and order aspects of the physical universe is to incorporate resonances between animals and tropes specific to sf's discourses. But at the Saudade event site, and through the operation of the rogue code in *Nova Swing* and *Empty Space*, the boundaries between the human, the animal and the machine are erased.

In *Nova Swing*, Vic discovers an artefact in the event site that spontaneously transforms from an animal, 'a one-off thing no one but him would ever see' with 'huge human eyes', to an object that 'was half bone, half metal, or perhaps both at the same time; or perhaps neither' (Harrison, 2009: 49). Vic's impression that the creature's eyes are human suggests the possibility for a hybridizing gaze that would make of them an amborg subject, yet the potential for a response between them is precluded by the undecidability of the creature/artefact itself. Like Anna's dream, the event site and the 'code' brought back from within its borders occupy a space that takes in all these states at once, a space of becoming that accords with Geoffrey Harpham's notion of the grotesque interval, described by Istvan Csicsery-Ronay (2008: 187–8) as that liminal space 'between the transmutative fluidity of the object and the classificatory uncertainty of the perceiver'. The entity Vic discovers vacillates between machine-code and biological-virus; it is able to replicate and spread, necessitating a quarantine of those who interact with it (through direct touch) and undergo trans-formations. In *Empty Space*, the *Nova Swing* is contracted to ferry a cargo, and 'by 10pm the same day, Bobby, Bella and Martha were a fully-fledged escape – translucent, infectious, a jelly part human, part virus, part daughter code straight from the local Event site' (Harrison, 2012: 157). The grotesque uncertainty generated by the vacillation between categories is pushed until all boundaries evaporate. The jelly to which the crew are reduced is an 'escape', a move beyond the cate-gory, containment and closure of their former, clearly-defined bodies. The *Nova Swing* becomes 'a quarantine dog' (Harrison, 2012: 158), evading attempts to re-establish the boundaries of the human world, to shore up the categories that have governed the organization of the interplanetary society.

Csicsery-Ronay explains that:

> The grotesque reduces to goo. As the body continues to withdraw from the human gaze, it loses more and more of its structure: first its body, then its organs, finally leaving only the protoform of plasma. The core is reduced to a formless jelly that yet has power: to con-taminate, to melt, to cause deliquescence by touch alone. (What deconstruction is to the sublime, deliquescence is to the grotesque). (Csicsery-Ronay, 2008: 195)

The effect of this deliquescence is to explore by analogy 'the decom-position of the solid bourgeois scientific sense of the separation of mind from embodiment' (Csicsery-Ronay, 2008: 195). In Harrison, grotesque deliquescence also explores the orientation towards the animal that many trace to Descartes's division of the organism into a mind and a body, and his parallel characterization of the non-human animal as purely reactive or instinctive, more like a reflex machine than a responsive animal.[8] Agamben's notion of the philosophical splitting off of the category of the animal from that of the human – a category which first occurs within the concept of the human – results in a gap that separates them. Harrison's grotesque aesthetic dissipates this radical exclusion. In the trilogy, the various transhumans and the alien New Men continually show how such dualisms cannot be sustained, and the rogue code collapses the boundaries separating bodies, human and otherwise, confronting individuals and societies with the threat, and possibilities, of deliquescence.

The sublime

While the dissolution of bodies is key to the trilogy, deliquescence and the grotesque are placed in counterpoint to moments of the sublime. In *Light*, Kearney and Anna discover Brian Tate – Kearney's colleague – and the physicists' white cat in their over-heated laboratory, which Tate has converted into a Faraday cage, inside of which he makes an important discovery. He passes Kearney and Anna a drive containing what will become known as the Tate-Kearney transformations, which will pave the way for quantum machines and massive parallel processing, and ultimately interstellar travel, but before he can explain what has happened, a fractal light, that takes the form of tears, begins to stream from the eyes of both Tate and the cat; their bodies dissolve into light. In another episode, Ed Chianese appears to hallucinate a white cat aboard the ship *The Perfect Low*, and sees the same fractal light streaming from the fishtank with which Sandra Shen trained him to prophesy the future. This light assembles itself into the figure of Shen, who turns out to be another iteration of the Shrander/Magician. Shen guides Ed to the site of Kearney's remains and the location where his sister, Seria Mau, transformed from a cyborg K-ship into a being capable of taking any form she desires. Ed takes her place as part of the K-ship, renaming himself the Black Cat, and pilots himself into the Kefahuchi Tract, thus changing the course of the future.

This sublime moment is preceded by Kearney's own experience with the Shrander, who takes him to the same mysterious location at the edge of everywhere – suggestively described in terms aligning it with the Aleph. He is surrounded by light: 'light unburdened, light like a substance: real light' (Harrison, 2007: 298). The Shrander tells him that 'everywhere you look it unpacks to infinity. What you look for, you find. And you people can have it. All of it' (Harrison, 2007: 298). In this sublime moment of enlightenment, Kearney finds a new understanding of himself, and the Shrander tells him that 'there will always be more in the universe. There will always be more after that' (Harrison, 2007: 300). Yet it is Seria Mau, brought to the same location by Dr Haends, yet another iteration of the Shrander, who is able to take full advantage of the promise made to Kearney. Transformed from the K-ship *White Cat* into a shape-shifting winged being, she becomes a 'bizarre organism' that is 'perpetually emergent from its own desires' (Harrison, 2007: 309), and thus an embodiment of boundary dissolution.

In *Empty Space*, Impasse van Sant – the last of the unmodified humans – encounters Seria Mau while he drifts alone in space, ostensibly for the purpose of studying the Tract. His solitary project, however, peters out and he is left observing wars that break out throughout the galaxy. His isolation from the (post- and trans-)human community, along with his observation of that community, lead him to reflect that humankind 'seemed full of madness and a direct rejection of anything he might have called humanity' (Harrison, 2012: 288). It is at this moment that he encounters Seria Mau, who he first experiences as empty space itself communicating to him in a whisper. Seria Mau explains to him that '"I can be anything I want ... but I don't want that. I want to be the one thing I am' (Harrison, 2012: 288), suggesting that the complete freedom of perpetual, radical becoming is at odds with the accumulation of experience and memory that makes a being situated and capable of responding to others. Van Sant, for his part, 'was never anything but myself. I was always locked in', and he looks to Seria Mau to discover the answers to questions that remain inaccessible to him, questions that can all be rephrased as 'will I ever go home[?]' (Harrison, 2012: 169). Van Sant's narrative thread thus turns on the sense of *saudade*, of a homesickness that cannot be alleviated. Of the region immediately surrounding the Kefahuchi Tract, he asks himself 'What was the Beach, after all, but a repository of fading memories?' (Harrison, 2012: 289). As the Tract is expanding and thus promises to transform the known universe, his sense of something lost is a premonition of the transformation the future brings, a transformation signalled by light and cast in terms of the sublime.

The relationship between light and the recurring animal motifs can be explained with an iconic episode from *Empty Space*. The unnamed youth who becomes Anna's lover shares, at her request, his passion for lamping, or nocturnal hunting:

> She could see how hard he found it – how emotionally clouded it was for him. How do you describe something you know so well? His focus was too close. It was a struggle to distinguish sensation from practice, to find sufficient distance without merging all the subtleties. (Harrison, 2012: 179)

This difficulty indexes – for him – a sublime moment of unity between companion species. 'I like it when the dog runs down the light' (Harrison, 2012: 179), he says, establishing resonances between the boy's lamp, the light-motes of *Light*, and the 'light' that Harrison writes of in his criticism. In an essay originally published in 1989, he describes a frisson, a sensation of re-inhabitation brought about by an individual's relationship to the objects that environ, moments that 'transfigured and intensified' (Harrison, 2005: 146) the objects of his childhood, during which he was able to intuit only 'the intense existence, the photographic actuality of such objects; of yourself and your encounters with them' (Harrison, 2005: 147). Familiar elements of the child's experience 'are reassembled as a way of looking at other things. It was this continual fusing and liquefying of accumulated experience which I had analogized as a light bathing the landscape' (Harrison, 2005: 147). Harrison's point is that such moments – what he at first identifies as 'self-awareness', 'awareness of time', perhaps 'the sexual trances of early adolescence' (Harrison, 2005: 147) – are also a property of Modernism and sf. For Harrison, it is not the objects revealed by the light, but the light itself that is of interest: the process of recombination that is central to metaphor's capacity for making connections.

The boy's description of lamping, then, resonates with Harrison's description of light as an analogy for moments of heightened awareness where experience is reassembled in meaningful and transformative ways. Of course, the companion relationships do not necessarily result in the flourishing of all the individuals involved. Dog, hare (or rabbit or fox; the boy is not concerned over the specific quarry) and human: all are united by the light cast by the boy in a relationship that is both troubling – Anna protests the cruelty of the sport – and uplifting, in that there exists a real sense of the sublime in the boy's characterization of this relationship. The light expands to block out the components of the scene in another gestalt, a unity that very strongly brings to mind the captivation of the animal and its openness to its circle of disinhibitors – a term Heidegger uses to refer to those external elements that impinge upon the senses of the animal. This triad enacts a dance of world making encounters; it is a moment of infolding that brings hunters and quarry together. The boy's 'merging [of] all the subtleties' recalls the sublime overrunning of reason that is the hallmark of the aesthetic, but Anna cannot share his enthusiasm for this moment (Harrison, 2012: 179). Her recognition of what feels to her like a cruelty serves to deconstruct the moment for the reader who is likely to view this marginal activity from Anna's perspective, given the narrative's consistent focalization from her perspective and contemporary opposition to fox-hunting, badger-culling and hunting of many kinds in the UK.

The boy's description of lamping resonates with the entradista's orientation to piloting in the Kefahuchi Tract, and with the injunction to 'go deep!' into its light. Liv Hula, herself a former entradista, recalls 'the classic entradista soul-fuck' with 'great contempt' (Harrison, 2012: 98), but Billy Anker attempts an explanation that in turn resonates with the boy's effort to explain his experience of lamping: 'That weird twist of light just hangs like a crack in nowhere. You can barely see it against the stars: but shoot through and it's like – ... Who knows what it's like? Everything changes' (Harrison, 2007: 260). The Tract's gaping maw is, in this context, a symbol for the orientation of the individual to the world. The careless abandonment of the entradistas is an attempt to open the individual to a space beyond the subjective *umwelt* and to respond to the other in its own right, and not simply as stimuli against which to react. Agamben describes the openness of the animal thus: 'For the animal, beings are open but not accessible; that is to say, they are open in an inaccessibility and an opacity – that is, in some way, in a nonrelation' (Harrison, 2004: 55). Animals thus cannot relate to other beings as beings, but rather as entities to which they react, rather than to which they respond. He later explains that, 'Insofar as the animal knows neither beings nor nonbeings, neither open nor closed, it is outside of being; it is outside in an exteriority more external than any open, and inside in an intimacy more internal than any closedness' (Harrison, 2004: 91). The amborg subjects of the trilogy orient themselves to the unknown in ways that allow them moments of captivation that open up the world while never making it accessible – a possibility that the trilogy consistently shuts down. Yet the trilogy challenges this property as belonging only to non-human animals by portraying the same dynamic at play in the examples of the reaction to olfactory stimuli that activates the memory and the absent presence of the animal, the captivation of the fighters and the Assistant to violence and the attempts to control the Kefahuchi Tract and the Saudade event site by shoring up physical and ontological boundaries. The trilogy refuses closure by opening up the narrative to an anticipation of something beyond the familiar human world. It points toward a mysterious externality that is inaccessible, but holds out the possibility of responding to the otherness of entities or the universe.

Conclusion

This essay has shown how the concept of the animal can help us to think about the relationships and the discontinuities in the trilogy, and how the amborg subject – infolding in grotesque relations and thus addressing the splitting of the animal and human – helps us to understand some of the novels' transgressions. These transgressions are discursive strategies that work to destabilize readings that posit certainty as a trait of the human relationship to the world, and which would thus close down the text's capacity to open up routes charged with possibility. The animal metaphors and the constant reminder of non-human animal presences likewise destabilize apparently coherent constructions of the world that fail to recognize that humans are, like other animals, restricted to an image of the world that is necessarily contingent and finite. As Agamben points out, for Heidegger, 'man' differs from animal in their capacity for being. 'Thus,' he says, 'the supreme category of Heidegger's ontology is states: letting be. In this project, man makes himself free for the possible, and in delivering himself over to it, lets the world and beings be as such' (Harrison, 2004: 91). Harrison's figurations of the animal thus create possibilities for new, posthuman relationships, and for amborg subjects that refuse closure through collapse into the human/animal division.

Notes

1 Mark Bould (2005: 20) explains that a 'good metaphor is one which implies equivalences between disparate things, but does not explain them. Rather, it is the reader's job to fathom the possibilities, complexities and ambiguities of metaphor'. Well-conceived and well-styled metaphors involve readers in a dynamic relationship that highlights the interrelatedness of 'reality' and the fantastic. Regarding the co-shaping of these two domains, Bould (2005: 20) suggests that it 'is through fantasising that we construct ontologies, including those which we take for reality'.

2 On resonance in Harrison's fiction, see Fraser (2005).

3 This is already evident in Harrison's much earlier space opera, *The Centauri Device* (1974). Rjurik Davidson (2005: 270–1), connecting Harrison's emphasis on the sensual to a rejection of the technocratic rationalism of Isaac Asimov's *Foundation* series and the 'gung-ho certainties' of Robert Heinlein's narratives, writes that in *The Centauri Device* 'spaceships become spiders, bolts and fish, implying a connection between things, a broader transcendent understanding concerned not with logic but with the sensuous'. Here, animal motifs work not only to draw together the technological and the biotic, but to affect a restructuring of space opera in an anticipatory mode that resists the closure of certainty.

4 The Assistant is likewise irreal, tailored for some mysterious purpose that is unveiled in *Empty Space*.

5 *Dasein* translates from the German as 'being there'. It refers to the possibilities of an entity's existence. It does not presume any categories for
that being's existence but directs attention to the pluriform possibilities
for being.

6 Captivation is the mode of being proper to animals, Agamben (2004: 52)
argues, and refers to the animal's instinctive response to stimuli that it is
capable of perceiving.

7 The machine is a category of non-human that is constructed in opposition to the organic and which parallels the human/animal opposition.
The category of the machine encapsulates a wide range of entities of different orders of existence. As Haraway (1991) explains, the human shares
qualities with the machine, and can potentially form hybridizing relationships that define them as cyborgs.

8 See, for example, Peter Harrison (1992) and Plumwood (1993).

Works Cited

Agamben, Giorgio (2004) *The Open: Man and Animal*, trans. Kevin Attell.
Stanford, CA: Stanford University Press.

Borges, Jorge Luis (1945) 'The Aleph', trans. by Norman Thomas Di
Giovanni, accessed 10 July 2015, http://web.mit.edu/allanmc/www/
borgesaleph.pdf

Bould, Mark (2005) 'Let's Make A Little Noise, Colorado: An Introduction
in Eight Parts', in Mark Bould and Michelle Reid (eds) *Parietal Games:
Critical Writings by and on M. John Harrison*, pp. 13–30. London: Science
Fiction Foundation.

Csicsery-Ronay Jr., Istvan (2008) *The Seven Beauties of Science Fiction.*
Middletown, CT: Wesleyan University Press.

Davidson, Rjurik (2005) 'Form and Content in *the Centauri Device*', in Mark
Bould and Michelle Reid (eds) *Parietal Games: Critical Writings by and on
M. John Harrison*, pp. 265–74. London: Science Fiction Foundation.

Fraser, Graham (2005) 'Loving the Loss of the World: *Tęsknota* and the
Metaphors of the Heart', in Mark Bould and Michelle Reid (eds) *Parietal
Games: Critical Writings by and on M. John Harrison*, pp. 299–318. London:
Science Fiction Foundation.

Gordon, Joan (2008) 'Gazing Across the Abyss: The Amborg Gaze in Sheri
S. Tepper's *Six Moon Dance*', *Science Fiction Studies* 105: 189–206.

Haraway, Donna (1991) 'A Cyborg Manifesto: Science, Technology, and Socialist-Feminism in the Late Twentieth Century', in *Simians, Cyborgs and Women: The Reinvention of Nature*, pp. 149–81. New York: Routledge.

Haraway, Donna (2008) *When Species Meet*. Minneapolis: University of Minnesota Press.

Harrison, M. John (2005) 'The Profession of Science Fiction, 40: The Profession of Fiction', in Mark Bould and Michelle Reid (eds) *Parietal Games: Critical Writings by and on M. John Harrison*, pp. 144–54. London: Science Fiction Foundation.

Harrison, M. John (2007) *Light*. New York: Bantam.

Harrison, M. John (2009) *Nova Swing*. New York: Bantam.

Harrison, M. John (2012) *Empty Space*. London: Gollancz.

Harrison, Peter (1992) 'Descartes on Animals', *Philosophical Quarterly* 167: 219–27.

Lévi-Strauss, Claude (1964) *Totemism*, trans. Rodney Needham. London: Merlin.

Mulvey, Laura (1975) 'Visual Pleasure and Narrative Cinema', *Screen* 16(3): 6–18.

Plumwood, Val (1993) *Feminism and the Mastery of Nature*. London: Routledge.

Santoro, Fernando (2013) 'Saudade (Portuguese)', *Dictionary of Untranslatables: A Philosophical Lexicon*, trans. Barbara Cassin, Emily Apter, Jacques Lezra and Michael Wood, pp. 929–31. Princeton, NJ: Princeton University Press.

Vint, Sherryl (2010) *Animal Alterity: Science Fiction and the Question of the Animal*. Liverpool: Liverpool University Press.

'The Geometry of Deterministic Chaos'
Fractal Structure and Recursivity in
M. John Harrison's *Empty Space* Trilogy

Nicholas Prescott

Disorder is infinitely deep. (Harrison, 2006: 180)

The structures and patterns central to this essay were initially discerned in a discipline quite distinct from that of literary study. In March 1963, research meteorologist Edward Lorenz published a paper that would become talismanic for many people working in physics and mathematics. Entitled 'Deterministic Nonperiodic Flow', it described a curious pattern Lorenz had discerned in the rendering of information that seemed to defy the very notion of patterns. Meteorologists – perhaps ironically – predicate their work upon the notion of predictability. In attempting to articulate the state of any given climatic system a month from now, meteorologists rely upon their understandings of the complex systems of heat exchange, air and sea currents, and so on, to predict the state of those systems at a given point in the future. This is a difficult feat to pull off accurately with any kind of regularity. While often the state of a particular part of a larger weather system can be quite accurately predicted one day out, by the time meteorologists project forward by a month or two, the predictions can and do become wildly inaccurate. This is, of course, logical: in a system with any degree of complexity, it is challenging even to measure the interactions of a myriad variables, much less predict the precise state of the system at a particular point in the future, when their interactions will all have had minute and significant effects on subsequent behaviour.

Lorenz, through his observation of the interactions of gases and liquids within closed vessels, demonstrated the curious fact that complex systems – with their multiplicity of variables, their myriad minute interactions, their immense challenges to accurate observation and prediction – nonetheless contained discernible recursive structures, or patterns within the noise, which suggested that something hitherto unseen and unrecorded was occurring within these extremely complicated systems. Lorenz's remarkable discovery, augmented over subsequent years by the work of physicists, mathematicians and other scientists, forms the basis of what we now know as Complexity Science or, more popularly, chaos theory.[1]

Describing Complexity Science for those without a background in mathematics or physics is certainly difficult, though for literary scholars the area at least possesses an extremely attractive lexicon: words and phrases such as 'non-linear', 'fractal', 'aperiodicity', and 'deterministic' abound, sometimes reaching apogees like the remarkable term 'folded-towel diffeomorphisms'.[2] The *OED* defines 'chaos' in this sense as the 'behaviour of a system which is governed by deterministic laws but is so unpredictable as to appear random, owing to its extreme sensitivity to changes in parameters or its dependence on a large number of independent variables; a state characterized by such behaviour' (Simpson, 2009: n.p.). This hints at the wonderful near-contradiction at the centre of complexity science: the systems being described here are *so* complex, and contain *so* many variables – any one of which can be seen to demonstrate its own nearly impossible-to-describe complexity – that predicting their behaviour would initially seem impossible. However, the study of these systems has revealed that *unpredictability* itself can be understood as an *operating principle* that can, in some way, be contextualized, observed and described. Non-linearity, then, can be seen as a structural principle as firm and lucid as linearity. Further, as Lorenz discovered, such non-linear systems frequently contain a seemingly contradictory pattern within their operation that suggests that complexity can render its own very beautiful – and meaningful – fingerprint.

This essay proposes the we can see in the work of M. John Harrison precisely such a complex system, a body of prose, plots, narrative devices, thematic obsessions and intellectual propositions that contains its own recursive structures, uncanny patterns, complexities of intertextuality, and other rhetorical and literary devices that form their own particularly elegant signals contained not within noise but within the more objectively visible elements of literary fiction. Harrison's work, whatever genre or mix of genres (or non-generic state) each novel or short story occupies, is very clearly a literature of complex ideas, wherein the articulation and examination of those ideas forms a deeply interconnected body of work, an oeuvre whose most recent manifestation contains tendrils of device, character, and idea that attach it like a living thing to its predecessors.

It is particularly fitting that the *Empty Space* trilogy – *Light* (2002), *Nova Swing* (2006) and *Empty Space* (2012) – upon which this chapter focuses, contains traces of hard sf, along with elements of other genres and styles of writing, including 'grim, gaudy space opera that respects the physics',[3] Gothic literature, 'contemporary fiction' (whatever that might be), realist prose, the literature of the uncanny, horror, the post-Lovecraftian Weird, and hardboiled crime fiction. Looked at with this multiplicity of genre conventions in mind, fiction of this kind can be seen to contain such a myriad of variables and pieces of information as to suggest that one can profitably take to its analysis ideas drawn from complexity science. Further, and importantly, in the trilogy Harrison himself both explicitly *and* implicitly acknowledges and engages with aspects of complexity science.

One of the ideas this essay will trace through Harrison's work is suggested by the phenomenon of the Lorenz attractor. Lorenz demonstrated that the mapping of the movements of a complex system driven by variables whose behaviour was non-linear, could reveal patterns that were not discernible without such detailed observation. Lorenz used computer modelling to track and render the moment-by-moment state of these systems, and to plot those states in a visual analogue. This rendering of that complex system,[4] whose moment-by-moment behaviours are, crucially, *non-linear* and unpredictable, looks like this (see Figure 1).

Visualizations of the Lorenz attractor are notable for their demonstration of the fact that within the complexity ('noise') they map lies a particularly beautiful pattern. In mapping the behaviour of a chaotic system, Lorenz created one of the first articulations of what would become known, enticingly, as a 'strange attractor'.

The Strange Attractor is a phenomenon that works within systems involving movement. To adapt James Gleick's instructive metaphor: if one imagines the pendulum in a grandfather clock as an object being

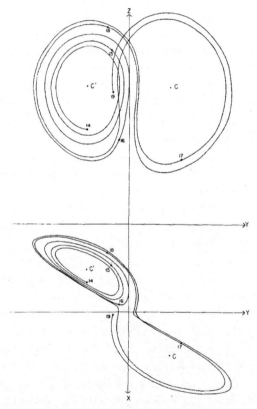

Figure 1. The Lorenz Attractor by Edward N. Lorenz from the paper entitled 'Deterministic Nonperiodic Flow', *Journal of the Atmospheric Sciences* 20 (1963): 130–41. © American Meteorological Society. Used with permission.

governed by a singular point of attraction (the point at the very bottom and centre of its swing) and labels that system as one describing a 'simple attractor', one can then consider a moving object without a fixed tethering-point, whose behaviour is governed by an infinite number of variables that thrust it wildly around in three-dimensional space, but whose apparently chaotic behaviour can be seen, upon close observation and mapping, to describe a recursive pattern like those visible in the Lorenz diagrams. Such a system would demonstrate a strange attractor.[5]

Strange attractors elucidate compelling patterns that exist inside seemingly chaotic systems. The recursiveness these shapes describe, the almost-but-not-quite identical repetition of gesture and line, also exists inside much of Harrison's writing. To elucidate his work, however, the notion of recursivity should be linked with that of fractal structuring, drawn from the work of the most famous of the chaos mathematicians, Benoît Mandelbrot. He coined the term 'fractal' in 1975, deriving it from the Latin *frāctus*, meaning 'broken' or 'fractured', and used it to describe an uncanny kind of self-containing structure he had discerned operating in both mathematics and in nature. 'Fractal Geometry plays two roles', Mandelbrot (1993: 122) claimed: 'It is the geometry of deterministic chaos and it can also describe the geometry of mountains, clouds and galaxies'.

Fractals – 'any shape that contains miniature versions of itself' (Bellos, 2014: 198) – and their visual representations have inspired generations of mathematicians, physicists, graphic designers and psychedelic musicians, and are famously represented through another visual analogue, the plotting of the Mandelbrot set. The expression of the Mandelbrot set (which, crucially, is an extremely simple algorithm), reveals to the naked eye a pattern which, even when magnified to enormous orders of magnitude, possesses infinite complexity. Figure 2 gives a hint of this.[6]

Like the Lorenz attractor, the Mandelbrot set shows an extraordinarily complex and beautiful signal buried within what initially appeared to be utterly chaotic noise, and asks us to consider the possibility that disorder, unpredictability and fragmentation are, as above,

Figure 2. Mandelbrot set. Public Domain, https://en.wikipedia.org/w/index. php?curid=2865253, accessed 14 July 2018.

the organizing principles of this kind of complex system. In this wonderful irony we can find another analogue for Harrison's work.

Harrison's particular style of recursivity operates in unusual ways. Not simply comprised of recurrent tropes or motifs, its strategies connect even his earliest novels to his most recent ones, demonstrating a continuity of theme and compositional technique. Years before *Light* appeared, Harrison made recourse to the language of mathematics as a means of exploring human behaviour. Early in *The Centauri Device* (1975), protagonist John Truck's origins are described:

> It was easy to see his own birth as a momentary lapse, a miscalculation. But again: had Annie Truck [his mother] answered some unconscious urge...? In dividing, to produce another vector, a small image of herself? – as if, by that multiplication of possibilities, the long

uncomprehending migration might be expedited; something lost to
her might be gained by him. (Harrison, 2009: 17)

The language and imagery of this passage revolves around mathematics and probability, exploring their connections with human behaviour and making explicit connections between literature and science.
This might be seen merely to demonstrate a continuity of authorial
interest, but in the inhabitation of the very particular lexicon of mathematics and physics, Harrison adds a remarkable element of realism
to these speculative texts. Furthermore, in the *Empty Space* trilogy, recursivity generates an unusual effect, an hallucinogenic sense of having been there before, of having heard particular descriptive phrases
earlier, of narrative time slipping beneath us in non-linear ways, of
'fractal structuring'.

Harrison's work can be seen as fractal in at least two distinct ways.
There are numerous passages and ideas that Harrison uses 'reiterative-
ly' in the trilogy. *Nova Swing* in particular has an internal resonance
that is set in motion through seemingly innocuous passages that crop
up again and again, in different contexts and from the mouths of different characters, as descriptions or observations that might have
passed as inconsequential if only used once, but which, in their repetition, gain an eerie power and significance. Mid-novel, for example, as
Edith Bonaventure is about to inform on Vic Serotonin, the narrative
voice notes that, 'A smaller ship left the ground on a line of light like a
crack across things' (Harrison, 2006: 148). Many pages later, after the
firefight in the aureole, the omniscient voice tells us 'the K-ship took
off on its line of light like a crack right across the solidity of things'
(Harrison, 2006: 185). A casual reader might note this correlation
and repetition unconsciously, and may therefore feel slightly uneasy,
wondering whether they had previously read the *latter* sequence, or
whether they had simply imagined the textual echo after all; this kind
of uncanny effect brilliantly reinforces the symptoms that the novel's
characters experience after trips into the Saudade event site – *déjà vu*,
an inability to remember things in the correct order, an inability to be
certain of anything at all. In this sense, Harrison instils his work with
an uncanny self-reflexivity that hinges upon the very notion of al-

most-perfectly-aligned recursivity, a strategy that might be described as a literary strange attractor.

Later still, Harrison returns to this image of a crack of light, as Liv Hula sees a ship leave 'A line of light across everything, then only the afterimage' (Harrison, 2006: 188). In addition to the uncanny resonance provided by this recursive technique, Harrison seems to be hinting at something through the repetition, suggesting that the reader consider the phrase more deeply. The use of the word 'light' in the passages above is suggestive, given the title of the first volume in the trilogy and the way in which 'code' is seen to work throughout the novels, yet there is also a quotidian quality to the descriptive phrase employed in each of those examples that suggests that the resonance itself, the internal echo, as it were, is what is important, not necessarily some deeper idea. The *possibility* of a deeper idea is left dangling before us, however, in an alluringly ambiguous way.

In another example of this recursive narrative looping, *Nova Swing*'s description of the detective Lens Aschemann recurs from person to person and from sequence to sequence, again with minor slippages. Chapter two begins with the phrase: 'A couple of evenings after these events a man who resembled Albert Einstein walked into a different kind of bar' (Harrison, 2006: 18). Later, when Aschemann speaks with his police assistant, 'The man who looked like Einstein smiled to himself' (Harrison, 2006: 27). Later still, Vic Serotonin sees a pink Cadillac: 'It belonged to Lens Aschemann ... a man who resembled the older Albert Einstein' (Harrison, 2006: 42). This recursive phrase also resonates in all sorts of ways, many of them clearly intertextual. Again, the repetition of the comparison of Aschemann to Einstein is the first element that makes this motif operate in an unusually complex way; as with the 'crack of light' example, when encountering these phrases, which sometimes occur many pages apart, one instinctually asks oneself: have I not read this before? Have I lost my place, or have I somehow inadvertently skipped back and am reading a sequence I have already read? Yet even more unusual is the curiously blank way in which each subsequent comparison is made, *as if for the first time*. That the authorial voice will not acknowledge the fact that it has used these phrases before suggests a device aimed at disorienting the reader slightly, at rendering their experience of the novel one that incorporates a kind of 'slippage of newness', a sense of *déjà vu* that again fits perfectly with the ideas associated with the Saudade event site, the zone of fragmented reality that is literally and figuratively the centre of the novel.

Further, in both of the above examples we see the repeated phrases delivered with minor but crucial variations; Aschemann 'looked like Einstein', 'resembled Einstein', 'resembled the older Albert Einstein', and so on. Quite apart from confirming the fact that the repetition is not simply an error of drafting, these minute differences render the recursive phrases a Harrisonian strange attractor: near-identical gestures, repeated over and over, weaving a complex pattern.

The recurrent comparisons of Aschemann to Einstein generate several more layers of intertextual correlation: concepts of time and relativity are central to the trilogy; in many ways these novels are as much *about* science as they are works of science fiction, and the invocation of the great physicist fits perfectly within Harrison's text. Further, as a detective, Aschemann is himself a kind of scientist, observing human behaviour and making evaluations, solving problems, enacting solutions: "'I always like to watch a little", he tells his Assistant, "before I do anything."' (Harrison, 2006: 21). In many ways Aschemann behaves far more like a physicist than a cop. His language, too, evokes both the hard-boiled worlds of Chandler and Hammett and the language of science and mathematics. He sometimes uses slang particular to the trilogy – describing a prostitute as a 'mona', for example – sometimes slips back into the language of scientific observation, discovering 'a kind of discontinuity in things at the Café Surf' (Harrison, 2006: 19), and so on.

Recursivity of description and the language of science are two elements Harrison wields, but a further analysis of the Aschemann passages reveals something else. The larger sequence from which an earlier quotation is taken is as follows:

Aschemann, who had been trying to light his pipe, threw another spent match out of the Cadillac. 'Look around you', he advised her. 'In the middle of the city we're less than two miles from the event aureole. No one is certain what happened in there. Anything is possible. What if crimes are motiveless now, whipped off the crest of events like spray, with no more cause than that?'

'A surprisingly poetic idea', she said. 'But the murders?'

The man who looked like Einstein smiled to himself. 'Maybe I'll tell you more later, when you learn to ask better questions'. (Harrison, 2006: 27)

Readers familiar with *Light* will recognize the incongruous presence of characters and plot devices drawn from hard-boiled crime fiction, working their way through this science fiction text; ironies and intertextual genre tropes thus present themselves. Further, Aschemann's haunting notion that the Saudade event site's disruption of reality may be responsible for the motiveless crimes engages once again with ideas about unpredictability and chaos. In a direct challenge to the causal imperative that is at the centre of any classical detective story, Harrison presents us with the idea that his detectives are operating within a realm of utter non-linearity, of un-knowable or non-existent causality, of true chaos.

This remarkably dense sequence also points us back to the short story from which sections of *Nova Swing*'s narrative have been drawn and reconfigured. 'The Neon Heart Murders' (2000), first published in *The Magazine of Fantasy and Science Fiction*, exists as a miniature of some of the Aschemann sequences in *Nova Swing*; the 'tattoo' murders and the relationship between Aschemann and his wife occupy the central parts of the story, which exudes the same kinds of wistfulness and existential melancholy we find in the novel. In *Nova Swing*'s case, the connection to the earlier text helps to create the skein of significance and obsession that knits one Harrisonian work to another, adding to the complexity and resonance of the entire oeuvre. Again, for the habitual reader of Harrison, the Aschemann sequences in *Nova Swing* may well evoke an uncanny *déjà vu*; for the analyst interested in identifying complex motifs and internal structures, the sequences reinforce connections and patterns that are essentially non-linear (which is to say they connect abruptly one discrete text to another) and reinforcing (in that they weave a fabric of authorial presence throughout the body of works).[7] Further, the fact that 'The

Neon Heart Murders' exists as a kind of miniature of *Nova Swing* renders the two works connected as fractals are: the larger text quite literally contains miniature versions of itself.

The intertextual gestures Harrison employs in the *Empty Space* novels are multilayered and deeply resonant, filled with further suggested meaning that seems to pulse beneath the surface of the text itself. We can see further evidence of complexity in narrative and narrative technique if we keep ideas of *déjà vu*, destabilization and nonlinearity with us while unravelling another intertextual device in *Nova Swing*, the use of a single and crucially ambiguous word to describe the key location of the trilogy: *Saudade*. It is a Portuguese word that has no direct English language equivalent. The *OED* traces its etymology through an evocative quotation from A. F. Bell's *In Portugal* (1912):

> The famous *saudade* of the Portuguese is a vague and constant desire for something that does not and probably cannot exist, for something other than the present, a turning towards the past or towards the future; not an active discontent or poignant sadness but an indolent dreaming wistfulness. (Simpson, 2009: n.p.)

The naming of the event site is, then, carefully calculated. As with any intertextual gesture of this complexity, in order to 'respond fully', a reader needs to be open to discerning meaning in this passage that operates on a number of levels simultaneously. The correlations between the word's ambiguous meaning and the un-knowability of the interior of the event site itself are clear. Moreover, the entire trilogy demonstrates precisely the difficult-to-define air of melancholy that Bell describes. Many of the novels' secondary characters (Vic Serotonin, Fat Antoyne, Liv Hula, Ed Chianese) appear as – if not outright tragic figures – at least as recognizably flawed human beings whose predicaments, desires, failings and compulsions are all daubed with the 'indolent dreaming wistfulness' of *saudade*.

Aschemann comes closest to describing what gave rise to the site itself:

'Come with me, then, let's stare this thing right in the eye, you can tell me everything you know about it'. He took Antoyne's arm and urged him to look across the old fence into the site, marvelling, 'A piece of the Kefahuchi Tract! A piece of the heart of things that fell to earth! I'm afraid of it, Antoyne, I don't mind admitting; I'm afraid of what it means to us, and that's why I asked you how you felt'. (Harrison, 2006: 143)

It is only at this point, more than halfway through the second novel, that we come to understand something of the nature of the site itself. The Kefahuchi tract, that mysterious part of space that begins to reveal itself to us in wonderfully ambiguous ways in *Light*, seems to have shed part of itself, to have suffered a breakage of some kind wherein a piece of that unknowable space has fallen to earth, bringing with it impossible physics and discontinuous time, creating a dangerous zone inside which 'reality' operates in entirely non-linear ways. This non-linearity resonates yet again with Bell's description of *saudade*, and with Harrison's masterful orchestration of slippages from the future to the past and back again. These slippages, occurring throughout the novels, help to render them works of complexity. For example, *Light*'s Michael Kearney, the physicist whose work sets up much of the far-future action of the books, encounters the name of the space site years before its existence will present itself to him. In late-twentieth century London, he hears a distressed woman utter a strange *non sequitur* on the streets of Soho:

He had heard words he didn't understand.
Kefahuchi Tract.
'What does that mean?' he said. 'What do you mean by that?'
(Harrison, 2002: 23)

This fractured notion of time, this disrupted, non-linear reality that haunts the novels, a reality wherein a crucial phrase sourced from a period in the future can be uttered by a complete stranger years too soon, where other groups of words can be uttered with the same sense of wonder and fear by characters separated by decades and light years ('Sparks! Sparks in everything!')[8] is one of Harrison's central tropes, and manages to make the word *saudade* resonate in numerous frequencies at once.

Finally, *saudade* appears in the titles of compositions by a number of noted jazz musicians: in particular, pianist and composer Bill Evans performed and recorded Antonio Carlos Jobim's *Saudade do Brasil* a number of times,[9] and the equally renowned bassist Ron Carter composed and recorded a languid, evocative track simply entitled *Saudade*.[10] Both artists are men whose work one would imagine is known to Harrison, given the frequent references to jazz in both *Nova Swing* and 'The Neon Heart Murders'. In the short story, a two-piece jazz band plays a significant part in the narrative, with the saxophone player providing a droll, existential point of reflection for the narrative itself. Harrison's description of the band's set refers to Charlie Parker and Johnny Hodges, two legendary jazz musicians from the early days of bebop, knowledge of whose work suggests a particular interest on the writer's part.

All of this resonance, all of these correlations and significances, manifest through the choice of a single word. It is through such densely constructed, multilayered signifiers in Harrison's work that we see complexity in operation. Further, and in a way that confirms the notion that complexity science is part of what Harrison is concerned with here, there are explicit allusions to the whole realm of complexity and chaos within *Nova Swing*. Early in the novel, Harrison describes the cats that leave the Saudade event site:

> Who knew how many of those cats there were? Another thing, you never found so much as a tabby among them, every one was either black or white. When they poured out of the zone it was like a model of some chaotic mixing flow in which, though every condition is determined, you can never predict the outcome. (Harrison, 2006: 13)[11]

Here Harrison seems to allude quite directly to the experiment that began complexity science, Lorenz's observations of the behaviour of mixes of gas and liquid that would become 'Deterministic Nonperiodic Flow'. A few pages later, Harrison describes the cats again:

Meanwhile the stream of cats flowed on like a problem in statistical mechanics, without any apparent slackening or falling away of numbers, until suddenly it turned itself off and Straint was empty again. (Harrison, 2006: 15)

Statistical mechanics, chaotic flow – such language confirms that the trilogy is, among other things, Harrison's response to complexity science. With that in mind that I want to look at a final allusive example from *Nova Swing* that again engages with ideas of recursivity and complexity in extraordinarily elaborate ways.

Late in chapter seven, a sequence explores the complicated relationship between Emil Bonaventura and his daughter, Edith:

Upstairs, Emil Bonaventure was propped upright against the pillows like a corpse, his skin yellow in the streetlight from the window ... Edith watched the pulse in his neck. She *could* almost see the life through the skin, the thoughts in his head, and what were they but the dreams he couldn't any longer have? Shallow water over cracked chequerboard tiles and cast-off domestic objects, books, plates, magazines, empty tunnels smelling of chemicals, a black dog trotting aimlessly round him in his sleep on some dirty waterlogged ground neither in nor out of anything you could think of as the world, while a woman's voice mourned open-throat from a house not far enough in the distance. (Harrison, 2006: 148)

Quite apart from its extraordinarily lyrical and heartbreaking description of a dying man and his emotionally fragile daughter, this sequence comprises an exacting evocation of several key images and motifs from Andrei Tarkovsky's enigmatic film *Stalker* (1979), whose own narrative – crucially – revolves around a deeply mysterious 'Zone' whose reality differs from our own, and at whose centre is said to lurk a kind of revelatory, wish-granting power. If we can catch this imagistic reference to Tarkovsky's film, our minds may be cast back to the very beginning of *Nova Swing*, which essentially 'opens' with Harrison's citation of a passage from Boris and Arkady Strugatsky's *Roadside Picnic* (1972), the novel upon which Tarkovsky's film was based. The connections between the three texts are startling in their multivalency and resonance. *Roadside Picnic*'s 'stalkers' attempt to guide pilgrim-like customers into and out of the Zones, just as 'tour-guides' Vic Serotonin and Antoyne Messner do in *Nova Swing*. *Roadside Picnic's* Zones also spawn artefacts (which operate somewhat differently to those in *Nova Swing*), and both locations, the Zone and the Saudade event, have a corrupting, madness-inducing effect upon the characters who enter them. Most importantly, perhaps, both locations are deeply and enduringly enigmatic, and operate as sites around which numerous ontological questions revolve.

In the passage quoted above, though, it is to the film that Harrison points. The immensely-detailed evocation of a very particular series of images and sounds from the film are chilling in their specificity, literally dream-like in their intensity (and we remember of course that the image in *Nova Swing* seems to be Edith's 'reading' of the dream that her father *can no longer have*). What is perhaps most intriguing about Harrison's evocation of the *Stalker* image is the fact that it comes from Tarkovsky's *adaptation* of the novel Harrison quotes at his book's opening. Again we see intertextuality operating in particular and complex ways; while we, as readers, are explicitly cued to the importance of the Strugatsky novel (through the opening quotation), we are never *directly* pointed to the significance of Tarkovsky's adaptation. The true and full extent of the significance of Edith's 'description' of Emil's dream is only discernible to those readers who are deeply familiar with the film in question. The reader who is able to apprehend the source of the image Harrison invokes will also likely know the sad history behind the making of the film; many of the technicians who worked on Tarkovsky's adaptation – along with the director himself – eventually died of cancers that have been linked to potent chemicals present at numerous locations used for filming.[12] This wrenching sadness-in-joy, this poignant, horrible realization that there is human tragedy lurking at the centre of a moving and enduring piece of art, fits, again uncannily, with the experiences of the characters that populate the trilogy. *Saudade* indeed.

This final complex example of Harissonian intertextuality that, in its precise evocation of a multi-layered pair of outside texts, in its power to force a retroactive reading of the novel's opening quotation, and in its bending of reality for both its central characters and its readers, demonstrates its author's delight in engaging with complexity both literary and scientific – and in thus providing us with one of the most fertile series of texts to have appeared in our new century.

Notes

1 Gleick (1988) remains the most lucid introduction to this field.

2 Gleick (1988: 5) mentions, though declines to elaborate upon, this phrase.

3 Ken MacLeod's endorsement from the front matter of *Light*.

4 This diagram is taken directly from Lorenz (1963: 137, Figure 2).

5 For a lucid introduction to strange attractors, see Gleick (1988: 132–7).

6 Image taken from University of Utah's Understanding Mathematics site, http://www.math.utah.edu/~pa/math/mandelbrot/mandelbrot.html

7 Another pattern emerges, too, when one notes the aural similarity between the names Aschemann and Ashlyme, the latter being the protagonist of Harrison's *In Viriconium* (1982). Ashlyme is a painter who is much concerned with a zone of his own (Viriconium's Plague zone), and is similarly surrounded – in the Viriconium cycle – by repetitions of description and phrase that work in much the same way as those described above.

8 This refrain is another of the phrases repeated by numerous characters, and the omniscient narrator, through the novel's many timeframes. For example, in *Empty Space*, Anna Kearney recalls she or Michael uttering the phrase while making love; later, as she investigates the strange fire in her summerhouse; she sees 'Something ... spilling off the shelves, in a shower of fantastic sparks! They were just like the sparks from a firework!' (Harrison, 2012: 29).

9 For a representative performance, see Evans's album *Eloquence* (1998).

10 On his album *Orfeu* (1999).

11 The significance of the black/white binary is clear to readers familiar with *Light*.

12 An account of the film's punishing shoot can be found at http://www.nostalghia.com/TheTopics/Stalker/sharun.html

Works Cited

Bellos, Alex (2014) *Alex Through the Looking Glass*. London: Bloomsbury.

Gleick, James (1988) *Chaos: Making a New Science*. London: William Heinemann.

Harrison, M. John (2002) *Light*. London: Gollancz.

Harrison, M. John (2006) *Nova Swing*. London: Gollancz.

Harrison, M. John (2009) *The Centauri Device*. London: Gollancz.

Harrison, M. John (2012) *Empty Space*. London: Gollancz.

Lorenz, Edward N. (1963) 'Deterministic Nonperiodic Flow', *Journal of the Atmospheric Sciences* 20: 130–41.

Mandelbrot, Benoît (1993) 'Fractals: A Geometry of Nature', in Nina Hall (ed.) *Exploring Chaos: A Guide to the New Science of Disorder*, pp. 122–235. New York: Norton.

Simpson, John A. (2009) *Oxford English Dictionary, second edition* (CD-ROM v.4.0). Oxford: Oxford University Press.

FLUTTER, FRACTURE AND FROTH
EVENT, OBJECT AND ACT OF
METAPHOR IN M. JOHN HARRISON

Fred Botting

Train Events

(*flutter; in which examples of significant metaphorical conjunctions from M. John Harrison are set out*)

The determining event of *Light* (2002) happens at a distinctly modern location – a station. It precipitates the radical mathematical reformulations which strip away the basis of modern reality. A recent encounter with Tarot cards has convinced Michael Kearney, protagonist, physicist, genius and serial killer, of an obscure link between mathematics and prophecy. At King's Cross, the connection is disclosed: 'a relationship between the flutter of cards falling in a quiet room and the flutter of changing destinations on the mechanical indicator boards at the railway station' (Harrison, 2002: 65). The meeting of randomness and determination – one fluttering conjuring another, he acknowledged, 'rested on a metaphor' (Harrison, 2002: 65). Further tests, he decides in honour of the metaphor, will all be conducted on trains. It is an apt choice: metaphor, etymologically, involves transport, carrying bodies and meanings from one place to another (De Certeau, 1984: 115). Kearney's train tests establish the possibility of

229

transforming the laws of physics. The flutter of cards and destinations condenses notions of chance (fortune and probability), cause and (mathematical–informatic–biological) code. Elsewhere, the event of metaphor conjoins economic and biological determination: in *Signs of Life* (1996) the 'flutter' of wings from a genetically-modified female human body realizes fantasies of personal fulfilment and neoliberal self-fashioning in a Petri dish of biotechnology, marketing and capital, all unleashed by financial (and ethical) deregulation.

Another novel, *Climbers* (1991) and another journey, this time from Sheffield: 'if you look straight down an Inter-City second class carriage, the landscape on both sides of the train flies past in your peripheral vision like images in a split-screen film. You have only an instant in which to recognize an object before it becomes a blur' (Harrison, 1991: 173). The fractured perspective in this image of blurred images alludes to quantum experiments on the uncertainty principle, according to which observation belatedly 'decides' the reality of the wave or particle reality. The com-position of train events undoes metaphorical unity: two realms remain in play in one moment and one, albeit mobile, place. Flutters and fractures reiterate. The Kefahuchi Tract hangs like a crack in the universe. In 'Running Down' (1975), set amid placid Lakeland hills, strange psycho–seismic energies make 'huge cracks and ruptures spread out across the cliff face' (Harrison, 2004d: 52). Cracked objects, cracked vision: in *The Course of the Heart* (1991), in which otherworldly conjurations wrench everyday reality apart, the narrator notes a 'visual fault', 'a neon zigzag like a bright little flight of stairs, kept showing up in my left eye' (Harrison, 2005: 29). No more than a migraine, it nonetheless gives image to a reality that is never itself. As in 'Anima' (1991), a kind of dissonant 'bi-focality' is at work, 'as if' one eye focused at eighteen inches and the other at twelve, leaving words and objects 'slipping naturally in and out of view' and suggesting a personality at once 'clear and sharp' and 'vague and impressionistic' (Harrison, 2004a: 282). In *Climbers*, a childhood experience in a department store cafeteria repeats the pattern in disorientating, reflective superimposition: plastic seating and customers, 'by optical accident' (Harrison, 1991: 18), are transposed to a dim, cold and rainy car park that seems inhabited by oblivious and ghostly diners. The play of reflections relaxes and then shocks the young observer: apparently addressed by a young woman, he moves in her direction only to crash into a plate-glass window! Perspective and reality do not cohere, yet life is lived, sometimes with a comic crunch, as if they did. *The Course of the Heart* describes the final days of a hospitalized woman haunted, since participating in an occult experiment at university, by two pale, shapeless, entwined figures: 'she could see right through *Celebrity Squares* or *Take the High Road* to where the white couple hung just inside every TV set, smiling out at her while they clasped and panted and turned to and fro like a chrysalis in a hedge' (Harrison, 2005: 171). Otherworldiness and extreme media banality hang together in indifferent disjunction. Screens enhance rather than occlude cracked vision, filtering unreality into rather than from framed discriminations of the world.

Cracked perspectives relate to articulation and transition. Tired of 'the constant talk of physics and money', Kearney flips channels in a Los Alamos hotel room, speculating that 'the moment of choice ... could be located very exactly as one image flickered, broke and was replaced by the next' (Harrison, 2002: 44). The moment remains elusive, though the attempt resonates with mathematical probability, Tarot and quantum code. It is broached four hundred years later as a pilot 'wired' into the controlling, sentient algorithms of her multi-dimensional interstellar 'k-ship' tries to grasp an image of a fleeting object–event that has just been registered by its computational systems: 'eventually it began to toggle regularly between two states. If you knew exactly how to look into the gap between them you could detect, like weakly reacting matter, the ghost of an event' (Harrison, 2002: 151). Missed, the object-event is retrospectively mediated, recuperated spectrally: a gap and an effect of gaps, it is both in and beyond the flickering of representational states and requires manipulation for the configuration to work. Metaphor, a split image, is retrojected, retaining physical effects.

Another train journey – this time to Euston: Kearney, in the sudden jolt of a busy commuter carriage almost falls into a woman and realizes, half-falling, half-righting himself, 'how good the body is at making metaphors' (Harrison, 2002: 122). In 'The Horse of Iron and

How We Can Know It' (1988), behind the plate-glass window of a video shop under a Glasgow railway bridge, an animated scene is replayed: a boy beside his father's body is watching a sword being struck in a forge, eyes wide as sparks fly; their reflected cathode glow illuminates the damp street outside and shines with the messages of so many tawdry advertisements in other shop windows. For the narrator, these scenes disclose the scandalous way that language can make connections, exemplifying both the work and exhaustion of metaphor: 'stories pass the experienced world back and forth between them as a metaphor, until it is worn out' (Harrison, 2004c: 245). While metaphor allows sparks of illumination, transforming (perception of) reality, its repeated usage leads to assimilation.

Emergence

(froth; in which episodes and figures from the Empty Space trilogy engage with transformative aspects of fractal iteration, probability, decoherence and singularity)

Decorative excrescence, accidental conjunction, bubbles of emergence: foam, in the *Empty Space* trilogy, marks quantum alternations and subjective, social and political transformation, tracking zones where matter becomes unstable and information solidifies. A child on a beach, collecting pebbles: the three-year old Kearney, already adept in numbers, notes how suddenly a 'shift in vision altered his perspective' so that 'he saw clearly the gaps between the larger stones made the same sort of shapes as the gaps between the smaller ones. The more he looked the more the arrangement repeated itself' (Harrison, 2002: 22). Focused not on things but on the spacing that distinguishes and organizes things, the observation marks an intuitive apprehension of the fractal underpinning of natural forms; it allows him to grasp a wider and recurrent pattern whose iterations have universal and, for him, prophetic, import. From pebbles beside the sea to waves making 'the shapes of a million small white clouds', he understands the 'condition of things': 'a boiling, inexplicable, vertiginous similarity in all the processes of the world, roaring silently away from you in ever-shifting repetitions, always the same never the same thing twice' (Harrison, 2002: 22). Living foam, reiteration at every level, chaos and order, pattern and randomness reshaping all relations.

The future that Kearney's vision portends and brings into being is similarly froth-ful: four hundred years forward, the Tract's radiation causes space-time anomalies on neighbouring planets, 'event-sites' in which things that happen without predictable pattern are cordoned off by a kind of froth, 'a whitish rolling strip like surf' and marked out by 'a stationary vapour of uncertain physics' (Harrison, 2006: 88–9). Both boundary and site of transformation, foam is neither solid nor completely amorphous but a line of emergence and uncertainty temporarily zoned off from a world in which objects remain in phase with the normal rules of reality. Inside – though notions of inside and outside make little sense – there is no such stability. Time becomes indeterminate and non-linear, space fluid, and objects assume arbitrary proportions: 'scale and perspective were impossible to achieve because the objects, toppling over and over in a kind of slow motion – or so the eye assumed – were domestic items a hundred times too large and from another age' or 'too small' (Harrison, 2006: 163). Outside the aureole it is possible to glimpse an 'unfamiliar object being tossed into the air by a silent but convulsive force' that was 'as impossible to understand as the objects themselves', but everything inside is 'so unconstrained by context that they seemed less objects than images' (Harrison, 2012: 78). Without frame everything is rendered as uncertain as the physics of foam. At the edge of an event aureole buildings seem to have 'lost confidence in their physical integrity' and streets manifest an 'inoperative geography' (Harrison, 2006: 5, 11).

The mathematical work carried out by Kearney and Brian Tate delivers data with its own foamy, luxile materiality. Searching for his research partner in a trashed laboratory, Kearney discovers, amid broken drives and monitors, 'a quiet spill of light, emerging like fluid from one of the ruptured displays and licking out across the floor' and 'shoal[ing] round his feet in a cold fractal dance' (Harrison, 2002: 138). It resembles a form that has haunted him for years, spectral yet with real effects. Later, in the house where the now uncontrolled experiment is relocated, a half-mad, quantum-data-irradiated scientist encases himself in a Faraday cage and aluminium foil for protection. To no avail: algorithms and data, foaming in light, leak from processors; his face and body are dissolving; a laboratory cat has already disappeared into the foam; the physics is '*off*' and fractals had begun to 'leak' (Harrison, 2002: 215). No discernible rules are in evidence, no predictable laws seem to apply. Information and light assume increasingly material form, confirming theoretical claims about the illusions of embodied reality: 'I'm not really here', Tate comments, 'None of us are' (Harrison, 2002: 216).

The experiment has, it seems, realized a fully quantum universe relieved of classical physic's restraints. At a subatomic level everything is governed by quantum energies and rules, but 'decoherence' allows those forces to recede and, at levels above the atomic scale, stabilize. In Schrödinger's thought-experiment, the cat in the sealed box with a vial of poison gas and a radioactive atomic trigger makes matters of life and death irresolvable: at a quantum level the atom has and has not decayed which means that the cat may be both dead and not dead. As an example of decoherence (cats are too large to be seen as both dead and not dead), the information about possible quantum superposed states has faded from an observer's access leaving only data relating to one – classical – state (Mullins, 2011: 8). Where interactions between atoms, objects, systems and environment are incessant and allow multiple possibilities at a quantum level, decoherence offers a 'selection process' that prevents excessive quantum variation in larger – macroscopic – objects (Zurek, 1999: n.p.). Decoherence protects a classical universe of objects by screening off multiple fluctuations and forces operating on a quantum scale. According to Kearney, it 'holds the world into place the way we see it' – 'But', he adds, explaining events to come, 'people like Brian Tate are going to find the maths that will get round the end of that' (Harrison, 2002: 92). Without decoherence there would be no recession of quantum forces, no objects able to emerge from frothing contexts, and no point at which the blur of things would resolve into meaning. There would only be numbers: 'that's all anything is. Nothing but statistics' (Harrison, 2002: 92–3).

The ordinary laws of the physical universe, too, screen off the forces manifested by a singularity. The Tate–Kearney theorem mirrors the effects of the Kefahuchi Tract, a 'singularity without event horizon' (Harrison, 2002: 93). As such it contravenes the usual attributes of a black hole: no longer does an event horizon operate as a 'one-way membrane' separating normal space–time from a region within where light cannot escape and where 'laws of science and our ability to predict the future break down' (Hawking, 1988: 88–9). In Einstein's universe no singularity is 'naked': an event horizon shields a singularity from external observation and prevents leakage of 'physical uncertainties' into the universe around (Penrose, 2011: 105, 336). Such a scientific 'fig leaf' need not remain in place: data from 'unexplained high-energy phenomena' suggests quantum forces, produced by hyperdense gravitational collapse, can leak from unshielded singularities, implying a breakdown in general relativity or evidence of space and time having an edge, 'a place where the physical world ends' (Joshi, 2013: 80). It might also be a site where the dense curvature and collapse of space–time produces 'huge quantum mechanical forces' called 'quantum foam' (Misner et al., 1999: 42). An event horizon works 'not as a limitation of human knowledge but as a *protection* against the breakdown of physical laws which might otherwise leak out into the universe' (Harrison, 2002: 93). Unshielded singularities, like the circumvention of decoherence, undo the world of stable classical objects, thus removing 'noumenon' or Thing: an 'absolutely objective' reality beyond sense is no longer separated from legitimate knowledge and no longer serves to 'curb the pretensions of sensibility' (Kant, 1929: 267, 272). The image Kant employs is of an enchanted island of understanding securely surrounded by natural limits where truth is protected by 'a wide and stormy ocean' from the delusion and deception of 'fog bank' and 'iceberg' (Kant, 1929: 257).

On Monster Beach, Kearney awaits the event his research has set in train: the 'shivering luminescence' of nocturnal sky, sea and winds roll out before him to offer a 'sense of things as endless' (Harrison, 2002: 247). The scene allows him to consider the spot as 'a metaphor for some other transitional site or boundary, a beach at the edge of which lapped the whole universe' (Harrison, 2002: 247). That beach is the Kefahuchi Tract, a 'weird twist of light that hangs like a crack in nowhere' (Harrison, 2002: 199). It obeys no known physical laws and resists scientific explanation while causing space–time disruptions on planets in the surrounding galaxy: its unfathomable energies uncontained, it is understood only as a place where 'the wrong physics' (Harrison, 2002: 237) are loose and 'where all the broken rules of the universe spill out' (Harrison, 2002: 316). As an edge, site of something entirely other, the Tract not only constitutes the limit of knowledge, it marks out new horizons of fascination and desire: in what becomes known as the 'Beach', an entire intergalactic culture – 'k-culture' – is devoted to its observation, with artificial star systems positioned as 'enormous detectors designed to react to the unimaginable forces pouring out of the uncontained singularity hypothetically present at the centre of the Tract' (Harrison, 2002: 140). Yet even the technological and imaginative prowess of species and cultures able to move stars and construct planets founders before the singularity. A dice game is as good a way of making sense of things as any theory. It serves as 'another device for trying to understand the place where the rules ran out' (Harrison, 2002: 318).

Metaphor

(crack; in which scientific uses of metaphor are examined in terms of literary theory as figures having a productive role in shaping perceptions of reality)

Scientific terms and ideas – already highly figurative in form and effect – constitute one rich seam for interrogations of metaphorical resonance in Harrison's fiction. The cats that populate the *Light* trilogy directly appeal to experiments in uncertainty. The flutter of cards and mechanical signs call up probability theory and iterations of fractal shapes, instances of underlying pattern in a world of apparent randomness. 'Code', too, marks a convergence of biology and information theory in the rewriting of life (see Kay, 2000). 'Quantum foam' postulates the space-time energies emanating from massive gravitational collapse; 'froth' signals the randomness enabling the adaptive interchanges of information in autopoietic or self-organizing living systems (Hayles, 1999: 286). As an exteriorization of metaphor as neural net, foam figures a fluctuating and dynamic 'frothing turbulence of the endocrine cascades bathing the synapses of our nerves' (Porush, 1996: 121). Metaphor, it seems, allows scientific understanding to radiate beyond particular spheres of technical expertise. For pioneer cyberneticist Norbert Wiener (1954: 97), it functions as an extension of human knowledge through communication, command and control: 'where a man's word goes, and where his power of perception goes, to that point his control and his sense of his physical existence is extended'.

Defined, in formalist theory, as 'thinking in images', art aims to 'recover the sensation of life' and renew feeling and perception through 'defamiliarisation' that disrupts habitual techniques of representation (Shklovsky, 1988: 17). Substitution allows a distinct new sense to emerge through the linking of the two different fields (or 'systems of related commonplaces'): without resorting to or trying to supplement literal inadequacies, metaphor, as a kind of necessary catachresis of normal usage, '*creates* the similarity' through a process of 'interaction' in which a new context extends meaning and thus 'organizes' a new view of the object; focusing and reframing sense through a condensation of fields, metaphor both 'filters and transforms' and 'selects and brings forward' new connotations (Black, 1954–5: 288–9). It can 'actualize' potential connotations held by two sets of properties and thus establish a new standard that, in turn, may become another dead metaphor (Beardsley, 1962: 302). Metaphor structures 'how we perceive, what we think, and what we do' (Lakoff and Johnson, 1980: 3). Altering linguistic conventions and habits, it discloses a new sense of reality, revitalising subjective appreciation of objects: its 'power of organising our perception of things develops from a transposition of our entire "reason"', a poetic conversion of 'language into matter', creating not just new images and connotations, but a 'solid object' able to give 'expression of itself' (Ricoeur, 1991: 268, 278).

Situated against an exhaustion of popular, generic and commercial language, metaphor involves the renewal of subjective vision, social significance and object-world: its importance lies in the way it interrogates relations of political fantasy and reality (Bould, 2005: 20). In *Nova Swing* (2006), retroporn – a nostalgic form of pornographic marketing – defamiliarizes sexuality to the point that it becomes – as if in answer to the mechano-erotic exhaustion of J. G. Ballard's fiction – interesting once more. In 'A Young Man's Journey to London' (1984), the light heightens an already hyperreal sense of the city's salient details, while, in *Climbers*, sunlight spreads an almost ecstatic brilliance on a cliff-side scene. Metaphor, like light, transforms both perception and things, reshaping objects in superpositions of surfaces. Though there are plenty of examples of things and images merging and mashing – the 'tailoring' of genes, the neurophysical fusion of pilot and spaceship, exotically 'cut' chimerical boxers – metaphor rarely occurs without residue, rarely conjoining in a new image without gaps remaining visible. The central metaphor – a collapsed star – shines as a crack rather than unified form: its event of metaphor, like the surprise of chance and the indeterminacy of foam, maintains polarized irresolution. Metaphor never quite seems to cohere. Or rather, it never quite allows the 'decoherence' that would fully distinguish object from energy, figure from ground, meaning from foam.

Surf Noir

(*froth; in which metaphors in the Empty Space trilogy are shown to articulate present and future in terms of different aesthetic, scientific and economic issues in the transformation of reality and meaning*)

Convergent and chaotic, foam conjoins aesthetic, scientific and economic effects. In *Nova Swing*, sociopolitical reflection meets genre, marketing and hyperrealism. The generic context is informed by geographical location and character: the sprawling spaceport fringes of a corporate planet, a black market hothouse of illegal new technological innovation, its exploitation and entrepreneurial speculative experimentation producing new bodies, goods and experiences. It is policed by a disenchanted yet thoughtful detective. At a sleepy bar, Café Surf, the pipe-smoking investigator sees a young child, clothed only in a T-shirt with 'SURF NOIR' printed on it. The motto is unclear but resonant:

meanings – all incongruous – splashed off this like drops of water, as the dead metaphors trapped inside the live one collided and reverberated endlessly and elastically, taking up new positions relative to one another. SURF NOIR, which is a whole new existence; which is a 'world' implied in two worlds, dispelled in an instant; which is foam on the appalling multitextual sea we drift on. 'Which is probably,' Aschemann noted, 'the name of an aftershave.' (Harrison, 2006: 27–8)

Collision and reverberation mark the metaphorical generation and dissipation of meaning. This scene of an accidentally productive encounter, throwing up and washing off meanings in a splash of foam, recollects postmodern plurality as a conjunction of discourses and metonymies linking genre and location (hard-boiled cyber-noir circa AD 2400) with advertising (circa AD 1985) in order to reflect on the convergence of economic, technological and aesthetic forces. The reading of the T-shirt presents a familiar late-twentieth-century multi-textual sea of polysemy and metonymy, its froth washing into dead-end hyperrealist marketing: 'Surf noir' is probably an aftershave, probably an old and spicy brand marking manhood in terms of a shining, muscled torso weaving in and out of curling waves to a bombastically dramatic soundtrack, from *Carmen* perhaps. The retrospection reiterates a shift that happened four hundred years before called 'the postmodern ironisation' (Harrison, 2012: 39). Preceded by definite article, it is truly evental, akin to the 'Death of History or the coming Singularity': 'Everything was changed by it. Nothing could be the same again' (Harrison, 2012: 39). Unanchored by representation, history or material contexts, postmodernism's evental rupture of modern frames accords with the unleashing of global fiscal fantasies and freedoms and the capacity of technological realization: the wrong money and the wrong signs are let loose in the universe along with the wrong physics.

Physics, capitalism and postmodern simulation are explicitly linked as un-real games of chance, prediction and prophecy in a future where mathematical code is mined like a natural resource for profit. In the contemporary setting, research is managed by 'Meadows Venture Capital' in an old annexe of Imperial College that has been 'orphaned recently into the care of free market economics' (Harrison, 2002: 116, 129). Two effects of the 'Big Bang' are conjoined, study of the original universal event meeting free market financial deregulation of the 1980s. Four hundred years on, illicit markets in neurochemical, genetic and digital technologies flourish around the Tract, trawled for saleable alien artefacts and advanced programming. Human explorers are captivated by the 'sense there was money to be made' (Harrison, 2002: 139). An ancient dice game rattles in bars and backrooms along the Tract: one has to 'pay to play', the gamble considered an 'ironic subtext to everything that happened in empty space', a 'narrative of capital' (Harrison, 2002: 174). Again, magic, money and maths converge in the flutter of chance and fortune, formula and code: speculators, worried that the Tract has been fully exploited, must be re-enchanted to believe it to be 'glittering in front of them like an affordable asset' (Harrison, 2002: 263). Physicists of Kearney's time are described as 'postmodern cosmologists' who are 'entrapped by self-referential mathematical games, habitually mistaking speculation for science' (Harrison, 2012: 147). On first receiving reports of the Tract, even Kearney considers the '24-hour news cycle, data massaged into fantasies for media consumption, less science than the public relations of science' (Harrison, 2002: 147–8). A generation later, however, cosmology and conjuring – Kearney's own method – seem inseparable, reinventing reality in terms of flights of formula, flutters of speculation. Theory and fiction precede and reshape things. The physics of space travel in the future is arbitrary, multidimensional drives operating according to different principles and assumptions:

> Every race ... had a star drive based on a different theory. All those theories work, even when they rule out one another's basic assumption. You could travel between the stars, it began to seem, by assuming anything. If your theory gave you foamy space to work with – if you had to catch a wave – that didn't preclude some other engine, running on a perfectly smooth Einsteinian surface, from surfing the same tranches of empty space. (Harrison, 2002: 139–40)

'Anything goes', the mantra of postmodern kitsch, becomes future reality (Lyotard, 1984: 41). Theory, no longer inhibited by matter, operates autonomously; mathematical code 'engaged whatever stood in for reality' (Harrison, 2002: 13). Planets, star-systems, alien arte-facts and ruins 'were alive with code' (Harrison, 2002: 186). Worlds are inhabited by 'algorithms with a life of their own' (Harrison, 2002: 50). Matter, code, life seem indistinguishable: 'information might be a *substance*' (Harrison, 2002: 273). Even tattoos are sentient. In this future, virtual promises pertaining to biology, digital technology and economy are hyperrealized in full.

The *Empty Space* trilogy seems to affirm a thoroughly postmodern universe: cultivars, twink-tanks, retroporn, chimera boxing, and the 'hyper-real' quality of objects in event sites (Harrison, 2006: 164). It concludes, close to where it began (early twenty-first century south-ern England), with a social and economic present of peak oil, financial collapse, constraints on conspicuous spending and a narrowing of the horizons defining wealth, comfort and success. Here a 'new econom-ics' implements cooperation, mutual association and social invest-ment, and banking is no longer the law: 'the financial sector, stunned by the discovery that money had been as postmodernised as every-thing else passively allowed the state to clip its wings. Bankers seeking explanations read Baudrillard forty years too late' (Harrison, 2012: 296). The reversal in financial fortune inaugurates a reversal of so-cial and political values. Given that so much of the trilogy's narrative seems enveloped in a hyperreal future, it is curious that Baudrillard – often considered an avatar of all things postmodern – is invoked as both explanation and belated caution to monetary and aesthetic post-modernization. Yet rather than condensing everything that is wrong with postmodernity – the wrong money (neoliberal deregulation), the wrong physics (quantum uncertainties), and the wrong signs (hy-perreality) – the invocation harnesses metonymies of foam and flutter to re-inscribe the possibility of a different – and political – fracture of perspective.

Like a metaphor

(fracture; in which Harrison's distinctive uses of metaphor are theorized as establishing a critical, active and productive stance in respect of scientific derealization and postmodern economics)

In *Nova Swing*, a discussion between two guides note how the event site is becoming 'newly elastic': something is changing deep inside, every occurrence feeling like 'it represented something else' (Harrison, 2006: 50). One almost makes a literary observation, but stays silent: 'it's like a metaphor' (Harrison, 2006: 50). Like a metaphor? A simile, a simulacrum, even, of metaphor? What curiously elided trope would that imply? Where iterations of foam, flutter and code converge on a hyperreal, transversal circulation of data, money, energy, the fiction stops short of total immersion in metonymic play. Its writing 'in honour' of metaphor attempts to make something of foam, flutter and, especially, fracture. Figure is sustained in an image of fracture, singular but divided like the crack in space. It is not a ready-made site of substitution and comparison, but a space of possibility, of gaps, tensions and potential sparks. Jacques Lacan (1977: 421–2) describes metaphor as the 'creative spark' ignited not from a simple juxtaposition of sounds or images but as a flashing 'between two signifiers' so that the 'occulted signifier' still flickers. 'Occultation' signifies an eclipse by one stellar body of the light radiating from another – but both remain, as does the gap between them –and thus metaphor should be understood not as a 'superimposition' of one signifier over another but as a matter of alignments and articulations. Metaphor involves place, gap, identification and knot, the latter the occulted point for any creative spark, and like meaning, it is both an *event* and an *act* (of performance and decision).

In 'A Young Man's Journey to London' an old man writes in his notebooks about how events 'are struck lightly' against their own significance, disclosing 'an energetic mote' at the core of metaphor and life (Harrison, 2004f: 172). In 'The Horse of Iron', the narrator ruminates on the 'scandal' of language, its monstrous capacity to make connections and engender repetition and exhaustion. At its crux, a further step is required: 'only then do we realize that meaning is an *act*. We must repossess it, instant to instant in our lives' (Harrison, 2004c: 245). Losses of meaning ensuing from repetition and habituation require active and vital renewal. Gaps remain, sites of impediment and precipitation: metaphor does not arrive wholesale but remains in process, mechanisms open to the scrutiny of a reflective and split position, a critical space defined precisely in the rupture of an event. The naked singularity, a fracture of space-time, is composed of dense but lawless flows of energies and association, site of imploding gravitational forces that continue to radiate. As such it constitutes a figure that inverts figure, a gap left open for metaphor's cracked perspective.

If a single perspective appears in Harrison's fiction, it does so under suspicion. References to video games, for example, expose a narrowness to single perspectival frames which elide and eclipse alternative objects, realities or desires. An aside, in 'Black Houses' (1997), a story of an amorous relationship composed of unsent letters and thoughts on the limits of writing, plots the narrowing of perspective and desire: 'It's like being in a computer game. One moment you have needs; the next, quite suddenly, they're satisfied or sidelined. The field of vision seems empty. Then you detect this faint serpentine flicker as the fractals grow and boil, and new needs have replaced the old. Desire is desire' (2004b: 429). Desire ... is desire ... is desire ..., conjunctive and connective and without break for reflection or meaning, it ploughs on forever. An empty monitor projects desire and screens off difference: the hot froth of fractals signal endless iterations of the same, desire recycled in the metonymy and monotony of a single perspective absorbing, without breach or rupture, a subjective, captivated gaze totally in thrall to continual virtual movement in virtual space.

When gaming meets climbing in 'Suicide Coast' (1996) not only does simulation occlude the risk and consequences of a very real activity, the absorbing lure of virtual perspective supersedes material existence: 'it's better than living' (Harrison, 2004e: 389), comments a paraplegic ex-climber now addicted to play (not without irony). Only briefly does a programming glitch interrupt the seamless flow invisibly conjoining the story's depiction of gaming – marked in opposition to the reality of climbing – as being entirely encompassed by another game. The break in perspective, however, only disrupts immersion for a moment until a repeated phrase signals that the story-game has reset itself.

Single perspective iterates sameness; cracks challenge seamless simulations of desire. *Climbers* offers a different perspective on perspective: climbing is a metaphor by which climbers 'hoped to demonstrate something to themselves' (Harrison, 1991: 79). Though its significance remains unstated, it is common to all, like the dream which, minor variations aside, is dreamt by every climber: moving in fine weather with pace and precision on a perfect route, high up, each dreamer follows holds provided by a long, secure crack running the entirety of the face. Timing, technique, climber and rock participate in an elevating experience: with 'empty space all around him', one describes the sensation as 'vibrant, receiving itself to his elation as he moved only to give it back as a blessing' (Harrison, 1991: 28). At the point at which the climb feels that it will continue perfectly forever, a horrific interruption occurs: a hand, only a hand, reaches out from inside the crack, or grabs the climber, or the crack itself traps the climber's arm leaving him dangling over the void (Harrison, 1991: 28). Smooth movement is suspended; fantastic elation stopped by paralysing anxiety. Climbing splits into complementary poles: desire–fear, elation–danger, joy–pain. They inform every climb, fantastic or otherwise. Climbing would mean nothing without them or the crack which articulates them. Like other examples of superpositioning – split-screens and fluttering images – the crack conjoins object and act in a division of perception and reality. More than passive alternation, polarities of desire–fear, elation–anxiety, form the conditions for the act that occurs in respect of a void, a crack tied to the decision of metaphor: one can remain hanging, suspended, or make a move that might risk injury. Fear and anxiety, palpable and incapacitating, evacuate subjectivity in echo of the empty space over which the body hangs. Yet that space and limit-encounter – internal and external – remains integral to the experience, whether outcomes are positive or negative: it involves confronting potential loss and at that point exercising a choice with unpredictable, but real, consequences. It strips away normal reservations and invokes a heightened, reinvigorated sense of life: climbing – a waste of time and energy without obvious material rewards – depends on losses that make no sense in terms of everyday calculations and interests and, evacuating these concerns, heightens, focuses and elevates existence in an experience, only temporary, of a different milieu of self, body, object and environment. One particular and 'exhilarating' climb sees the climber overcome initial trepidation and difficulty to cling 'magisterially to nothing' in a controlled and hypersensitive absorption in movement and surroundings, losing himself in an effortless flow of details, holds, feelings and smells while continuing to climb with superlatively attuned reflex and reflection and becoming 'the idea or intuition that sat cleverly at the centre of all this, directing it' (Harrison, 1991: 51). Still amid (his own) motion, self and more than self, lost in space, time, things, the articulating position is no longer that of discrete body, object or subject, but an evaporation in continuity where event, decision and act come together. Such exhilaration is rare. More often climbs involve waiting, soaked with rain, at the bottom of crowded routes; or slow rehearsals of painful holds; or cursing broken equipment; or dangling uncomfortably on a nylon rope. Yet, its joyous instant realizes a different sense of life, an instant when, in the crack of perspective and things, objects are produced and meaning made in acts of metaphor.

Works Cited

Beardsley, Monroe (1962) 'The Metaphorical Twist', *Philosophy and Phenomenological Research* 22(2): 293–307.

Black, Max (1954–5) 'Metaphor', *Proceedings of the Aristotelian Society* 55: 273–94.

Bould, Mark (2005) 'Let's Make a Little Noise, Colorado: An Introduction in Eight Parts', in Mark Bould and Michelle Reid (eds) *Parietal Games: Critical Writings By and On M. John Harrison*, pp. 13–30. London: Science Fiction Foundation.

De Certeau, Michel (1984) *The Practice of Everyday Life*, trans. Stephen Randall. Berkeley: University of California Press.

Harrison, M. John (1991) *Climbers*. London: Paladin.

Harrison, M. John (2002) *Light*. London: Gollancz.

Harrison, M. John (2004a) 'Anima', in *Things That Never Happen*, pp. 281–302. London: Gollancz.

Harrison, M. John (2004b) 'Black Houses', in *Things That Never Happen*, pp. 417–30. London: Gollancz.

Harrison, M. John (2004c) 'The Horse of Iron and How We Can Know It', in *Things That Never Happen*, pp. 237–52. London: Gollancz.

Harrison, M. John (2004d) 'Running Down', in *Things That Never Happen*, pp. 23–54. London: Gollancz.

Harrison, M. John (2004e) 'Suicide Coast', in *Things That Never Happen*, pp. 385–404. London: Gollancz.

Harrison, M. John (2004f) 'A Young Man's Journey to London', in *Things That Never Happen*, pp. 159–18. London: Gollancz.

Harrison, M. John (2005) *The Course of the Heart*, in *Anima*, pp. 1–226. London: Gollancz.

Harrison, M. John (2006) *Nova Swing*. London: Gollancz.

Harrison, M. John (2012) *Empty Space*. London: Gollancz.

Hawking, Stephen W. (1988) *A Brief History of Time*. New York: Bantam.

Hayles, N. Katherine (1999) *How We Became Posthuman*. Chicago, IL: University of Chicago Press.

Joshi, Pankaj S. (2013) 'Naked Singularities', *Scientific American* 22(2): 74–81.

Kant, Immanuel (1929) *Critique of Pure Reason*, trans. Norman Kemp Smith. London: Macmillan.

Kay, Lily E. (2000) *Who Wrote the Book of Life?: A History of the Genetic Code*. Stanford, CA: Stanford University Press.

Lacan, Jacques (1977) *Écrits*, trans. Alan Sheridan. London: Methuen.

Lakoff, George and Johnson, Mark (1980) *Metaphors We Live By*. Chicago, IL: University of Chicago Press.

Lyotard, Jean-François (1984) *The Postmodern Condition*, trans. Geoff Bennington and Brian Massumi. Manchester: Manchester University Press.

Misner, Charles W., Thorne, Kip S. and Zurek, Wojciech (1999) 'John Wheeler, Relativity, and Quantum Information', *Physics Today* (April): 40–6.

Mullins, Justin (2011) 'When the Multiverse and Many-Worlds Collide', *New Scientist* 2815: 8–9.

Penrose, Roger (2011) *Cycles of Time*. London: Vintage.

Porush, David (1996) 'Hacking the Brainstem', Robert Markley (ed.) *Virtual Reality and its Discontents*, pp. 107–41. Baltimore, MD: Johns Hopkins University Press.

Ricoeur, Paul (1991) *A Ricoeur Reader: Reflection and Imagination*, ed. Mario J. Valdes. London: Harvester Wheatsheaf.

Shklovsky, Viktor (1988) 'Art as Technique', David Lodge (ed.) *Modern Criticism and Theory*, pp. 16–30. London: Longman.

Wiener, Norbert (1954) *The Human Use of Human Beings: Cybernetics and Society*. London: Eyre and Spottiswoode.

Zurek, Wojciech (1999) 'Decoherence is our Ticket out of the Quantum World'. *Science Daily* (2 Feb), 9 April 2018, https://www.sciencedaily.com/releases/1999/02/990202072053.htm

Spread Pages

Tim Etchells

'What you've got to recognise, Ed, is that they want you dead. All prophecy is a sending-on-before. The audience need you to be dead for them.'

Ed stared at her.

On the night, he wasn't sure what the audience wanted from him. They filed into the performance space in a kind of rustling hush, ... quieter than a circus audience ought to be, they had bought less food and drink than Ed had expected. They were ominously attentive. They didn't look as if they wanted him dead. He sat on the wooden chair in his tuxedo in the coloured spotlight and stared out at them. He felt hot and a bit sick. His clothes felt too tight.

'Ah,' he said.

He coughed.

'Ladies and gentlemen,' he said. Rows of white faces stared at him. 'The future. What is it?'

1. Topographies

In a series of works titled simply *Pages* made between 2009 and 2012 the artist Vlatka Horvat examines, cuts and opens the flat plane of a series of blank A4 pages.

Through a set of crude grid-like dissections, in which the pages in question have been cut into parts and then joined to once again make A4 sheets, to a series of later works in which the page is sub-jected to a series of incisions, openings and foldings back on itself, Horvat draws the quotidian paper surface (blank container for writ-ing, drawing, printing) into question, marking its whole as a number of parts, re-framing its everyday unity as a mere surface, a problem-atic suspension, beneath which lurks an infinitely complex arrange-ment of buried possibilities. The page refigured in these works as a rough composite grid, soon gives way to more complex mosaics and subdivisions, the lines of Horvat's cuts alluding in particular works to less immediately graspable and in any case irregular logics of divi-sion, with the intersecting straight lines of the grid-pieces replaced subsequently by longer, more wayward paths that score the pages into a series of oblique dysfunctional territories. It is not long either in the development of Horvat's Pages project, before the base gestures of flat plane cutting and refixing are joined by the more complex spa-tial gestures of bending and folding, actions which drag the flat plane of the paper emphatically into three dimensions; sometimes form-ing the single surface into one containing concertinaed peaks and troughs, falls and rises, and at other times revealing, in different ways and in different proportions, the reverse plane or underside surface of the pages in question. These excursions into three dimensions of course, only serve to further complexify the question of the page's surface, revealing it not only as a constructed territory which may be marked, cut and even *made* from any number of smaller parts, but also as a three-dimensional object-as-question whose front and back are opened into a mutable state of intertwining and entanglement.

In a conceptual if not temporal sense these works prepare the ground for Horvat's concurrent minimalist sculptural project *Spread Pages*, also 2009–12. For each of these works Horvat has approached the page through a similar gesture, namely that of purposefully exca-vating the middle of the rectangular page-object and folding it out, more or less systematically, to the sides, in the process reversing the surface on display. Through this process – a kind of shifting, or dig-ging out – the middle of each page becomes its edge or outermost point. In this work the question is not only one of emptying the famil-iar limited zone of the A4 page, but also of exploring its potential for territorial expansion and dispersal in different forms and directions. Viewed from above, as they rest on the gallery floor during exhibition, Horvat's spread pages are problematic objects – unsuitable for their intended use as pages and at the same time – unruly, irregular, unplaceable – escaping (or cast out from) any zone of formalised aesthetic contemplation. Scattered on the floor they appear as rejected, discarded and disrupted materials, problematic and in some sense wounded objects whose utility has been suspended. At the same time they share certain generative properties belonging to biological virus and computer code, in that each page-object proceeds from a simple instruction set followed *mise en abyme* – if not replicating as such then at least unfolding continually according to a rule and within a limit prescribed by the physical properties of the material.

Horvat's even later work, *Topographies I–X*, first shown in her exhibition *Beside Itself* at Zak|Branicka Gallery in Berlin in 2011, shifts and multiplies the material form of her pages enquiry, creating as it does, a series of modified A6 notebooks, the plain brown covers and virgin gridded leaves of which have all been subjected to a range of interventions (cuts, folds, bends) designed once again to elaborate the problematic of dimensionality, as well as drawing our attention to the proliferation of surfaces in each of these familiar objects made strange. Whilst certain of the A4 *Pages*, and indeed the *Spread Pages,* work as a group, proposing an inquiry about the three dimensionality of the page, it is this later series of the altered blank notebooks that brings this topic most to the fore, steadfastly and repeatedly marking the plurality of surfaces contained in these objects, as well as calling into question the nature and completeness of our view (or lack thereof) to them.

Topographies, as the collective title for these works suggests, are notebooks (sites of one representational matrix via drawn line, grid, letter or number), which simultaneously enter another regime of representation in the form of putative and unlikely three-dimensional models, though of what precisely or to what end we cannot quite be sure. There are amongst these *Topographies*, certainly, several which might be taken for models either of geographical or data landscapes, or models of a space or as codices of an argument which we can only imagine or infer, whilst yet others bring to mind complex data-visualizations that might figure as part of a presentation concerning some newly imagined and highly speculative physics.

The blank notebooks of Horvat's *Topographies* are treated not as containers to be filled, but as physical entities reimagined and reconstituted via a series of contortionist acts – turning and twisting around axes, tucking sides one beneath another, wrapping around their centres, or exploding, spilling from quotidian confines. Each of these unstable and malleable objects appears to be caught in the midst of a particular spatial compression or extension, shifting flat planes and rectilinear spreads into curving, spiralling and bending forms which conjure organic movements and morphologies.

Indeed, even while these works self-evidently retain their identity as notebooks, potential containers of information (notes, texts, drawings, maths), albeit modified and in some cases thoroughly stripped of all possible future utility, they are at the same time (via the designation of Horvat's title and through her sculptural interventions on the objects themselves) promoted and re-categorized as three-dimensional models of another space – physical or conceptual.

2. A Reading

Crammed into a small central London venue for *The Weird Reading Evening* late in 2013 M. John Harrison joined a handful of other writers to perform stories to a packed crowd. The scrum, heat and strange energy of the event's location, itself a kind temporal and cultural interzone, framed the readings in peculiar ways from the outset. A former 1797 equine hospital complete with cobbled floors, cast iron pillars and tethering rings, the Horse Hospital became an arts centre in 1992 and during *The Weird Reading* event simultaneously played host to an exhibition presenting maverick early 70s artist Jacques Katmor, whose 'The 3rd Eye Group' drew on the Situationists and the Surrealists to create a unique and isolated counter-cultural phenomena in Israel at that time. Gloomy, rough and somehow vibrant all at the same time, the Horse Hospital performs its pastness very presently, dragging work shown there into a kind of violent temporal collage, made all the stronger on this occasion by the juxtaposition of the diverse uncanny readings with Katmor's drawings, sculptures and text works, many of which comprise modified maps of one kind or another.

To read aloud is clearly another matter than writing. In it the arrangement of words on page or screen via keyboard or pen implies, generates or gives rise to, a subsequent arrangement of words in time, through the embodied physical processes of voice (vibration), gesture and social triangulation. Watching and listening to writers as they read their own material can be excruciating since lamentably, their language skills often exist largely in a specific modality and kind of understanding, focused on the page and its energy/economy of space, printed text and time. No matter how tuned to dialogue or speech such authors might be in their writing, they are tuned at the same time, you might think, to an inner voice and ear of the reader, to the silent negotiation of meaning and unvoiced voice that takes place between writer/reader and the page, a private (non-public) transaction which has minimal (if profound) relation to questions of actual voice or physical embodiment.

In a performative sense many writers lean to *fill* what they have written, persuaded perhaps by their own unique knowledge of their texts, adding while reading inflections, accents, interpretations, embroideries, characterisation and, worst of all (for this listener), opinions about the text they are reading. But when Harrison reads his own writing, it is another physics altogether.

As reader he clearly knows the language in front of him but does not anticipate or judge it; knows how and where to sound it, but at the same time, refuses to fill it or 'enact' it. I am not talking about flatness, but about a certain kind of precise and technical relation to the speaking out of a text, a relation that refuses to overdetermine or assume the affect of what is said and that avoids the temptation to play act. Words, in Harrison's reading, are measured and sounded out, placed, allowed place and space in time; a move which allows the set of tensions, energies, narratives, dynamics and ideas already present in the texts to find manifestation in the event of his reading, step by step. The words are a clockwork, a set of beads on a thread that need to be counted, a machinery that needs to be spoken into motion, an existing argument and trace object whose transparency and clarity requires no further comment. In this particular, precise and because of it evocative approach to reading – a mirror to the economy and clarity of his writing of course – there is a trust both in listener and in text – trust that the text will do its job, and trust that if allowed to do so, the listener will do her work.

The text is a code, a precision sequence, an algorithm, a procedure whose efficacy was made before this moment of speaking out, but whose execution, in the moment of reading, in the moment of performance, requires a combination of clarity, commitment and restraint. The work of the reader (become listener) is that of letting in the code; the work of listening, simply put, is that of letting the code act.

3. On Twitter

August 6th

Stand in the doorway 10.30pm & watch rain fall on the deserted street & think how suddenly you can be happy with no more reason than that.

4. Bodies/Code

Code runs everywhere in the *Empty Space* trilogy, perpetually jumping the gap between abstraction and material form, arcing between the conceptual and the physical/actional, expressed as a kind of meeting between Burroughs-esque language virus, nano-computer virus and engineered biological virus. It is there in the mathematical space of the K-Ship 'where code runs without substrate in a region of its own', it is there in the Shadow Operators, endless whispering, gathering, massing and commenting in the peripheries of spaceships, bars and offices, it's there running up and down the walls, running up and down the flesh of the characters like the Assistant with 'discrete code flows rippling up the inside of one forearm like smart tattoos', it is running into and out of people, it is there in the early EMC experiments described in *Light* as 'running code in the substrate of proteins and nano-mech', it is there in the whole of the K-Tech cargo cult, with its compromising intersection of human and alien biology and technology; code 'like having a wave of luminous insects spill out of the machine, run up your arm and into your mouth before you could stop them.'

It is there too in *Nova Swing*'s highly infectious daughter code too, viral code which the protagonists think emanates from the Event Site, carried by figures who are 'half-flesh, half-artefact', 'speaking in tongues' and 'spilling code out of their mouths like light to infect a whole city block'.

> The worst things we ever brought out of there, we called them 'daughters'. Bring out a daughter and you had nothing but trouble. A daughter would change shape on you. It wasn't alive, it wasn't technology either: no one knew what it did, no one knew what it was for.

Perhaps mirroring terminology from both typesetting and computer coding – widow/orphan text, orphan events – Harrison's gendering of the daughter code, and his positioning it within the logic of biological, familial lineage and parenting, poses it as a kind of uncanny, dreaded opposition – an unruly, shape-shifting daughter that threatens the stability of the still-ubiquitous-yet-always-precarious masculine binary.

More broadly, code in Harrison's trilogy is something external and at the same time internal, something that can be seen, read, discussed, but also felt, touched, tasted, smelt, ingested, internalized. It exists in numerous physical and auditory forms, running on or into human beings. It is, pretty much, everywhere, having an existence inside and outside of the human subject, as both exterior/object and as a kind or modifier of interior consciousness itself. It is something known, manipulable, authorable and the same time (literally) alien, unknown and unknowable, even as it may, at the same time, be inside or in some direct causal link to the subject.

Code blurs the line between thought and computational process, linking human consciousness with landscape and built environment, the connection operating not so much as a feedback loop but as a kind of fluid, switching and expanding process of displacement and dispersal.

Indeed, code is only *one* means or mode through which the human is extended or dispersed in the *Empty Space* trilogy. In Harrison's future – a unique construct which nonetheless follows those of Burroughs, Dick and Gibson among others – bodies, consciousness and identity are substantially remixable and retrofittable. Significant enhancements for appearance as well as for physical and mental skills, capacities and aptitudes (via chops or tailoring) are everywhere in all three books, whilst individual consciousness/presence is routinely extended or displaced from its 'usual place' in the body of the subject via or through any kind and number of potential doubles, avatars and projections. Running their identities on vat-grown temporary cultivars, appearing via 'holographic fetch', plunging themselves into the immersive fictions of the Twink Tanks the populations of New Venusport and Saudade are in a constant double dance of presence and non-presence.

The frame of these enhancements to, and dispersals of, the human body and mind is that of an extended and amplified version of our own Late Capitalism – perhaps Very Late Capitalism – in which opportunistic entrepreneurial, corporate and military interests set the pace for technological innovation and change that are reflected, refracted and exploited widely and without mercy in the deregulated (and in this case intergalactic) markets of the inhabited universe. This generative field, especially in combination with the wild card technologies and code innovations of the Kefahuchi Tract and the Saudade Event Site makes for a fiction in which many of the characters struggle with the open question of their humanness and that of those around them.

When Ed Chianese kills one of the Kray Sisters in New Venusport, there is a short time in which he is unsure if the person he has shot is a unique biological 'person' or simply a consciousness running remotely at a distance on an artificial body or cultivar. Somehow the idea of the temporary uncertainty is more disturbing than that of the death itself. Seria Mau meanwhile, one of several identity-troubled central figures in *Light*, maintains, for most of the book, a tangible anxiety about her relation to humanness. Compromising and all but destroying her human body in order to enter a state of apparently irreversible merger and symbiosis with the K-Ship, the physical body of Seria Mau is a crippled biological form, floating in a tank from which wires, tubes and neural connections link her to the ship. From this position – drilled through the spine and cut through the neo-cortex – she can access and directly control the spaceship's instruments, nanocams and other tools as well merging, when she needs to, with the ships mathematics, entering K-space to control more complex aspects of battle and navigation. Throughout the bulk of the book, traumatized by separation (bodily, familial and existential), Seria Mau is 'looking for traces of herself' in the crew she reluctantly takes on board and later kills, drifting between their corpses in the vacuum into which she has expelled them, staring, grieving for a childhood that she failed to complete and which she can only partially remember; a non-narrative childhood that is coming back in fragments only, out of sequence and partially transformed in her dreams.

While Harrison's world of hulking Rickshaw girls, figures bedecked with sentient tattoos, heavily 'tailored' agents with reaction times in micro-fractions of a second, identical monas in high heels and bobbed hair, cultivar fighters with distorted bodies and the like, demonstrates some of the more extraordinary possibilities for the human body on offer in the legal and illegal free markets in New Venusport and Saudade, his depiction also insists that for the most of the inhabitants of that region of space and time, the preeminent feeling appears to be one of confusion or deep loss. It is no surprise perhaps, that Saudade, the port city in which much of *Nova Swing* is set, famously takes its name from a Portugese word describing a deep state of melancholy and longing for an absent loved one or thing.

When Seria Mau finally has a body to inhabit, lovingly built for her by the shadow operators that haunt her ship, she inhabits it for a while but soon professes disappointment. The daydream of embodiment was more potent and psychically gripping than the playing out of its fantasy in material form. What was gone is irretrievable.

She felt no more 'alive' than she had in the tank. What had she been frightened of? Bodies were not new to her, and besides, this one had never been her self.

'The air smells like nothing in here,' she said. 'It smells like nothing.'

For many of Harrisons other characters it is not so much the spectacular dimensions of human bodily possibility or machine and chemical altered consciousness that obsesses them so much as the pull they feel from the missing mundane. The pumped and ripped giant Rickshaw girl Annie who falls in with Ed Chianese, remakes herself as small and 15, a Mona that affords her a less grotesque scale-invisibility, while Tig Vesicle, the guy that runs the Twink Farm stays off his own virtual reality merchandise in favour of old fashioned holographic porn. Most of the stories he watches on the channel he's addicted to end with the heroine being sexually used by some unlikely cultivar – 'all tusks, prick the size of a horse' – but Vesicle typically skips that part of the narrative, preferring her to 'do ordinary things, like trying to paint her toe nails naked, or trying to look over her shoulder at herself in the mirror'.

When the eccentric Site Crime Officer Lens Aschemann is goaded by his nameless Assistant, she yells at him, mocking him and his faux late period Albert Einstein appearance: 'I don't understand why you have to pretend to be old, and get driven around in a car from the historical times. No one in this culture has to be old anymore.' Later he replies, speaking of the loss of his wife, very likely a strange less-than-fully human artefact of the Event Site: 'No one has to lose anyone now...,' he says. 'Perhaps I wanted to know what it was like.'

The yearning pull to banality – as nostalgia, as proof of presentness and superiority or simply as ground to stand on – is also found in Sandra Shen's The Circus of Pathet Lao – in which the Observatorium freakshow suggested by the name in fact comprises a collection of 'everyday scenes' presented as melancholic tableaux.

In a time like that, who needed a circus? The halo was a circus in itself. Circus was in the streets. It was inside people's heads.

...

But in the face of the uniform grotesque, the Circus of Pathet Lao had been forced to look elsewhere for the cheap thrill at the heart of performance, and – through a series of breathtaking acts of the imagination devised and sometimes performed in by Sandra Shen herself – present the vanished normal.

'Brian Tate and Michael Kearny Looking into a Monitor in 1999', 'Toyota Previa with Clapham Schoolchildren, 2002', 'Novel Reading, Early 1980's', 'Having Breakfast, 1950', 'Buying an Underwired Bra at Dorothy Perkins, 1972'.

These gemlike tableaux – acted out behind glass under powerful lights by the clones of fat men about to have heart attacks on a Zurich metro platform, anorexic women dressed in the Angelino sport-fuck wear of 1982 – brought to life the whole bizarre comfortingness of Old Earth. Such desperate fantasies were the real earners. Like fairy godmothers they had blessed the Circus at its inception, funded its early whirlwind travel across the Halo, and now supported its declining years in the twilight zone of New Venusport.

Here and throughout the books, Harrison mocks and critiques the relentless drive through which anything, especially the boredom and clichés of previous eras can be newly commodified, fetishised and monetised here, again and again, in the futuristic jaws of Experience Economy capitalism. He also points to the window of course. And to the rain outside of it, since, to stand there at the window, and watch the rain fall on the deserted street outside, can make you happy, with no more reason than that.

5. The Window

Dear M,

You know the scene because you've been there.

I'm sitting at what was once the loading window of the warehouse place we're renting on Belfast Road, the battered red paint-peeling half height double doors which must have been used to bring stuff in here, back in the not-so-long-ago days, when it was a clothing sweatshop. These doors – when open at least – are really the best place to sit here, so long as the temperature isn't too low outside, great for the light and for a sense of connection to the world, even though I'm effectively buried in work here these last few days, hardly moving.

While I'm so still, so landlocked these days, the weather is so changeable, sunny, bright one moment and then cold overcast the next. It's now raining outside, the rain falling at 45 degrees across the frame of the window, the wind starting to blow and the light in the whole scene is dispersed completely, soft, but not dull – the sky still bright and luminescent in fact, glowing behind the unbroken covering of flat cloud, even as the rain comes slanting down.

I've been sitting here for the last few days, reading, writing and from time to time slipping to sleep in this same chair. I'm tempted to say that the books are scattered around me but that's not true in any real sense, only as metaphor, since all the books are on the laptop here, as are the notes I've been making. Everything criss-crossing and piling in this digital space. Somewhere beneath the open Word document I'm typing into, I have *Climbers* open, and *The Course of the Heart* and *Empty Space* plus assorted documents of notes, synopses and other stuff I think might be relevant; *Roadside Picnic, Solaris,* a few Wikipedia pages on neuroscience.

The sound score here is complex – rain patterns the most of it, beat out on the corrugated roof of this large former warehouse and somewhere beneath the rain there is the London drone of the planes, one every five minutes or so passing over, and beneath all that there is the pulse and throb of the African church of El-Bethel downstairs. At first it seems like it's just drums, regular steady, in no hurry, pulsing in the background of the rain, the plane drones and the occasional cop car sirens phasing in the distance, but sometimes voices are audible with the drums too, singing, chanting, never too loud for the moment, at least not since the last bout of ecstatic preaching came to an end an hour or so ago.

The rain has stopped now. And the sky has cleared. And from the church the singers have gotten louder – the pulse of the drums and the high voices and low voices are braiding around each other, and braiding around the drums.

From time to time out there a cat emerges to the rooftops of the buildings on the other side of the yard outside; winding through the gap between the roofs, one at a time, an hour or so apart, sometimes more, sometimes less. The cats emerging, venturing out and across to left, tracing a line across the sloping horizon of the corrugated asbestos and tin, moving slowly and disappearing over the top to the other side again.

6. Folded out and folded over

In two linked sets of collages – *For Example (Folded Out)* and *For Example (Folded Over)*, both from 2009 – Vlatka Horvat again cuts and folds paper, in this case to repeatedly transform a single enigmatic self-portrait image into a series of emphatically three-dimensional objects. Each piece in the series, in its own way, tests the borders between her own inkjet image and the blank reverse side of the paper it is printed on, confusing the relation between image and frame, figure and ground. The ur-image for this series, taken from an earlier purely photographic sequence titled *Hiding*, shows Horvat as though caught in a perfunctory and ultimately unsuccessful enactment of the title – standing in the corner of an anonymous room, attempting to hide her face by concealing it with the upturned collar of her jacket.

In the first set of collages making use of this image – *For Example (Folded Out)* – Horvat partially cuts around the figure, folding and bending it back on itself, revealing the blank unprinted underside of the paper, and at the same time excavating a hole in place of the figure. In this way Horvat's original image is doubly punctured; both evacuated entirely in one portion and obscured or covered in another of identical shape. No matter which part, parts or zone of the figure Horvat excavates in this way the result is always a partly readable figure interrupted and in a certain sense combined with these varieties of missing image; part photograph, part vacated outline, an unruly hybrid of figure and negative space.

In the second sequence of collages making use of the same image from the *Hiding* series – *For Example (Folded Over)* – Horvat again cuts around her own figure in a variety of ways and places, but instead of folding the body itself back over itself she now folds the plane of the paper back over the figure in a variety of ways, exposing the underside of the paper, and in the process substantially obscuring parts of the original image whilst leaving other parts of it exposed. These images – a series of figure studies in which the figure both merges with and is bisected by the background and by the underside of its own image – present a human being warped and remade though a process that calls at the same time to the transformative possibilities of the geometric mathematical and the magical uncanny. She is a figure in, become, and bisected by landscape. She is figure as image folded into, become, and bisected by the paper ground she stands on. A diagram of possible and impossible human prototypes. A figure caught in the twisting and turning event site of the page.

7. The Tract/The Event Site

They stared across at the event site. You were never sure what you were looking at. Beyond the wire, beyond the remains of the original wall, with its fallen observation towers, prismatic light struck off the edges of things. There was a constant sense of upheaval. Loud tolling noises, as of enormous girders falling, or the screech of overdriven machinery, competed with the sudden hum of an ordinary wasp, amplified a million times. It was like a parody of the original function of the place. But also there were snatches of popular songs, running into one another like a radio being tuned through some simple rheostat. You smelled oil, ice cream, garbage, birchwoods in winter. You heard a baby crying, or something clatter at the end of a street – it was like a memory, but not quite.

Sudden eruptions of light; dense, artificial-looking pink and purple bars and wheels of light; birds flying home against sunsets and other sweet momentary transitions between states of light. Then you saw things being tossed into the air, what looked like a hundred miles away. Scale and perspective were impossible to achieve because these objects, toppling over and over in a kind of slow motion – or so the eye assumed – were domestic items a hundred times too large and from another age, ironing boards, milk bottles, plastic cups and saucers. They were too large, and too graphic, drawn in flat pastel colours with minimal indication of shape, capable of liquid transformation while you watched. Or they were too small, and had a hyper-real photographic quality, as if they had been clipped from one of the lifestyle-porn magazines of Ancient Earth: individual buildings, bridges, white multi-hull sailing ships, then a complete city skyline toppling across as if it had been tossed up among flocks of green parrots, iron artillery wheels, tallboys, a colander, and a toy train running around a toy track.

Everything in a different style of mediation. Everything generating a brief norm, reframing everything else. At that time, in that instant of watching and listening, in a moment savagely and perfectly incapable of interpretation, they were all the things that fly up out of a life, maybe your own, maybe someone else's you were watching. Day to day, you might have more or less of a sense that the things you saw were describable as 'real'. In fact, that wasn't a distinction you needed to make until you crossed inside.

At the heart of the *Empty Space* trilogy there are the twin zones of confusion and upheaval, the vast Tract itself, and its landfallen side effect, the smaller, grounded schism of the Saudade Event Site. Filling the sky like a vast tear in a curtain the former proves a dynamic engine for the sweeping soap opera narrative of change and revelation on a grand scale begun in *Light*, stretching back aeons to a time way before human life, to its origins and pointing to futures far beyond. The latter is a more intimate zone – an urban planning eccentricity, arising from the Tract but by virtue of its material base in the city of Saudade allowing the possibility of *Nova Swing* and *Empty Space*'s more human scale, or post-human scale encounters with the Tract and the upheavals it creates, in relation to more mundane questions of love, the law, identity, desire and loyalty. The same thing in a sense, reworked in a different scale, and a different key.

Tumbling through the books there are also a series of echoes of the Tract – the suitcase brought by Gaines to Lens Aschemann's unnamed Assistant in *Empty Space*:

> We call it the Aleph ... an artefact at least a million years old ... constructed at the nanometre length, the purpose of which was to contain a piece of the Kefahuchi Tract itself.

And the cracked monitor, spilling light into Michael Kearney and Brian Tate's laboratory playing their q bit experiments, the screening of which proves an endless fascination for their cats.

> 'The fractals started to –' he couldn't think of a word, nothing had prepared him for whatever he was seeing in his head '– leak. Then the cat went inside after them. She just walked through the screen and into the data.' He laughed, looking from Kearney to Anna. 'I don't expect you to believe that,' he said.

8. A Moment's Clarity

At various points in the trilogy diverse protagonists are offered glimpses of another reality – of a logic behind, or within or parallel to the Universe. Usually taking the form of 'unintelligible' visions, confusing light shows, delirious combinations of images and events as well as mathematics, code and other more abstract materials, these glimpses are the cause of anxiety in each of their recipients even as they aspire to them, and very often arrive with an explicit warning or summation that they may not be endured for long. Ed Chianese's first Prophecy Act with Sandra Shen is what she calls 'a short show':

> As soon as you put the fishtank on your head, you had some sort of spasm. ... They weren't convinced,' she went on, 'until you got out of the chair.' He had got out of the chair, she told him, to stand facing the audience for maybe a minute in the shifting light, during which time he trembled and slowly pissed himself. 'It was a real twink moment, Ed. I was proud of you.'

When both Billy Anker and Michael Kearney get their views of the Tract from the Sigma End, neither of them can bear it. Anker tells Seria Mau:

> 'I didn't stay, I wasn't up to it. I saw that at once. I was too scared to stay. I could feel the code, humming in the fabric, I could hear the light pour over me. I could feel the Tract at my back, like someone watching.'

Later, when Kearney is taken to the same place by the Shrander, the first thing he says is, 'Too bright.'
He's astonished by what he sees.

> 'Where is this? Are these stars? Is there anywhere really like this?'
> Now the Shrander laughed too.
> 'Everywhere is like this,' it said. 'Isn't that something?'
> ...
> 'That's the one thing we never seemed to get,' it said: 'How unpackable everything is.'

Before he leaves he has 'turned up his face to the sky' and 'imagined he could see among the clouds of stars and incandescent gas, the shapes of everything that had been in his life'

> 'You understand?' said the Shrander, which, having remained courteously silent through this process, now came to his side again and stared up in a companionable way. 'There will always be more in the universe. There will always be more after that.'
> Then it admitted: 'I can't keep you alive for much longer, you know. Not here.'

These brief glimpses of what's behind things find a mirror in the brief dangerous trips into the Event Site undertaken by generations of so-called travel agents like Vic Serotonin and the dying Emil Bonaventura. They also find a parallel in the short time that Seria Mau can withstand in direct connection with her ship's mathematics, a union which drags her into the ship time of q-bits and which gives her access to the raw quantum data that the ship negotiates constantly. It's a direct contact that cannot be endured for long and Seria Mau resents it, caught as she is between the crippled frame of her human body and consciousness and the pure space of data that underlies the universe.

This split or tension between the surface universe as it's seen and sensed by human beings and the underlying universe of maths and data flows is at the heart of these works, especially in the sense that so many of the protagonists are endlessly caught in the space between these systems of perception. The tailoring that so many of the human figures sport is a small ramp up towards a perception of this hidden space. Meanwhile Harrison's key characters – Kearney entangled with quantum physics, the Shrander, the Tarot and the dice, Ed Chianese propelled into the space and practice of Prophecy, as well as Brian Tate, Vic Serotonin, Emil Bonaventura and Seria Mau – are all, in their own ways and by their own means, driven and consumed by a quest for some other deeper vantage or position.

There's an explicit mirroring in *Light* between two conversations; one towards the start of the book between Michael and Anna Kearney and one between Seria Mau and her K-Ship's mathematics. In the first of these Michael Kearney derides his wife's enthusiasm for the newly released pictures of the Kefahuchi Tract.

> 'It is beautiful, though,' she objected.
> 'It doesn't look like that,' Kearney told her. 'It doesn't look like anything. It's just data from some X-ray telescope. Just some numbers, massaged to make an image. Look around,' he told her more quietly. 'That's all anything is. Nothing but statistics.'

And later in the same conversation:

> 'It sounds awful. It sounds undependable. It sounds as if everything will just –' she made a vague gesture '– boil around. Spray about.'
> Kearney looked at her.
> 'It already does,' he said … 'Down there it's just disorder … Space doesn't seem to mean anything, and that means that time doesn't mean anything.'
> He laughed. 'In a way that's the beauty of it.'

In the second conversation I'm thinking of, the K-ship consoles a weary Seria Mau.

> 'Shall I tell you something?' the mathematics said.
> 'What?' [said Seria Mau]
> 'Display up,' said the mathematics, and the Kefahuchi Tract exploded into her head.
> 'This is the way things really look,' said the mathematics. 'If you think ship-time is the way things look, you're wrong. If you think ship-time is something, you're wrong: it's nothing. You see this? This

isn't just some "exotic state". It's light years of blue and rose fire, roaring up out of nowhere, toppling away again in real, human time. That's the way it is. *That's* what it's like inside you.'

9. Gone Midnight

It's gone midnight Mike and there were so many things I wanted to write.

About the fact that your work, all of it really, not just the *Empty Space* trilogy, appears to be this extended essay insisting on the unknowability of things, a universe in which the characters know themselves so poorly, and know the world poorly too, resolutely mistaking things, or not learning at all, like the central figure in *Climbers*, clinging to poorly grasped ideas and theories, like Michael Kearney fleeing the Schrander without having the slightest understanding if it's interested in him. About how as readers we're also forced back into not knowing so often in your work, invited to imagine worlds, experiences that in one sense are so very far from our own, and yet which in other ways are strangely familiar. About the habit you have in your writing of leaving the reader to infer so much from so relatively little, about the rather provisional approach to world-building that you have, which is more about placing ideas, images, fragments in constellations than it is about constructing brick by brick supposedly coherent histories or physics, about the determination you have to undo certainties, to throw the reader back on herself, to form the object of the text from a set of finely worked tensions and vibrations. About the small observation you made concerning your own work, back at the Horse Hospital last year, about being interested in 'the subtlest possible rupture of the mundane by the uncanny and the subtlest possible rupture of the uncanny by the mundane.' About this question of transformations of the body and what they do to human consciousness, about the increasing mediatization, alteration and dispersal of ourselves. About the fact that you chose that beautiful old word – fetch – as a name for the holographic avatars that the characters in the trilogy sometimes deploy, that the word itself comes from folklore, referring to a double, the double of a living subject, the arrival of which is sometimes taken to indicate the coming demise of the subject. I wanted to write you about the reading I did this week concerning programming language, half convinced that the 'daughter code' was an actual term, something I'd heard before and how for one brief moment I was really excited because one online page I found with an account of Unix programming terms and forms talked about daughter process alongside the more ubiquitous terms used in that context such as 'parent', 'child' and 'orphan' code and processes, but it was only that one page I found which had the 'daughter', so in the end I more or less abandoned my pursuit of it.

I wanted to write you about magic in the books. About Sprake, the 'greatest magician in London', about the Tract and the Event Site and their relation to conjuring and vaudeville and about the links between your conjuring spaces and my own work with Forced Entertainment that has created something related, in the zone of performance. I wanted to write about the death of the comedian Tommy Cooper – did you see that? It was 15 April 1984, broadcast live on television from Her Majesty's Theatre. Cooper, dressed up in an absurd 'Egyptian' robe, was presenting one of his numerous absurd appearance and disappearance routines. As he stood in front of the curtains, a series of objects were fed through from backstage so that in some absurd suggestive way they appeared from between his legs, through the folds of his costume. Somewhere there, in all the mock shambolic slapstickery, face pulling, birth and sex organ innuendo, he fell back, suffering a heart attack, heading backwards, heading down then clutching at the curtain to lie dead or dying, prone in centre stage. Some people, remembering that night, say that the curtain came down over him, cutting him in half, others that it was cloaked around him. However, all agree that whilst dying he remained partially visible for some time, his legs sticking out from under the drape. I thought of this scene, reading the Dr Haends routine in *Light,* white gloves and gold topped ebony cane, 'Mathematics itself was loose, like a magician in a funny hat, and nothing would ever be the same'. There's a similar feeling in the description of the Event Site at some point in *Nova Swing*, though somehow, for the moment I cannot find it – I'm thinking about a line that describes these outsized props, and again this moment of conjuring.

I wanted to write to you about another death, the killing of Michael Brown in Ferguson, and the protests which have followed it, which have formed a strange and strong unfolding counter narrative this week as I've been buried in your writing, sitting in that chair by the window, reading and making notes and feeling the light change. In this time, caught in that far-off trauma, I somehow became pretty much addicted to Twitter again, following people in the crowd of protestors there in Ferguson, reading the tiny micro narratives and speculations from inside and around that situation of anger and oppression, the protestors surrounded by police, the scene riddled with journalists and commentators of one kind and another. There's a vanity perhaps to the attention on that scene from such a distance that social media allows, a pornography of sorts to the shadow of proximity if affords, and yet, on the other hand, the connection person-to-person even if dispersed via digital platform, has a vividness that I feel something for, it seems important, confronting, or at least hard to let go of. I don't know. I lost hours to it this last week. Reading, watching, reading again. Angry, bewildered.

What a distressing cross current that unfolding story from Ferguson has been to rereading your texts and writing this week, that unfolding present, very rooted story of race, economics, history and police violence set against your futures. It drew me to something you said in the discussion at the Horse Hospital event, where you spoke about the world 'transforming transfixing and tormenting us' – I don't remember the precise context of, but I have been certainly been transfixed and tormented this week.

And I wanted to write to you about the haunting image of the floating corpses in *Empty Space*, and about the strange figures that appear from out of the nightclub toilets in *Nova Swing*, reverse tourists as I think they are described, 'people' that are in fact just artefacts from the site, 'emerging tentative, unsure of what was required of them or of what they required for themselves', figures with 'appetites but [who] did not yet know what they were'. Those disempowered, almost-abject figures are somewhat comical, slapstick presences in the book as well as rather sad or empty. I was thinking that, somehow it feels like you're sympathetic to them and reading back I began to wonder why, exactly that might be? Is it their lack of ego, the way they tune to and ride on the situation, the way they don't need to know or fix understanding, the way that in their blundering forwards without frame or plan they might be, as Lens Aschemann seems to suggest at one point, as human as we are.

> He thought about the damp sand at the back of the Café Surf, squeezed together daily by the implacable shaping forces of the Long Bar – improvisation, iconolatry and red light – to make new inhabitants for the city. What if he were part of that cycle too?

I wanted to write those things, and many more and of course I'm realising way too late that I forgot to say how funny the books are. But there is no time anymore, the red doors to the loading window are long closed now and the light has gone and the night has gathered itself outside. It's cold. I'm ready to sleep.

But before that I wanted to bring in this passage from *Nova Swing*.

> It was one of those things. They loved paper suddenly. The nostalgia shops were full of it, all colours of cream and white, blank or with feint lines, or small pale-grey squares, shining softly from the lighted windows which were like religious cubicles or niches. There was every kind of notebook in there, paper between covers you could hardly believe ...
>
> Everyone suddenly loved paper ... But it was more practical for some than others. Emil Bonaventure kept the habit where others kicked it, and wrote everything down until the day he went into the Saudade site for the last time. He didn't trust his memory by then. He'd been in there once too often. The stuff he had to remember was complex – directions, bearings, instructions to himself. It was data. It was clues. It was everything you daren't forget in that trade.
>
> ...
>
> Emil wrote it all down in that water-stained letter – as if he had to convince himself of something – in a kind of slanting disordered scribble which did not reflect his personality. Then he hid the book.

and then from later in the same book:

she brought the journal to her own room. It looked worse in the light. Her father's adventures had aged it the same way they aged him. Its covers were bruised and greasy; like Emil's, its spine was rotten. Every page was stained, spattered, slashed; some had been torn in half longitudinally, to leave only curious groups of words – 'emergent behaviour', 'sunset of the amygdila' and 'outputs accepted as input'. But these were just problems of legibility. The site being as it was, an electromagnetic nightmare, writing was the only way to get anything out: but how do you write the fakebook to a place that is constantly at work to change the ink you write with, let alone the things you see? Her father's script tottered into the gale of it, stumbling off the edge of one page to fall by pure luck on to the next.

10. A Fakebook

Dear Mike. It's this very same notebook mentioned above – that of Emil Bonaventura – with its form of torn and folded pages, its fragmentary narratives, its erasures and its omissions, that in this final section of the prophecy I will claim to have possession of.

Or I will state, that I have, here in my possession, a more complex object – an impossible amalgam of Bonaventura's notebook described in *Nova Swing*, combined with various topographical sculptures of Vlatka Horvat's, themselves made entirely from notebooks and referred to at the beginning of this text.

It seems that somehow, thinking between your work and Vlatka's, I got to thinking, Mike, that another version of the Tract, another version of the Event site, another version of the crack in the universe from which this all unknowable disorder is emerging, might be language itself, or if not language, then simply the page; that page, the blank page that is simple only in its absolute complexity, complex only in its absolute simplicity.

The rest of this text then, the remainder of this prophecy if that's what we can call it, all that follows from here, all of it in any case borrowed as fragments from your work, will be taken from that imaginary notebook, that non-existent source.

It's been fun. It's been heartbreak all the way. It's never been less than a trip.

'The air smells like nothing in here,' she said, 'It smells like nothing.'

You knew it would come to that. You knew.
You always knew it would come to that.

Breakfront cabinets whose glass doors were etched with exotic scenes from Ancient Earth.

Come here Vic, and look at this.
Come here Vic, she said, and look at this.

I was so innocent.
That's unjust of me.

The room smelled of standing water, electricity, darkness.

Rocket ships, shooting stars, snowy mountains.

Whatever comes out I have to deal with the consequences.

A daughter would change shape on you.

'I don't like to travel. I don't like these cheap seats.'

'Two miles from [illegible] Point'

'It wasn't a beach. They weren't dogs.'

She turned her back on him and began to walk away. 'I'm going in, whatever you say.'

'Elizabeth, you're already in.'

Whose story was he telling when he said these things?

It's been fun. It's been heartbreak all the way. It's never been less than a trip.

'If I'm predicting the future, how come I always see the past?'

half-flesh, half-artefact,
falling to pieces,

speaking in tongues

His eyes went out of focus very suddenly and he let go her arm. 'A year passed in there, Billy boy,' he shouted, 'less than a day out here. What do you make of that?'

'The air smells like nothing in here,' she said, 'It smells like nothing.'

We lost the [illegible] & had to walk out.

'Four days in here, a week passed outside.'

We believe it is very old.
We believe it is very old.
When we use the word 'constructed', we don't rule out the idea of self-construction.

You can't see it for longer because its already in its own future.

Satnav and dead reckoning both unreliable.

Sparks, in everything.

Stand in the doorway 10.30pm.

Scribbled across this, in a hand so distraught it looked like someone else's, was the instruction, 'Forget it.'

The bits of music you thought you knew.
The sense you had of a voice reciting something.
The sense of everything fallen away from sense.

It was one of those memories that folds itself quickly out of sight.
It was one of those memories.
It was one of those memories that folds quickly out of sight.

Tim Etchells, London and Sheffield, 2014

Acknowledgments

This is an artistic and critical response to M. John Harrison's oeuvre, rather than a strictly scholarly one. As such it draws directly on and reproduces, both faithfully and in distorted fashion, fragments of text from across Harrison's body of work without attribution.

Notes on Contributors

Fred Botting is Professor of English and Creative Writing at Kingston University. He has written extensively on Gothic fictions, and on theory, film and cultural forms. His current research projects include work on fiction and film dealing with figures of horror – zombies in particular – and on spectrality, the uncanny and sexuality. [email: F.Botting@kingston.ac.uk]

Mark Bould is Reader in Film and Literature at UWE Bristol. He co-edits the *Studies in Global Science Fiction* monograph series. His most recent books are *Solaris* (2014), *SF Now* (2014) and *Africa SF* (2013). [email: Mark.Bould@uwe.ac.uk]

Vassili Christodoulou is Head of London Programmes for The School of Life, an international organization dedicated to helping individuals and businesses cultivate emotional intelligence. Before joining TSOL he ran the *HowTheLightGetsIn* festival of philosophy and ideas, and *Crunch*, a contemporary art fair. [email: vassili.christodoulou@gmail.com]

Ryan Elliott is an independent researcher, writer and critic based outside of Seattle. His work has appeared in *Strange Horizons*. [email: ryantelli@gmail.com]

Tim Etchells is an artist and a writer based in the UK. He has worked in a wide variety of contexts, notably as leader of the world-renowned performance group Forced Entertainment and in collaboration with a range of visual artists, choreographers, and photographers. His work spans performance, video, photography, text projects, installation and fiction. He is currently Professor of Performance & Writing at Lancaster University. [email: Tim@timetchells.com]

Graham Fraser is Assistant Professor of Modern and Contemporary Literature at Mount Saint Vincent University. He has published work on J. G. Ballard, Samuel Beckett, Jean Rhys, Paul Auster and Virginia Woolf, as well as M. John Harrison. His current work explores the intersection of spectrality, metaphor and modernism. [email: Graham.Fraser@msvu.ca]

Nick Freeman is Reader in Late Victorian Literature at Loughborough University and the author of *Conceiving the City: London, Literature, and Art 1870-1914* (2007), and *1895: Drama, Disaster, and Disgrace in Late Victorian Britain* (2011). He has published on Crowley, Swinburne, Wells, Wilde and serial poisoners, as well as Gothic and Weird fiction. In 1996, he published the first academic article on M. John Harrison. [email: N.Freeman@lboro.ac.uk]

Timothy Jarvis is a writer and a lecturer in Creative Writing. His research interests, as a practitioner and critic, include the Gothic, speculative literature, innovative writing, digital storytelling, and Creative Writing pedagogy. His debut novel is *The Wanderer* (2014). [email: timjjarvis@gmail.com]

Paul Kincaid is the author of two collections of essays and reviews, *What It Is We Do When We Read Science Fiction* (2008) and *Call and Response* (2014), and *Iain M Banks* (2017). In 2006, he received the SFRA's Thomas Clareson Award, and in 2011, the BSFA's Non-Fiction Award. [email: paul@appomattox.demon.co.uk]

Rob Latham is an editor of *Science Fiction Studies*. He is the author of *Consuming Youth: Vampires, Cyborgs and the Culture of Consumption* (2002) and editor of *The Oxford Handbook of Science Fiction* (2014) and *Science Fiction Criticism: An Anthology of Essential Writings* (2017). He teaches at California State University, Long Beach. [email: rob.latham@me.com]

James Machin is a postgraduate researcher and associate tutor at Birkbeck. His thesis on early weird fiction (1890–1940) examined the connections between literary decadence and genre fiction. The editor of *Faunus: The Journal of the Friends of Arthur Machen*, he provided the introduction to Tartarus Press's edition of Machen's 1936 collection *The Cosy Room and Other Stories* (2016). [email: jmachi01@mail.bbk.ac.uk]

Chris Pak is the author of *Terraforming: Ecopolitical Transformations and Environmentalism in Science Fiction* (2016) and the editor of the *SFRA Review*. In 2011, he co-founded the annual *Current Research in Speculative Fiction* conference. [email: chrispak650@hotmail.com]

Nicholas Prescott teaches in the School of Humanities and Creative Arts at Flinders University, and is ABC South Australia's weekly film reviewer. He chairs the Adelaide Festival Awards for Literature's fiction panel, has served on the Sydney Film Festival FIPRESCI jury, and has written for the *Australian Book Review*, the *Independent Weekly*, the *CRNLE Review* and *The 100 Greatest Films of Australian Cinema*. [email: nick.prescott@flinders.edu.au]

Christina Scholz is a Research and Teaching Associate at the Centre of Intermediality Studies at the University of Graz, where she is also writing her PhD thesis on M. John Harrison's fiction. Her research interests include Weird fiction, hauntology and the gothic imagination, and depictions of war, violence and trauma in the arts. [email: c.scholz78@gmail.com]

Rhys Williams is Lord Kelvin Adam Smith Research Fellow at the University of Glasgow. He has published in *Science Fiction Studies*, *Paradoxa* and *SFFTV*, and co-edited *SF Now* (2015). [email: rhys.williams@glasgow.ac.uk]

Index